"There, But for the Mindless Whims of Chance, Go I"

The Thurstonian Theory of Life

And

"The Anatomy of a Rape: It Took Two to Tangle"

John R. Thurston, Ph.D.
Clinical Psychologist
2014

Jennifer Geiss, Editor

First published by Dog Ear Publishing
4010 W. 86th Street, Ste H
Indianapolis, IN 46268
www.dogearpublishing.net

ISBN: 978-1-4575-3043-2

Library of Congress Control Number: has been applied for

This book is printed on acid-free paper.

Printed in the United States of America

Cover images by Jennifer Geiss aka Darkest Artist
"Tango"
http://www.fineartamerica.com/profiles/darkest-artist.com

This presentation provides an opportunity for the reader to test out his or her understanding of a man and woman who were involved in a vicious crime. Do your previous beliefs help or hinder you as you proceed?

In the pages herein, explore with us Thurstonian Theory.

Hopefully, your knowledge of Thurstonian Theory will be useful in that pursuit.

The Thurstonian Theory of Life

You're truly one of a kind. But then, so is everyone else.

There, but for the mindless whims of Nature, Nurturance, and Chance, go I.

Stuff happens, and so did you.

We're all tethered to our pasts.

You're more dynamic process than person.

A Magnum Opus – 2014
By John Thurston, Ph.D.

There But for the Mindless Whims of Chance, Go I.

The Thurstonian Theory of Life

By John Thurston, Ph.D.
Clinical Psychologist

Table of Contents – Part I

PROLOGUE

Of Bugs and Men—and Women!

Once upon a time, there was a bug, known locally as a "piney bug." It and hundreds of his kind spent a 2012 summer on the pines of my property doing "bug things," eating, resting, reproducing, and surviving. It's not known if it thought, experienced emotions, or had any political affiliations.

I, a human, was spending a summer allegedly maximizing my human potential as I thought, experienced emotions, and developed a few more beliefs about many things. Among these was a conviction that a "bug" had no business on my property. The appropriate reaction was a quick execution of any trespassing bug.

We—the bug and I—passed a reasonably tranquil and rewarding summer. Then, the cold winds of autumn may have triggered ancient instincts in the bug. It apparently sought shelter in my home.

On a fateful day (most assuredly fateful for the bug), it and I had an encounter. Both of us were standing on the kitchen floor. I know not of his motives. It was just there, doing its bug thing, probably luxuriating in the warmth of my home.

As I entered the kitchen to get a cup of coffee, I saw it. My belief system kicked in. Armed with a fly-swatter, I delivered what proved to be a fatal blow to the bug. It was squashed on the floor. I scooped it up and deposited the remains in the garbage can. I then went my way, unaffected by this incidental experience. My life went on; the bug's didn't.

Stuff happened! Are there human parallels? Yes. By the galore!

Encounters take place between living beings and other living beings and their environments on a 24/7 basis throughout their lifetimes. "If" and "Chance" may play a large part in these encounters. If the bug hadn't felt the cold and I hadn't needed a jolt of caffeine, the event would never have occurred. You're convinced that you're in control of your life. But think of the role of "Chance" in all events of your day, every day. Is there the possibility that you may be living a very chancy life over which you have little say?

Read on.

INTRODUCTION

"Stuff Happens"—and So Did You!
An Exploration of Your Personal Complexity
Who Are You and How Did You Get That Way?

My position is that no living thing really has any choice/control/responsibility in doing anything. This includes what I'm about to do in the exploration of this topic. I really have no real choice or control in regard to anything I do.

The person I am at this split second of time—I am constantly changing and will continue to change until I die—together with all aspects of the world around me impel me into undertaking and recording this point of view.

Choice and any real control over one's conduct are illusions. I find that we are all "inadvertently programmed" to do anything—and I mean <u>anything</u>.

Now, reader, consider for a moment your reaction to that statement. If asked about it, and you answered, you'd probably be convinced that your statement of acceptance or rejection resulted from personal thinking followed by acceptance or rejection. Not so! The person you are—and are always becoming in the situation in which you find yourself at this time could have made no other response.

Your answers or responses are merely awaiting a question or a situation requiring some response. The responses lie in wait for that which will stimulate their expression. They have been acquired knowingly and unknowingly over the course of one's life. You are living in a world chock full of potential questions and other stimulating situations requiring responses.

A few of these have been selected for illustrative purposes:

Do you prefer apple or cherry pie?

Shall you visit Cancun or Maui or stay at home this year?

Is the person you've been dating the one you intend to marry?

In the course of your life, a very large number of other questions and situations keep popping up and you keep supplying the answers and responses automatically. You change in the process. You may believe that you are thinking and in control, but you are merely a conduit for these reactions. And anyone, everyone, anything and everything in contact with you constantly changes you and adds to your armamentarium of answers and reactions. You are not even the same person you were when you began to read this paragraph!

Inasmuch as you never had any choices regarding the formative processes that resulted in the current "you," you really make no choices. You have no control over the conduct of your life. You never have. You never will. To further complicate this matter, no one could ever identify the determinants of your answers/responses and their interactions.

You may continue to believe that you are making choices and asserting control, that you are making thoughtful independent judgments. That belief has been established by the same processes that I have suggested and will now attempt to illuminate. You could not believe otherwise. Your resistance to changing that belief has been established in the manner I've suggested, and you will continue to hold those and other beliefs. Your resistance to change is incredibly resistant to change.

Almost as an aside, I must point out that my approach, while concentrating on human beings, encompasses all living things. While some anthropomorphic souls might endow some animals with an element of choice and control, its absence in plants seems obvious. In my formulation, no living thing ever has any real choice or control over its behavior or future courses of action. It's always been that way. It will always be that way.

It would be best from my standpoint if you would adopt an open-minded, free-swinging approach to understanding what I am about to say. And while I suggest this, I realize that you really have **no choice** in this matter. You are who you are, forever more dynamic process than person. Either you will entertain my notions, reject them out of hand, or respond in some way in between, but your stance was established prior to my statement and any consequent need for a reaction. For some, my position will make "common sense." For others, it will be the product of the wild-eyed hallucinations from an inhabitant of some Never-Never Land or the pronouncements of an Anti-Christ. For most, the viewpoints will be so highly individualized that they cannot be categorized. And think hard as these others might, none of the above will have any choice in their beliefs in this matter.

Basic Positions: The Thurstonian Theory of Life

1. You are an incredibly complicated, unique individual. There is no one else in the world like you. But before you get unduly proud about this, you must realize that this can be said about each and every other person in the entire world and any person who has ever lived. Furthermore, no one has ever had any real independently-generated input into the process. You just happened. You are continuing to happen. You cannot really take any pride—nor experience any guilt—regarding the person you are and are constantly in the process of becoming. At any moment, one is a product of one's past and current circumstance. Each of us is a unique and constantly developing person. This development results from experiences that we fortuitously encounter in the course of living. To paraphrase Barnacle Bill, the sailor, "We are what we are, and that's all we are." (As should be obvious; you have no choice as to whether or not you'd be pumped up or downtrodden by this revelation. You may not even understand what is involved.)

2. While you may willingly accept my statement regarding your uniqueness, you very probably have never delved into the matter deeply. While you will probably disagree, you really don't know very much about yourself, and you certainly haven't a clue as to most of the specific important determinates of the person you have always been in the process of becoming.

3. I propose that you delve into this matter deeply. But as I've proclaimed before, you don't really have any choice in the matter. It's already established whether you will or won't engage in this self-study. In this treatise, you have already read and will read this message that I repeat again and again. You may or may not find this tiresome. You might reject it out of hand. But before you engage in that rejection, you must realize that I myself really have no choice in stating that position repeatedly. I must make such repetitious statements. They were there all along, merely awaiting the appropriate opportunity for expression. That opportunity was before me at this time. I have no "choice."

4. You will have to "mind boggle" if you continue. Maybe you can't do that. You really don't have any choice in the matter. If you proceed, you will have to consider a mind-boggling, mind-blowing complexity of determinants of your personality that are clearly beyond your understanding and anyone else's as well. As I've suggested before, it's my intention to identify three very general classes of determinants: Nature, Nurturance, and Chance. Virtually all of the specific ingredients of these determinants can never be explicitly identified, described, or defined.

5. This attempt to understand your complex uniqueness and that of all other living things as well, represents nothing new. Asking "Why?" about oneself and others has probably been going on since the time man began to think. An ancient example: "Why doesn't Og want to share his fire with me?" On a much more current note, why of all the things in the world I might be doing at this moment, am I composing this "Magnum Opus" and why do I facetiously call it that? Why do I listen to an abundance of classical music selections and hear something new in them each time? Why are you reading this when there are so many other things that you might be doing? The list of examples is endless. The answers are superficial at best. "I do these things because I do them," is both accurate and devoid of any useful insights or understanding.

6. It might be useful to look at yourself as a kind of "point man" in the contact of your life. At any time, you are chock full of near infinite number of responses or reactions that are awaiting an appropriate stimulation for expression. The stimulus often appears on a Chance basis. The response in turn occasionally changes the individual. The same stimulation later on may or may not lead to the same response.

7. Religiousi have heavy instruments and beliefs regarding this matter of uniqueness. "You are made in the image of God," is one of them. They claim to know so many things about people. Many philosophers, psychologists, psychiatrists, and a few laymen have spent lifetimes developing theories designed to understand people and their problems. Many of these alleged authorities have prospered by supplying answers. They claim to <u>know</u>. And they probably believe that they do <u>know</u>.

At best, their controversial positions have provided mere opinions and untestable hypotheses. In response to a great and continuing need, they set forth purported answers to important questions. Some have attained great fame and status as they meet this great need to know. And of course, most have rarely, if ever, been held accountable; required to tell what they know and their justification for that belief. "In the land of the blind, the one-eyed man is king." If they ever were put in the cross-hairs of a scientifically-based examination of their belief system, they would come up short, maybe empty. The conclusion of such investigations would be inescapable: **No one really knows much of anything important about themselves or any other living thing**.

8. Religious believers rarely lend themselves to rational discussion, and if you have gotten a bit of the drift of where I'm coming from, I really have had no choice regarding this position. The person I happen to be at this moment makes that statement and all other decisions for me. The beliefs of the Religiousi are similarly determined although they will reject this position as out of hand. I don't condemn them; for them the rejection was automatic. No real choice was involved.

   A succinct statement of the differences between the Thurston position and that of the Religiosi is in order.

   Religious statement: "There, but for the grace of God, go I." Usually the statement refers to a criminal or ne'er-do-well, although it could apply to a nuclear physicist, Sister Theresa, or anyone else in this world.

   Thurston statement: "There, but for the mindless whims of Nature, Nurturance, and Chance, go I."

   In either formulation, no individual is seen as having any real control over his or her life. In the former, an omniscient and omnipotent God really calls the shots; prayers merely create the illusion of control. In the latter, Dame Fortune or Chance is the determining factor. Chance enters into the determination of the Nature of both Nature (genes) and Nurturance (experience). Chance can trump either or both on occasion, i.e. a single Chance event can significantly alter an individual's life in important and unpredictable ways. Said in a different way, the behavior of the "you" that you are at any split second is determined by your genetics and personal experience as you respond to the situation confronting you. You then become a different person because of the consequences of your act. You react and change constantly throughout your life.

   "Free will" advocates have unwittingly come to believe in "free will" because of highly individual forces and factors beyond their control. To be convincing regarding the validity of their position, they would be required to identify the time and circumstances under which individuals become emancipated from programming ("shackles") imposed upon them by their Nature, Nurture, their worlds, and Chance. And they have never done this. Nor will they ever be able to do so.

9. Freud and other personality theorists have developed their views in response to a great and persistent need on the part of people to understand themselves and the people who surround them. They promise far more than they can deliver. Their theories are simplistic, simple as in simple-minded, i.e. naïve, pretentious, incapable of surviving even mild critical scrutiny.

Some theorists have produced useful techniques that are helpful in understanding and resolving personal problems. Albert Ellis' ABCs and Carl Rogers' client-centered approach are good examples. When employed, they sometimes work well and at other times, they do not. Protestations of the proponents of any school of thought notwithstanding, there is little understanding of the basis for their successes or their failures.

Freud has always been over-rated, albeit venerated. While seemingly complicated, his views are simplistic and close to being useless in any practical sense. For example, he would have us "understand" a great deal about the behavior of women because they were "pining for a penis." Freudians believe that the lack of that valued organ determined and controlled a large part of women's lives.

Where did he get that nutty notion? The source lies in Freud's contact with a few disturbed women whose problems may have stemmed from competition with males. He then generalized this highly questionable assertion to apply to all of womankind. Freud's theory, all dressed up in the words of psychobabble, was supposed to provide an understanding of people and their problems. That never really came about.

The medical establishment has employed its medical model in its efforts to understand people and deal with their issues. While this approach has worked well with physical diseases, it's pathetically ineffectual in trying to understand the complexities and problems of people. In it, people are diagnosed (compartmentalized) and then treated on the basis of their diagnosis. Individuality is lost as people are crammed into diagnostic categories such as schizophrenia and depression solely on the basis of ill-defined similarities in behavior.

In the past, there have been relatively few of these categories. There has been a virtual explosion of psychiatric diagnoses in the latest Diagnostic and Statistical Manual (DSM). If a person cannot be crammed into a category, a new "mental illness" is provided, e.g. Post-Traumatic Stress Disorders, bipolar disorders, shyness, hoarding syndrome, and Attention Deficit Disorders. People inhabiting these categories are then accorded essentially the same sort of treatment. Sad to relate, the treatment is usually drugs. The incredible uniqueness of the individual and the issues confronting him are lost in the process. **But then, a complete, in-depth understanding of each individual is impossible. Psychiatrists seem to have given up trying to understand the people they treat.**

Within the constraints of ignorance and stratospheric prices, responsible mental health care is impossible for almost anyone. The customary prescription of pills is cost-effective while creating the illusion that treatment is being provided. At best, serious personal problems are quelled rather than cured.

CHAPTER 1

Perspective
A Comprehensive View of the Determinants of the Behavior of All Living Things

Part A
A History

On April 16, 2008, Edward Lorenz, the father of Chaos Theory, died at the age of 90 in his home in Cambridge, Massachusetts.

Lorenz was a professor at the Massachusetts Institute of Technology when he came up with the scientific concept that small events lead to big changes, something that he called "The Butterfly Effect."

He explained how something as miniscule as a butterfly flapping its wings in Brazil began a long and complex chain of events that could eventually trigger tornadoes in Texas or Hurricane Katrinas. It should be pointed out that other forces immediately interact with this butterfly and change the impact of its flapping. In many forms, these impacts and change continue to operate in an incredibly complex fashion that powers and changes the dynamic process all the way from the butterfly's flapping to the cataclysmic events in the example.

Meteorologists of today are said to base their forecasts on Lorenz's theoretical formulations.

In principle, this makes common sense, but its application is another matter. It improves weather forecasting, but that may not be saying much. Maybe the preceding one-line paragraph should be changed from "to base their forecasts on" to "to have their forecasts influenced by" Lorenz's theoretical formulations. When and where can the meteorologist take measurements or make observations that are useful in making predictions regarding the next steps in the sequence and ultimately the event? Currently, this is an important unanswered question. Ongoing studies may very well provide answers.

Specifically, regarding Hurricane Katrina, what were the crucial signposts and when could they have been noted? No one talks about butterflies. A dropping barometer in Cuba? Selected measurements in the eye of this hurricane? Increasing the lead time—the time from awareness to onset—by even a few minutes can have significant consequences in the case of cataclysmic events. With computers, visual representations, and a Chaotic stance, we have come a long way from simply looking at the Gulf of Mexico south of New Orleans, noting a huge cloud, and concluding that a big storm is about to descend upon us. However, we haven't come as far as some meteorologists would lead us to believe.

Chaos Theory tells weathermen where to look, and most importantly, humbles them with its formulation of the enormity and complexity of the process that they must evaluate as they predict the weather.

Part B
A Continuing Thread

I suggest to you that the same theory may be applied to human behavior as well. Any behaviors of yours—and I mean any and all, ranging from refusal of a second cup of coffee to career decisions to proposals of marriage—can, in theory, be traced to very distant and recent personal "butterflies" in your past.

But if you have been impressed by the enormous difficulties weathermen have and will continue to have in predicting tornados and Hurricane Katrinas, they are insignificant when compared with what is involved in understanding and predicting the actions of humankind. The identification of that single Amazonian butterfly is simple in comparison to determining the distant, early butterflies of human behavior.

It is virtually an impossibility to determine even one or two of the distant butterflies in your personal background that relate to your current behaviors. Attempting to connect such dots is both interesting and challenging.

But Chaos Theory seems to make a lot of common sense in its application to human behavior. It acknowledges our incredible ignorance. We really know only bits and pieces of the determinants of our behavior.

Let's make this analogous to assembling a jigsaw puzzle. It would be challenging to complete the puzzle if you had all the pieces. But you won't. In addition, someone has supplied you with thousands of other pieces that are unrelated to the puzzle you are attempting to put together.

Chaos Theory also indicates clearly that significant progress in understanding ourselves and others is and will always be impossible to accomplish.

Part C
Thurstonian Theory

I'll now begin to explore Thurstonian Theory, a considered, rational way of looking at human development. I'd like to call this a theoretical formulation, but it lacks the precision that that would demand. It is Chaos Theory as it would be applied to humans and other living things. The reader might think that this Thurstonian title is a blatant, transparent exercise in self-aggrandizement. He may be right; he may be wrong.

Thurstonian Theory borrows freely from largely-undefined Chaos Theory, capitalizing on the broad sweep of this "outside the box" thinking while at the same time attempting to make its components reasonably explicit, understandable, and meaningful.

Observations:

1. You, the reader, are an incredibly complex individual.
2. There is no one else in the entire world who is exactly like you.
3. There has never been anyone else exactly like you nor will there ever be one of you again.
4. The same thing can be said about every individual on the face of the earth.
5. How did this come to pass?
6. You haven't a clue as to how incredibly complex you really are (See numbers 1-3 above), but you probably think that you have a pretty good idea.
7. In no sense are you now a finished and complete personality, nor will you ever be. You are more dynamic process than person. You will agree that you are not the same person you were five or ten years ago; the experience of living has accomplished that. You are not the same person you were five minutes or even five seconds ago.
8. You have only the foggiest idea as to who you are and the processes that have been involved in your personal development.
9. You're of the opinion that you're in control of your life and all of the "decisions" and "choices" that you make.
10. You think you have a pretty good understanding of all this.
11. You are wrong on numbers eight through ten.

12. You very probably agree or disagree with the previous statements even partially or en toto. This is understandable. While an ignorant point of view, it's reassuring to believe that one is in control of his behavior, that you are making a controlled judgment in this and all other matters. You look around and may envy others who appear to have that capability.

To face and accept the Thurstonian Theory may make one insecure and fearful. Theory states the "control" you believe you exercise is pure illusion. "Choice" and "free will" are clearly self-serving deceptions. The various conceptions of God, while useful and reassuring to many worshippers, are illusions as well. (It follows from Thurstonian Theory that people on opposite side of religious arguments, including atheists, really had no choice in whatever religious position they espouse.)

13. If you disagree with any of the basic assumptions of Thurstonian Theory, your position has been established without any considered thought on your part. You may think that you thought all this through and that you can mount unassailable arguments as to why you are right. That is nonsense; the determinants for your decision were in place before you ever read a word of this. Your judgment was just lying there in wait for an opportunity for you to express it. The same thing is true of all of your other behaviors as well.

14. You feel that you have developed a basis for your disagreement with the Thurstonian Theory, but if asked, you couldn't possibly identify and define any of its alleged sources or "butterflies" and how they interacted over the course of time. You probably have never thought about it in those terms or any others. Most likely, you have uncritically and unknowingly accepted a frame of reference supplied by other people or organizations, and you never knew that as it was happening. Your framework is never established in one fell swoop; these components have been acquired in bits and pieces over the course of your entire life, often without your knowledge, awareness, or control. According to Thurstonian Theory, there is a near-infinite number of such "butterfly" components in each and every one of our backgrounds.

15. You may have latched onto some psychological/psychiatric theory to provide a framework for understanding yourself and others. Freudians emphasize the role of the family in your personal development, particularly that of the mother. Psychiatrists tend to emphasize the brain and the effects of medication and surgery upon your "abnormal" behavior. Dr. Phil has his own notions. There are as many different points of view as there are people expressing them.

16. **Any frame of reference you have selected in standard or modified form (12-14) is incredibly simplistic, irrational, and indefensible. If you rely upon it uncritically, you will be misled.** No one could possibly identify and utilize the enormous number of the determinants, "the "butterflies" and their incredible interactive complexity that would be necessary to understand who you are and how you got that way.

17. Thurstonian Theory poses an infinite number of questions. They provide no answers. If understood, the determinants of your behavior are mind-boggling in their complexity. If you think that you really know what I mean by this, think again.

Thurstonian Theory depicts a complexity that clearly surpasses our ability to understand. Its basic ingredients can never be explicitly identified nor defined. Even if they could be, the complex nature of their interactions would forever escape identification and definition.

18. As you have no real control over your actions or thoughts, you have no responsibility for them.

But if one reads this and thinks about it a bit, one can develop awareness of how very little we can ever come to know about ourselves. It follows then, that we can never truly understand much about others as well.

Part D
The Need to "Mind-Boggle"

We will now return to the familiar "butterfly to hurricane" development that was used to exemplify Chaos Theory. If a specific butterfly hadn't fluttered, a complicated, continuing series of events would not have followed, and a hurricane would not have taken place. All one has to do is retrace all intervening events in sequence and the true source and course of the hurricane can be ascertained. Like so many things, the wisdom of "the retrospect" gets higher grades than any thoughts employed in prediction.

Now, the preceding paragraph describes some major league mind-boggling, but it's nothing compared to what is involved in the Thurstonian Theory regarding personal development. A hurricane would be child's play. That deals only with physical factors and forces. (For the mind-boggler, the analogy between a hurricane and a person is already apparent.) By way of comparison, the step-by-step sequential development of personality would have to take into consideration **everything** that is going on in the world during the time frame of that development, and most importantly, *before* as well.

To get something of a grasp of the deep and widespread implications of the Thurstonian Theory, you must "mind-boggle," a term for thinking creatively "outside the box." An initial admission of your ignorance is an absolute necessity for useful mind-boggling. You must be willing to consider anything and everything freely and openly in a maximum effort to address and remedy your incredible ignorance. However, Thurstonian Theory contains an element of "Catch-22" within it. They say that by the very nature of the person you are in the process of becoming, you have no choice regarding your mind boggling as well as any of your other behaviors. At this moment, you can or cannot mind boggle. Only mind-bogglers can proceed from this point.

If you miss the cut, but still stand in there and try, you'll come up with some half-assed, inhibited, and unsatisfactory mind boggling. Genuine mind-bogglers should not be smug. The Thurstonian Theory states that if any one of a thousand of truly significant events in the person's life had not taken place, he or she might have been rendered incapable of mind boggling.

In summary, two of the ingredients of Thurstonian Theory are **Nature** and **Nurture**. There's nothing new in this. The former is sometimes called genetics, or "the way we're wired." The latter refers to the human and physical environment surrounding us. **The third, really a form of Nurturance, is the under-emphasized factor called "Chance," "Dame Fortune," fortuitous and unpredictable events.**

Chance has never been accorded the attention it deserves.

Part E
Nature/Heredity

I may have misled you into thinking too simplistically about heredity, e.g. understanding your heredity in terms of that which you believe you inherited from your father and mother. ("You have your father's fixtures and your mother's features.") Let's go far beyond this superficial approach.

In Thurstonian Theory, your heredity must go all the way back to include **all of your ancestors**, even the earliest ones, i.e. Adam and Eve, cavemen, apes, reptilians, primordial ooze, etc.

Now, as we try to become mind bogglers and mind-boggle along, it should be pointed out that the genetic component of the Thurstonian Theory has little practical significance in answering basic and important questions of who you are and how you got this way. Trying to relate any ancient or more recent genetic material to your current circumstance isn't feasible. But in theory, such an ancestral connection remains a possibility. Concentration on more recent ancestors will be more rewarding, but never forget that each of these men and women had ancestors who may have had genetic impact upon them, and inferentially, upon you, and the Nature of these impacts is generally unavailable to you.

This goes far beyond skin or eye color. Some say that you may be genetically programmed to develop problems such as diabetes, a heart condition, breast cancer, or depression. Current research in this area is very promising.

You had no say or choice in any determination of any of the genetic components of your personality. Most people would agree with that statement. (To introduce a bit of facetious commentary, I'll repeat the statement alleged to be told by grand-grand-grand-grand-grandfather of the reader. Although its source is open to mind-boggling speculation, Grand-daddy is said to have said sometime in his life, "If I'd known how he—the reader—was going to turn out, I'd have 'opted out' of participating in intercourse on that occasion of long ago.")

You have already made a judgment about my theory and perhaps about me. You think or have thought that you had a choice or a decision regarding this.

You have not! All determinants for that "choice" or "decision" were in place, pre-determined or programmed, if you will. You understood or didn't understand my Grand-daddy joke. Once the question was posed, you simply articulated the appropriate, pre-determined words or thought. All determinants were in place. Considering the person you were at the moment of that decision, your judgment could not have been otherwise.

I'm neither offended by your disagreement nor made happy by your agreement with the foregoing statements nor by any position you have taken or will ever take. As you have no control nor say in whom you are, you have no choice or say in the making of any "decision." I had no choice in any judgment that I have just made. "It just happened. It had to be this way." I will repeat this over and over, again and again, during the course of this treatise. Some might refer to this as a litany of mine.

Part F
Nurturance

When we come to environmental determinants or **Nurturance**, they are really "complexity compounded." By way of comparison, genetic or ancestral determinants of an individual and his behavior are relatively simple. The reader must shift into the highest of gears of his mind-boggling mode.

Environmental determinants include **all internal or external contacts the individual has ever had with people and his physical universe**. This statement is truly mind boggling.

In theory, this also includes all the past internal and external contacts of all individuals who come into contact with the individual we are trying to understand. If you understand and accept this, you are truly into mind boggling. You must continue on and on until you have exhausted not only the current population of the world, but previous populations of the world all the way back to the beginning of time. Now that is real mind-boggling. "Ask not for whom the bell tolls, it tolls for thee."

Isn't it clearly understood why some current theories of personality are much more acceptable than mine? **My theory, correctly stating the complexity of the matter, poses profound questions while you want answers**. For example, Alfred Adler promises you answers about a person based mostly upon the person's birth order, and answers will be forthcoming as this approach is employed. They can be used in making important decisions about that individual. They will be wrong. Things just aren't that simple.

If nothing else, Thurstonian Theory should make the reader very humble regarding how much he or she can understand himself/herself or anyone else for that matter.

It speaks directly to the uniqueness of each and every individual who has ever been on earth.

Part G
Chance

Chance cannot be overestimated as an important factor in understanding how people become the individuals they are.

I'll provide some examples to illustrate the part that **Chance** plays in Thurstonian Theory.

1. Conjure up some of your own. You must have hundreds of examples when something out of the blue occurred that had important impact upon you and your life. It is the ifs and the ifs that didn't take place that need identification. They occur at important forks in the road of an individual's life. Life is never the same again.

   If its and buts
   Were candy and nuts
   We'd all have a Merry Christmas

   If ifs and coulds
   Were sticks of wood
   We certainly could
   And most assuredly should
   Have a big bonfire.

2. If for any reason any ancestor of yours hadn't shown up for intercourse on that night, s/he wouldn't be your ancestor and you would not be here today. Where you would be is another question!

Intelligent Design, favored by those given to a God and religiosity, pretty much rules out Chance. They believe that there is something or someone up or out there somewhere who has a handle on all the factors, forces, interactions, and outcomes that I have included in what I call Thurstonian Theory. It's reassuring to believe that "There's someone minding the store."

In Summary

In what I regard as an exercise in grandiosity, I'll attempt to gather and systematize my thoughts and misgivings regarding the development of an individual's personality. After all, my theorizing addresses the topic long thought to be the territory of alleged "experts" such as Freud, Maslow, Albert Ellis, and more recently, various biochemists. All of these have something in common: They believe that they "knew." They have something else in common: They didn't "know."

I shall approach this theorizing with a listing of self-evident truths and some assumptions which are anything but self-evident. The reader is encouraged to attempt to make these distinctions.

1. You, the reader, are an incredible, complexly-determined individual. You are clearly one of a kind. I'm in absolute agreement with this.

2. You may have spent some time trying to understand yourself and how you got to be this way. I whole-heartedly applaud introspection and attempts at self-appraisal. Success in such ventures is required if one is to "accentuate the positive, eliminate the negative" elements in one's lifestyle.

3. In acknowledging that you are "one of a kind," some people would be satisfied in saying that "they threw away the pattern" after you were created. While that has a nice sound to it, there was no pattern.

4. A lot of people have tried to understand people. This search has occupied the time and attention of endless numbers of psychologists, philosophers, religionists, politicians, Ann Landers, Dr. Phil, etc. Some attain an enduring fame as they become Freudians, Darwinians, and the like. Some have fashioned lucrative careers based on these searches and the positions they take. I applaud their efforts. I then dismiss their findings as simplistic and unhelpful. They're of little use to anyone who is seriously trying to understand self. The reader might find that these statements smack of grandiosity, but as we shall see shortly, "That's just the kind of guy/psychologist I am." I really had no choice as I developed and expressed these opinions.

5. Speaking of grandiosity, I summarily dismiss out-of-hand any notions that some God created you. For some readers, my statement is the equivalent of a "stop order." You'll read no further. But if you did, you might find out why I think that you should consider stopping.

6. You were idiosyncratic, special, and unique in a genetic sense from the get-go. That makes sense to me, but that genetic determination was accomplished in an incredibly complex manner that has never received the attention that it deserves. I shall mention it, at least.

7. Your "persona" or personality never stops growing from the time of your conception until the moment of your death. While you may readily accept this statement in principle, you may have some difficulty in applying it to your everyday life.

   a. You are not the same person that you were ten years ago.
   b. You are not the same person that you were five minutes ago.
   c. You will be a different person five minutes from now and most assuredly five or ten years down the pike.

Let's back up a bit and contemplate what went on to produce your DNA.

   a. You had no "say" or choice in the determination.
   b. Despite this, your DNA will be an important determinant of your personality, the "self" that you are becoming. If it were different, you would be and become a different person. I believe that to be a self-evident truth.

Your eye or hair color is determined in this manner, but is of little consequence.

Race and gender are so determined and are of great consequence.

It is a rare month that goes by without new scientific discoveries involving the impact of genetic makeup upon important aspects of one's life. There appears to be a genetic link to one's longevity, Alzheimer's, and a host of physical ailments. At the very least, it can be said that the genes contribute to a predisposition to develop physical problems. Whether or not there must be a "psychosocial" trigger for them is still under investigation.

Your genetic history goes a long way back.

Genealogists will tell you how difficult it is to find out what went on even a few generations ago.

Your family history required a lot of matings. If any one of these thousand upon thousand of matings and consequent conceptions had not occurred, you, the reader, would not be here today.

Why did all of these take place? We'll never know! I can state that with absolute assurance and authority. Knowing what you don't know is an important first step toward developing understanding of virtually anything.

Keeping it relatively simple, why did you parents hook up? We can be general in our approach to answering that question or, being inquisitive, why did they hook up on a special day or night? There are real problems in getting these answers. It may be clearly "no-no" country for many, a topic that's not to be discussed. Your parents might not know the answers. Some may never have thought about it. Many would never talk about this subject. "I just looked at him across the room and knew that he was the one," does not stand up to scientific scrutiny.

Each parent was at one time conceived. Their respective DNAs were established, and then the environment took over. If their experience in the womb would be characterized as "intrauterine bliss," they would be born as individuals quite different from those born to a "crack head" or who had suffered from some disease during the course of her pregnancy, e.g. rubella. There are probably as yet undetermined factors which could complicate a pregnancy.

Each child is born of these parents and eventually became an adult. What was involved in this? Once again, we do not and cannot know. All parents participate in a huge and unknowable number of interactions with people and their physical environment.

It seems reasonable to believe that all people and all of their predecessors had been subjected to a similar huge and unknowable number of such interactions.

Your background thus involves an enormous number of other people, your ancestors and all of the people each interacted with...and all of the people who had interacted with them...and on ad infinitum.

Do you truly realize the enormity and complexity of these interactions? I'm talking in terms of billions.

The ancient Greeks would have had great difficulty trying to figure out interactions associated with their origins. They tried the idol, Gods, and star routes, but their efforts are simple in comparison with yours. You have so many more interactions to consider.

Probably most of these distant interactions with people and the physical environment had no impact upon the nature of your personality, but some might have. You will never even know about almost all of them, let alone which ones were influential and why they were.

Now, scientists would like to have us believe that it is possible to develop a formula and identify these interactions and cram it all into a computer that will then disgorge both understanding and predictability of human behavior.

On the face of it, such a computer-oriented formula would be impossible to establish. Many scientists proceed as though it were feasible. They defend their piddling studies on the grounds that they are but first steps toward achieving that noble objective. The problem with these studies is that there is rarely a second or third step. The scientists often sidestep or step back or step aside and take another first step in another area. As a consequence, they are going nowhere. The formula seems to be an illusory part of an impossible dream.

Even if this grandiose formula became a reality, it could never be used to predict behavior. Why? It's because Chance factors intrude. "The best laid plans of mice and men often go awry." Chance rules! All the understanding and planning we can generate regarding ourselves and others can be overridden by a single fortuitous, absolutely unpredictable event.

Accordingly, we'll never know what makes us tick.

At best, we can come up with a working hypothesis regarding our personality development. With it, it's possible to develop a framework that we can use to identify our strengths and weaknesses, capitalizing on the former and eliminating the latter as much as possible.

8. I hold that we really have no real "choice" involving anything we do. You, the reader, really had no choice in believing or disbelieving that statement. All of your thoughts and behavior, including this one involving your beliefs, are pre-determined by "Chance factors" interacting with your genetics as they interact with your experiential background.

This holds true in simple matters. If I were to ask you who were the best President of the United States, you might pause and consider the matter before responding. My position is that your response was pre-determined as was your consideration, contemplative pause, and your answer. You may have thought that you had a choice, but you didn't.

This also holds true regarding such complex matters such as selection of marital partner or occupation.

As I've said, this holds true for all of your thoughts and behaviors.

Does this suggest that you are complexly floating through your life sans real control over your conduct and what becomes of you? Yes!

You might protest. You would like to think that you have "free will" or "independent choice," or that you are the captain of your ship. To establish this, it would be incumbent upon you to state the time you sprang free from the shackles of your past and the circumstances that enabled you to do so.

CHAPTER 2

Three Determinants of Personality

For the purposes of discussion, I choose to identify three major classes of determinants:

A. **Nature** (genetics)
B. **Nurturance** (environment)
C. **Chance**

You, at this very moment and during the moment that you just experienced and the next moment up the line, are a complex collage, the momentary end result of the intermingling of your genetics, environmental experiences, and Chance. Chance is far more important in this determination than anyone realizes.

Nature and **Nurturance** have received the bulk of attention over the years. In the main, they and their basic elements have been studied separately. Although it would be common sense, their incredibly complicated interactions—Nature working with Nurturance—have not received much attention. Perhaps more importantly, Chance has been ignored in most theoretical formulations.

But it would seem reasonable that all of the many ingredients in each of **Nature, Nurturance,** and **Chance** interact, intermingling, constantly in an incredibly active, dynamic process, changing every millisecond, that continues from the moment of an individual's conception to his death.

A brief sketching of some of these ingredients and their interactions allow the reader to fill in the blanks and explore the possibilities of the aforementioned scenario.

A. Nature (Genetics)

My knowledge of genetics is anything but sophisticated, complete, and current. One's genetic pool and all that derives from it is determined by your ancestry all the way back time immemorial. Sometimes genetics is referred to as "wiring." One's genetics have long been thought to be fixed and immutable. That view is out of date and wrong.

Genetics is the element of your being for which you are programmed or "wired" by your ancestry. Its near infinite complexity is only now beginning to be studied. Not too long ago, the genetic, "wired" component of your being was exemplified by such characteristics as eye, hair, and skin color—all clearly observable at birth.

Now, with DNA studies, research into the genetic component of your personality extends a multiplicity of observable and non-observable physical and mental characteristics that become manifest at varying times throughout the life of the individual. Examples include diseases such as cancer, Alzheimer, or depression. The basis for these and many other diseases may lie in wait for expression at some later age. Scientists now hold out the possibility that these genes can be modified. This suggests that many diseases are not inevitable and can be prevented through such interventions.

In the 2009 Presidential Election, some even suggested that a liberal point of view was genetically determined, and there is a developing body of evidence that genes can be modified **in a negative sense** by one's lifestyle (*Newsweek*, June 23, 2008). "Lifestyle influences a person's risk for cancer by generating growth-promoting signals that affect cells primed to become cancerous. What primes these cells to become cancerous in the first place? What are the changes in their genes?" For example, it's hypothesized that red meat cooked at high temperatures generates potent mutagens called heterocyclic amines that could alter genes and possibly cause cancer.

For your strongest consideration, your genetic "wiring" is the result of untold numbers of matings that took place over millennia. If any one of those had not taken place, your "wiring" would be different. The you that you have selected for self-study would be very different in a multitude of knowable ways. "You" wouldn't be able to make any such selection because "you" wouldn't exist.

It may be helpful for you to consider yourself as the top card of a tall house of cards that is perhaps 50 or 100 or 1,000 feet high. The horizontal cards represent mating. The supporting cards represent a male and a female ancestor. If any one of those cards was displaced and the mating of two of your ancestors did not take place on a given day of the month, then your current house of cards would not exist, and you would not be sitting on top of it.

Admonition: Any in-depth, complete understanding of the important genetic element of your being, your wiring is beyond you or anyone else. Undue contemplation of the genetic contribution of your ancestors, while inherently interesting, can't add much to your self-understanding.

B. Nurturance

This determinant includes anything and everything that has ever happened to you from the moment of your conception until your death. To wrap your mind around this concept requires uninhibited mind-boggling. As mentioned before, you may or may not be capable of doing this.

Your Nurturance includes all interactions you have had with people and elements of your physical universe.

Focusing on people for a moment, it must be remembered that each of them is as complex as you, as complexly-determined products of their Nature and Nurture as you, and in the same constant state of flux/change/growth as you. This volatility holds true for your forbears, your family, and all others who have ever been in contact with you.

Admonition: It's obvious that any in-depth, complete understanding of these important formative factors in your personality is beyond your capabilities and those of anyone else.

In line with this, it's okay to admit that there are many things that we can never know. One of them happens to be the details of the process by which your "being" was formed.

C. Chance

Your life may be an "exercise in serendipity." Like it or not, you are forever making plans which will bear only a minimal resemblance to what you will eventually do.

Consider the fortuitous, happenstance encounters of varying duration involving you and Nature/Nurturance. Mind-boggling thought is required yet again to consider in depth all the incredible implications of that statement.

The impact can be positive or negative.

The importance of Chance in the formulation of your personality is too often neglected or omitted by personality theorists. They have enough trouble trying to impose a semblance of order upon events and circumstances that they can readily identify.

By definition, Chance events cannot be anticipated. Their occurrence introduces further chaos into the chaotic process that is personality development. The importance of various Chance events may or may not be understood at the time of their occurrence. They certainly interfere with the simplistic orderliness of most personality formulations. Some Chance events are trivial; some may be of monumental importance.

Consider if you will what would you be if you had been born into the Eighteenth Century as opposed to the Twentieth or Twenty-first Century?

Comment

Professionals and laymen alike who are interested in understanding themselves and others have simplistically divided the determinants of personality into two very general classes: Nature and Nurturance. It is interesting to note that so many simplistically frame this as a Nature **versus** Nurturance debate as they attempt to understand individuals. This either/or classification of determinants belies the truth that every action on the part of any individual at any time is the product of both Nature and Nurturance working in complex interaction...and **more.** The "more" is Chance, the fortuitous factor that is missing or lacks emphasis in the formulations of most, if not all, attempts to understand the human condition.

Chance involves the happening of important, personally-impacting events that lack apparent cause or design. The word "apparent" deserves some attention for there is always a cause for every action or event. We simply don't know what it is; "Stuff happens."

People have no monopoly on complexity. All other living forms are complex as well, but lack human strengths, i.e. some lack mobility, language, intelligence, capacity to learn, early death, etc.

Every living thing from ant to zebra is far more complexly determined than people realize. This important, all-inclusive truth won't receive any additional attention in this treatise that is to follow. I shall concentrate on the reader and humankind. My plate is more than full. I'll run the understanding of human complexity into the ground in this writing. Its importance, magnitude, and range cannot be exaggerated.

Summary

Now is the time that I step aside and allow you the opportunity to consider the validity of my assertions. But at the same time, you are reminded that the kind of person you have become and are becoming is the result of the incredible, continuing interactions of Nature, Nurturance, and Chance. Those interactions have already established your reaction to this opportunity to consider and challenge the aforementioned validity of my assertions. **You really have no choice or control in the matter. You really have had no choice or control regarding any decision you're making at this split second that you've made in the past or that you'll make in the future.** This includes opining about my viewpoints.

"There, but for the grace of God, go I," or looking at this matter in the **Thurstonian** way, **"There, but for differing genes and experiential (all of the experiences since conception) background and whims of Chance, go I."**

Your being or self constantly evolves. As a result, you can't possibly come to a complete understanding of your being or self. If you are denied the ability to fully understand yourself, it would follow that you cannot possibly understand others. Many of the ingredients necessary for such understanding are simply unavoidable to you. **Ignorance of self and others is inevitable.**

CHAPTER 3

Nature

I have been sorely tempted to leave this entire chapter blank. That would convey to the reader the enormity of my ignorance regarding up-to-date information regarding the current and developing role of genetics in understanding how people grow and develop. It deserves more than any superficial treatment I might provide by checking out Wikipedia or some newspaper headlines.

Genetics (Nature) contains many demonstrated and potential determinants. This discipline provides the basis for some useful insights, but these pale into relative insignificance when compared with what might lie ahead.

Now that the reader has been forewarned and forearmed regarding my credentials or lack thereof, I shall proceed with some thoughts I have had about Nature and its role in understanding living things.

By way of background the incredibly complex development of your personality; let us begin by conceptualizing your "self" as a tangible, dynamic, active, growing, ever-changing, evolving, pulsating, ill-defined "being." You—and everyone else—are indeed one of a kind.

This "being" originates from the interaction of two other beings, your parents and other ancestors. They supply the genetic component (Nature), the DNA, genomes, that are crucial in your being's development. They were supplied by their parents', who were supplied by their parents' and on and on back a very long ways. This makes sense to the general public. For example, people can readily believe that eye and skin color are genetically determined. "It runs in the family." It is harder for people to believe that this DNA contains incredibly complex encoding and potentially a time table for the development of truly important events in one's life, e.g. the development of liver disease or Alzheimer's, one's religion or political affiliation. The last two sound especially far-fetched, but they cannot be ruled out. It's my belief that we've only begun to scratch the surface of what Nature supplies in the form of determinants of our personality.

Time (October 22, 2012) is enthusiastic in its endorsement of genome research and the importance of its findings. National Geographic (February 2014) finds "The New Science of the Brain" to be a most promising field.

It would make explanations simpler if DNA were the sole determinant of your being. Even though your genetics are complexity incarnate, it would simplify matters in comparison to the degree of complexity I suggest during the entirety of this treatise. DNA is but one very complex component amongst many others.

There is something of a "Catch-22" involved in some of the uninhibited thinking and creativity that I advocate for the reader. My point of view is that you, as an adult reader, have had your illusion of "Choice" in this matter and many others, already determined by the "being" you have become over these many years. You really have no choice in anything you do even though you believe that you do this routinely. This latter misconception is thoroughly engrained in your ever-developing "being."

Let's talk a little bit more about your DNA with an eye to exploring its incredibly complex determination. You received your DNA from your parents, who in turn got their DNA from their parents, and on and on back to maybe Adam and Eve. Your highly-individualized DNA is the end result of an incredibly long and complex chain of human interactions. That chain, called "Chain One" for my purposes, could have been broken fortuitously many times along the way, but it wasn't. It any of your forbears, for whatever reason, had not been available for mating, perhaps on a given day or night, then the "being" that you think you know and understand would not be here reading this book.

If you think about this deeply and at length, and I urge you to do just that, consider the infinite complexity of this "causal chain." Consider if you will the role of Chance in this extended, complicated process. What if any one of your forebears had died of yellow fever or was killed in an accident on the way home?

Chain Two suggests another key ingredient in the determination of your DNA. In addition to Chance, there are individual differences in the way your forbears reacted to an opportunity which presented itself. While their DNAs may have provided some input, the more crucial factors undoubtedly involve their experiences with their environment. **Nurturance** is an all-inclusive term containing anything and everything that involved an interaction of the developing "being" and his surroundings. While physical surroundings are part of this, the most important interactions involve people. And as I would hope to emphasize elsewhere, each of these developing "beings" with whom you interact is also being formed because of the aforementioned **Nature** and **Nurturance** factors.

If you take the time to consider this matter fully, and I urge you to do just that, you are bound to be impressed by how truly unique you are, not only in a genetic sense. Go back beyond your parents and grandparents, perhaps to the beginning of time. You might be very surprised at who some of your relative are. In the 2007-09 election campaign, Barack Obama and Vice President Dick Cheney were alleged to be related. It has been reported rather conclusively that all the descendants of Thomas Jefferson include a large components of blacks.

As long as you are thinking about this matter a bit, consider again the role of Chance in this chain of matings. If even one of your ancestors, for any reason, had not been available on a certain conceptual night, the "you" that you know might not be here. The alternate night for mating might have involved a different sperm and/or ovum. You may engage in endless conjecture as to where you would be if that mating had taken place as originally planned.

Your development as a "being" is a function of genetic components supplied by the parents interacting with its environment. In effect, this "being" and its ingredients constitute all that is you/yourself/self. Eventually, the "being" that is you, like all other "beings," will die and vanish (said "being" and its varying manifestations will cease to exist). I'll leave it to theologians to speculate as to where this "being" will end up.

As we shall see, this "being," along with millions upon millions of others is but a miniscule part of a far larger physical/psychological universe, but let's keep it relatively simple for a while. As you might come to realize, there is nothing simple about your personality development and that of others.

Your personality "being" contains all of its genetic components, all the DNA materials that were bestowed upon you by your parents. And I mean all of them. It's difficult for any individual attempting to understand himself to find and employ any useful information in this area. It's something that can only be accepted as a truth, an incredibly complex truth. While one would like to find the "bad seed" in his past that is responsible for his shortcomings, one would find it hard to justify that position on any rational basis.

As with all progress, there are drawbacks associated with the acquisition of knowledge:

1. If a conclusive linkage has been demonstrated between a given gene of yours and the development of Alzheimer disease at 40, would you want to know this at the tender age of 20?

2. If that gene were identified with a child **en utero**, would it be advisable to consider an alteration or elimination of the gene or a possible abortion?

CHAPTER 4

Nurturance

Your "being" is molded by all of your environmental interactions with people and the natural world as well. Pause for more than a moment to consider how much learning that statement encompasses. **I do mean all**. This is Nurturance. This process begins immediately after your conception and continues uninterrupted until your death. This includes the indirect results of all the environmental contacts that all of your predecessors had as well. Had these events not taken place, your predecessors would have been different and their impact upon you would be different as well.

All of this makes you an incredibly unique and complex person. You are one of a kind. You are also lucky to be alive.

Again, take considerable time in contemplation as you try to understand the enormity of your complexity. You may not do this. That decision is determined by the kind of person you are at the very moment you read these words. Some will attempt such introspection; others will not. Still others will not even seriously consider this possibility.

Let us consider an interaction between the complex beings that you and I represent. This interaction between an aspect of our beings is usually oral or visual, although all other senses may be involved singly or interactively.

Let us pause for a moment. Have you accepted or rejected the major tenets of this approach? Or are you somewhere in between? You really believe that you are making enlightened rational personally-controlled decisions in this regard. As you will see later on, my approach indicates that the Nature of your current "being" determines this acceptance or rejection. You have no control regarding this decision. The Nature of your response is well-established long before the questions are posed.

The same holds true for all decisions you make about anything, ranging from trivial (ordering coffee or not) to consequential (selection of occupation or life partner). You have no awareness that this is the case. You very probably reject the possibility.

This position is the basis of all of your decisions and actions. You may think that you are the captain of your ship when in reality, you are a mere passenger. You are pushed and directed by your past (Nature-Nurture-Chance). Free will is an illusion.

Consequences: You have no basis for experiencing pride in or guilt regarding any aspect of your conduct. You are not responsible for anything that you have ever done or will ever do. You had no choice or control.

Interactive Chain

You need no convincing about the importance of family and close friends in the development of your being, and you're right on this count. People you've never known—and never will know—very probably have indirectly impacted your life as well. These strangers may also have impacted your family and close friends. There's no way you can identify any one of these distant strangers, let alone describe just how that individual's actions fit into the interactive chain of events, the linkage to the past that led to the "being" you have become and are still becoming. You might just have to accept the idea that there are important determinants of your "being" that you will never know, and that amongst these is a significant understanding of yourself and those around you. An admission of ignorance is a necessary, crucial step on this road to understanding. It is a gift to be humble.

The concept of an interactive chain is central to my thinking. An example might illustrate how this chain becomes involved in a person's development. If you think about this matter, you'll find hundreds of examples in your own life.

In 1914, an Eau Claire, Wisconsin mother proudly looks out into her backyard at her teenage son who is in the company of his friends. He is handsome. She bursts with pride. At that very moment, another young man in Yugoslavia prepares to leave his home on a mission to assassinate Archduke Ferdinand of Austria. He succeeds.

The successful assassination triggered the beginning of the incredibly complex interactive chains that led to World War I. The Wisconsin mother's son eventually was caught up in that war and died in France during the Battle of the Somme.

The Wisconsin mother never fully recovered from her son's death. Although she lingered on for fifteen years, it could be said that she too died on that French battlefield. That event changed her. She was my grandmother, a woman who was incredibly important to me in my formative years. Thus, that distant event/assassination impacted me as well.

"If" figures prominently in this kind of thinking. "If" the assassination had not taken place, there would have been no World War as we know it. Accordingly, the Wisconsin boy would not have died on a battlefield in France. What would have happened to him if that assassination had not taken place? What would have happened to me if he had been around during my childhood and my important grandma would not have been chronically depressed? We will never know, but a studied contemplation of such questions might allow us to explore one aspect of the incredible complexities involved in the development of our "beings."

Some people are aware of the hypothesis that Hurricane Katrina began with the fluttering of a single butterfly's wings in an Amazon rain forest (See Chapter 1). Some promising research has attempted to identify what happens during the complex "interactive chain" between two such disparate events.

My uncle/grandmother example was selected out of an ongoing chain of billions upon billions of interactions that potentially contribute to the development of each of our "beings." I am an end product of the interactive chain. While you and I are now interacting as you read my writings, I have become part of your chain. Whether or not this becomes significant in the process of your continuing development remains to be seen.

There is no end of examples.

1. A Chinese girl dabbing poisonous lead paint on a doll could lead to the death of your child in the USA.

2. Islamic extremists studying the Koran reached a conclusion that led to the death of nearly 3,000 people in the 9/11 destruction of the World Trade Center.

These interactive chains appear reasonable, i.e. in broad terms; you can accept the concept of linkage. However, consider:

3. Linking the success of an African Watusi hunter to your dinner tonight would be more than challenging, if not impossible.

4. Try linking the behavior of the Yugoslavian assassin to yours as you're reading what I've written, but even such far-fetched examples as these are possible and meaningful under my scheme of things. You might conjure up a few examples of your own, ranging from the reasonable to the flat-out nearly impossible. To tantalize you a bit, I believe that you haven't any choice in deciding whether you will enter into the introspection that I've just suggested. The world and its people are incredibly complex.

John Donne put this sort of thinking in another wondrous yet more limited way. "Each man's death diminishes me, For I am involved in mankind. Therefore, send not to know for whom the (funeral) bell tolls, it tolls for thee."

I'll extend this further. It could be said that each living or any deceased woman or man who has ever lived, known or unknown to me, influences me, for I am involved in all of mankind. Furthermore, as I am one with Nature, anything in the physical world that has ever happened (and I mean everything) has the potential for influencing me. If all the implications of this statement are fully understood, it will boggle your mind. It says that everyone living on earth and every plant and every physical feature at this time and all those who preceded them could have some direct or very indirect impact upon you and your life. That clearly outdoes Donne. I go further, as I say that in theory, anything that has ever happened or is happening in the entire universe may exert influence upon you in your life at this very moment in the determination of your "being."

JNDs and JNNDs

Let's take an example or two of how Nurturance impacts you and your psychological development. And let's subject you to the "Dullsville" that is Experimental Psychology's contribution to your understanding of you as a "being" and how you got that way. If this area smacks of redundancy to you, I shall be eternally grateful. Why? Because you remember something I've written, and that's the kind of redundant guy I am!

You will be endlessly changing throughout your life. As has been suggested throughout this treatise, this can take the form of robotic, automatic change. If change is to take place, it's likely that it will take place slowly. "Epiphanies," the sudden, intuitive revelation or development of insights occur rarely, if at all.

As suggested elsewhere in this treatise, most change takes place in JNNDs: Just Not Noticeable Differences. The person in the process of change has no awareness that it is happening. Later on, when the change grows and becomes more obvious, JNDs (Just Noticeable Differences) may be noted. JNDs need not be outgrowths of JNNDs. They can be devised on their own.

An example may be in order yet again. Initially, people successfully involved in weight loss programs have no evidence that they are losing weight. This can be most discouraging. For such people, the scale may seem stuck. Any weight loss that is occurring can be described in JNNDs. Something is happening; but the difference on the scale is Just Not Noticeable. Fewer weigh-ins may be recommended for the faint-hearted. Weekly weigh-ins are more likely to produce encouraging JNDs (Just Noticeable Differences). If a successful program is being implemented, clearly Noticeable Differences on the scale will be noted eventually along with indiscernible JNNDs.

The same process takes place when an individual is undertaking a personal change, e.g. a significant change in a belief that has long been basic, but not beneficial. There are no scales that measure this change. Any relevant measures of personal change in JNNDs and JNDs simply aren't available.

Nevertheless, the process goes something like this throughout the entire life of an individual. **If you understand nothing else in this treatise, make sure that you understand the following:**
At this very moment, you are a being in the process of development as you read these words. **Nature, Nurturance,** and **Chance** have been in play and continue to be in play. For the purposes of discussion, let's call your current momentary "being" UR-1. UR-1 will inevitably (and probably immediately) encounter a stimulating experience; a bell rings in the distance, a hot cup of coffee falls in your lap, your fiancée tells you that the marriage is "off," you have a heart attack. This list is varied and endless.

You then react to the stimulating circumstance. Your personal reaction can be categorized roughly as positive, negative, or insignificant. If your reaction is positive (even subliminally), or insignificant, you'd respond in the same way when confronted with an identical situation next time. You'll remain a UR-1. But if any negative significant reaction has taken place, **even subliminally**, you will have changed. By definition, you'll remain unaware of any positive or negative subliminal reaction. You are now different; you are now a UR-2. Another inevitable, stimulating event occurs and as a result, you may remain a UR-2 or become a UR-3.

All of this may have taken only a few seconds, and this dynamic process continues again and again and again throughout your life. It has occurred throughout your reading of this paragraph. You are not the same person you were at the beginning. You may or may not be aware of it, but you have changed. Consider the number of "beings" you have been during the course of this reading of a paragraph or two. Let's say that you started as a UR-1. Are you now a UR-55 or UR-85, or UR-?

There are no free passes, although the person has no responsibility for any of the processes that are producing him, his behavior, or misbehavior, which does have consequences. This is part and parcel of the learning process (UR-1, etc.). If his reactions are well-received by members of his society, they or similar ones are likely to be repeated when he is confronted with another situation requiring a reaction. If they are not well-received (prison, shunning, fisticuffs, etc.), they may be supplanted by more acceptable reactions or retained in spite of the negative reaction.

Shifting for the moment to older family members, especially your mother, who holds much sway over you and your Nurturance during your early years. **You are reminded that each one of them is engaged in the same personal developmental process that you are involved in. They too had no control or choice in this matter.**

Shifting further ahead, any and all of the people you will ever meet are personifications of this same ongoing dynamic, developmental process. **None of them ever had or will ever have any choice or control regarding any ingredients of this process.**

Any person attempting to engage in a significant, personal metamorphosis both negative and positive, might be one of the last to notice any evidence of change…change that is perhaps obvious to very close friends and relatives. Seeking out such observations from time to time may allay the discouragement that is part and parcel of the process of change. But the "being" you are at these moments just might not "choose" to reach out for such assistance.

As an example, the progression of an individual from social drinker to becoming an alcoholic takes a similar form. Many different determinants are involved in this. The social drinker begins to drink a bit more and then more. It often takes places in JNNDs to the developing alcoholic but the JNDs for friends and family who become convinced of the need for an intervention. "The man takes a drink, the drink takes a drink, then the drink takes the man."

Change isn't a smooth process. There are many bumps in the road. The person positively engaged in this journey must fight against the well-entrenched support systems of a previous style of life. Important personal beliefs are highly resistant to change. Discouragement must be anticipated and accepted as part of the cost of proceeding into some new and more fulfilling "Promised Land."

The Role of JNDs and JNNDs in Marriage, Divorce, and All Points in Between

JNDs: Just Noticeable Differences
JNNDs: Just Not Noticeable Differences

The USA divorce rate is close to 50 percent and many who remain married are unhappy with their circumstance. Each current generation thinks it knows a great deal more than the people of the previous one, and that could be true. But in light of the changing and challenging times, that might not be enough; people may continue to lack the know-how to identify and deal with marital problems.

Despite the emergence of no end of modern pre-marital behaviors and learning experiences, marriage too often continues to be the union of two strangers. Problems may develop almost immediately as the couples get to know one another. While the newly-discovered facets of the partner are sometimes wondrously positive, too often they are not. During the early "shakedown" of a marriage, some of the discoveries occasion "buyer's remorse" or "Oh, God, what have I gotten myself into?" These warning signals could provoke constructive discussions, but they usually are ignored, papered over by small talk in the hope that things will eventually work out to everyone's advantage.

I'll single out the powerful expression of "I love you" as a statement that people contemplating marriage should study very seriously. It can be a ticket to paradise or to the chains of enslavement/despair/unhappiness, or some point in between. The listener dearly loves to hear another say, "I love you." It makes him or her feel special, lucky, happy, emotional, and swept away. And saying "I love you" is serious business even though the speaker often has little idea as to how serious it can be. All too often, the saying has no meaning *per se*. It means what the listener would like to believe about the partner.

"When I use a word," Humpty Dumpty said, in a rather scornful tone, "It means just what I choose it to mean—neither more nor less." "The question is," says Alice, "whether you can make words mean so many different things." *Through the Looking Glass*, Lewis Carroll.

"I love you." "I love you, too." A kissing, fondling, grappling couple may be swept away in the romance of the moment. An opportunity to know the other a little better is lost.

I suggest, facetiously, that couples would be better served by substituting, **"I glompf you." "I glompf you, too."** Each would immediately provoke rational inquiry, i.e. "What in the hell do you mean by *that*?" This could then lead to an in-depth discussion of each other's personalities, individual and mutual goals, and how well they are suited to one another. That sort of information is essential in making decisions regarding marriage or any long term personal involvement.

Janet Mills on "Marriage"

"Two trees
A portion of your soul has been
entwined with mine
A gentle kind of togetherness, while
separately we stand,
As two trees deeply rooted in
separate plots of ground,
While their topmost branches
come together,
Forming a miracle of lace
against the heavens."

The above has a wondrous, romantic sound about it. Potential marital partners might be misled into thinking that this "forming a miracle of lace" is automatically on their agenda. It may take more time, energy, and talent than most couples possess.

A cynic might point out that even one of the trees better not be a weeping willow. Over the course of time, in JNNDs, its invasive roots would kill off the other tree. If they were both willows, the process could take the form of a competition with a dreary ending. If the reader can't see an analogy between these willows and some marital partners, this treatise is in serious trouble.

The Fugees illustrate this point with Norman Gimbel's lyrics to the song: "Killing Me Softly," that illustrates another facet of a marital relationship:

"Strumming my pain with his fingers,
Singing my life with his words,
Killing me softly with his words,
Killing me softly with his words,
Telling my whole life with his words,
Killing me softly with his song."

JNDs and JNNDs provide an understanding of how two people may grow apart, but they may sound so abstract that the average reader won't take the time necessary to understand and apply them to himself. Maybe a simplified definition of these terms is in order.

1. JND (Just Noticeable Difference) refers to a noticeable change. One partner does something clearly notable (positive, negative, or innocuous). If "innocuous" rules, there is no change. If either positive or negative have impact on the interchange, then there may be a noticeable difference or change in the relationship. There is a Just Noticeable Difference! Differences that are ignored are the source of problems.

2. JNND (Just Not Noticeable Difference) refers to subliminal change. The partners may be unaware that anything has happened. But something *has* happened: a Just Not Noticeable

Difference is now in place. Both JNDs and JNNDs influence the relationship. If there are problems, those involving JNDs can be addressed and resolved. Those involving JNNDs by definition can't be addressed rationally and may introduce problems.

Each partner is more process than person; both are constantly learning and changing. Too many partners report that that the other partner has changed, that the girl or the guy they married isn't the same one they're living with now. When asked about this, the complaining partner may not be able to identify any specific determinants.

"Buyer's remorse" may linger on; i.e. if I had only known what I learned later on, I wouldn't have married this person in the first place. And now, to compound any problem, he or she has been changing ever since. This change can be conceptualized in terms of JNDs and JNNDs, the happenings that are the agents of change. Very few husbands or wives go to bed on a given evening and awaken to find a complete stranger in his or her bed. But Thurstonian Theory indicates clearly that both the partners of the morning are inevitably different in tiny, indiscernible ways (JNNDs). The process involving such change takes place unceasingly throughout the duration of the marriage.

Sometimes, the change is identifiable (JND) by the changed person or an onlooker, but often it's subliminal (JNND) and unnoticed by anyone. A few random JNNDs might not impact an individual's life, but JNNDs in the aggregate could have significant consequences. These partners might be helped if they could realize that this really happens. Unless the process is acknowledged, they may not take the steps necessary to avoid negative consequences. Arguments about a checkbook balance may have little to do with a checkbook balance *per se.* Life is complicated; marriage is <u>very</u> complicated.

Chaotic genetic and environmental determinants including Chance: The true basis for personality determination.

The formulation is all-inclusive. The genetic (Nature) component is there along with all of the contacts with people or your physical world (Nurturance) you have experienced from the time of your conception to the present moment.

Now, let's see if I've got this straight. You, the reader, have your "being" determined in part by your genetic makeup/DNA.

You never had any choice of your ancestors nor the genetic contribution they provided. They too had no choice in this matter.

From the moment of your conception, you were dumped into an environment (Nurturance) that wasn't of your choosing. Contact with others and your physical surroundings became a continuous and never-ending learning process. Through these learning experiences, you developed your personality. Over the course of your life, the elements of this experience number in the millions or even billions. You are aware of only a few. Try to consider the probability that many other experiences unavailable to your recollection might be truly important determinants as well.

If you have a problem in contemplating the number of such experiences, consider what you have done in the last minute. You may have looked around, overheard a conversation, shifted a bit to get more comfortable in your chair, fiddled with a pencil, etc. You may have even had a thought or two, an experience triggered by the environment in which you found yourself.

You very probably have no awareness of the first year of your life, but by the time that birthday rolled around, you were already a complex "being." And as you grew and your experiences multiplied exponentially, your complexity, your uniqueness, grew enormously.

Possible Practical Implications

In the main, you should not dwell upon your past as you seek to gain an understanding of yourself. The crucial determinants of your "being" are incredibly complex and unavailable to you. You cannot find the "Nurturant dots," let alone be able to connect them. Anything other than a superficial understanding is impossible for you to achieve.

Estate planners and insurance agents notwithstanding don't dwell upon the future and what it might hold for you. Chance events or your DNA may be the crucial determinants.

Live fully in "The Now." Enjoy the pleasures of the moment and endure the unhappy times. The former may be rare and unrepeatable. "This too shall pass," a truism, is a useful belief in dealing with the latter.

While they're right on target, none of the aforementioned admonitions or recommendations are offered with any expectation of your implementing them.

The "being" that you have become will proceed as before. You may be set in your ways. You never had any significant control over your personal development and you never will. Chance and the Nature of your being will fashion your future, sans any meaningful control on your part.

Old Russian proverb stating the likelihood of success in producing personal change:

Up to the age of five, he may be shaped,
From five until nine, he must be bent,
From nine until seventeen, he must be broken,
After that, the only solution is the grave.

Is this proverb unduly depressing? I surely hope so, but how do you break out of the closet of your mind? Chance might offer a solution, but if you simply wait for some Chance salvation or epiphany, you might become involved in a wait without end. Maybe it could be better phrased as an "opportunity." Maybe you can prepare so when opportunity knocks, you'll be ready.

"Opportunity" might take the form of something on a TV commercial, a prolonged, in-depth conversation with an "emancipated friend," a book such as the one you've been reading, a feeling one morning that something special is going to happen, or something only you would know and act upon.

You know what you would have done in similar situations in the past, and you will be strongly tempted to do that again. It's a moment of truth. Odds are strong that you would remain mired by the Nurturance of past experience.

But you just might hesitate and try something new. It might be comparable to a young bird on its first flight with its initial awkwardness and discomfort. In relatively short order, the bird takes flight and soars into a new, breath-taking and challenging sky. You and your life can take wings as well.

The Development of Beliefs

Now is the time when I can give you the full benefit of my bias. It's my belief that you (and I, or anyone else) are in no way "predestinarianists," those who are fulfilling some destiny ordained and governed by a God. I don't believe that there is "Chess Master" in the sky dictating your behavior with His eye on the sparrow and all that, and at no time did I have any choice as I developed that belief. "Destiny" can be ruled out as well. For example, the romantic notion that you are destined to marry a person who was made for you is utter nonsense. You may find ample support for this in romantic prose and poetry, but little in the scientific literature.

In a recurrent vein, I believe that "free will," choice, and control are illusions as well. You've never been in charge of your life. You've never been the captain of your ship or the master of your soul. It's incumbent upon those who believe in "free will," i.e. personal freedom of choice between alternatives, to state the time and the circumstances when he cast off the shackles of his past and stepped forward boldly and freely to chart the course of his life. And they will be unable to do this.

Why do you believe in such nonsense? You "learned" to believe this. Have you ever really challenged this or any other of your basic beliefs? Probably not. It's likely that you've never attempted to rigorously define your belief system, let alone questioned any aspect of it. Your religious beliefs were determined by your Nature/Nurturance and the whims of Chance by the same process that you developed a fondness for the color blue and a membership in the Republican Party.

Choice Points

Let's add a little class to this discussion. It takes the form of Robert Frost's "The Road Not Taken." Hopefully, the reader is familiar with this poem. It might even have caused him to veer off his well-trodden path and embark upon a new, challenging, and anxiety-provoking venture. Or more likely, he might visit and revisit his past and find no end of choice points where he made the wrong decision. Just maybe his guilt might be alleviated a bit if he buys into my view that at any of those moments, he really had no choice.

The Road Not Taken

Two roads diverged in a yellow wood
And sorry that I could not travel both
And be one traveler, long I stood
And looked down one as far as I could
To where it bent in the undergrowth.

Then took the other, as just as fair
And having perhaps the better claim
Because it was grassy and wanted wear
Though as for that the passing there
Had worn them really both the same.

And both that morning equally lay
In leaves no step had trodden back
Oh, I remarked the first for another day!
Yet knowing how way leads only to way
I doubted if I should ever come back.

I shall be telling this with a sigh
Somewhere ages and ages hence:
The roads diverged in a wood, and I,
I took the one less traveled by,
And that has made all the difference.

I hold that all the ingredients of that decision were within him as he came to that fork in the road and that his decision was in place before he was in the position of having to make it. He had no choice. He and you are chock full of responses that are in place, waiting to be stimulated into expression. Those were established by a lifetime of living, the determinants roughly categorized as Nature, Nurturance, and Chance.

Dig deeply into your own personal recollections now for examples. You'll probably come up with the "big events," those happenings that clearly influenced and changed your life. But these are but the tip of a very large iceberg. During your life, there were millions upon millions of other life-changing events that you weren't aware of or that you have forgotten about because they seemed to have so little consequence. In deference to Freud, some may be excluded from your memory because they were repressed. Every decision that you make is made in advance, produced by some combination of your personal determinants.

CHAPTER 5

Chance

"Luck be a lady tonight"
-*Guys and Dolls*

"I know how it feels to have wings on your heels
And fly down the street in a trance.
You fly down the street on the Chance that you meet
And you meet—not really by Chance.
("Hello, Young Lovers," from *The King and I*)

By now, the reader has been thoroughly apprised as the importance this treatise places on the role of Chance as a determinant of one's "being." Little things sometimes become all-important.

For Want of a Nail

For want of a nail, the shoe was lost.
For want of a shoe, the horse was lost.
For want of a horse, the rider was lost.
For want of a rider, the message was lost.
For want of a message, the battle was lost.
For want of a battle, the kingdom was lost.

And all for the want of a horseshoe nail.

To paraphrase Robert Burns a bit, "The best laid plans of mice and men oft go astray." Chance events occasionally interfere.

However, Chance has been under-emphasized TO THE POINT OF OMISSION in virtually all attempts to understand the nature of man and his development.

There's good reason for this. Psychologists shy away from Chance because it undercuts their comprehensive personality theories that purportedly allow them to fully understand people and their personal development, and most importantly, predict what will happen during the course of a person's life. Chance is a messy, unpredictable, and important determinant of personality.

Chance clearly relates to Chaos Theory and the sensitive dependence of lives and processes upon prior conditions. A time-honored example of this links the flutter of a butterfly's wing in an Amazonian ran forest to Hurricane Katrina's destruction of New Orleans (See Chapter 1).

Chapters 2, 3, and 4 present material relating to the rule of Chance as it interacts with Nature and Nurturance.

Of course, "Chance events" can be earth-shakingly negative or positive or somewhere in an inconsequential middle.

Chance gets a bum rap from those relying on religion to understand mankind. They state that everything has a cause and purpose; that everything is known and understood by an omniscient and omnipotent God, e.g. His eye is on the sparrow and He knows that sparrow's flight pattern. Events that others might ascribe to Chance are said to be "blessings" or "curses." The religious typically kowtow to that God's incredible strength and wisdom, humbly stating that mere mortals couldn't possibly understand what He understands so clearly and easily. It's almost as though they brag about their ignorance in deference to the strength of this God.

While there is little doubt about the ignorance and the humility surrounding it, there is no doubt that an individual's life can be given some sense of rhyme and reason by a reliance on religion. A religious framework also gives a person a means of accepting and justifying events that seem utterly devoid of meaning and purpose, e.g. the accidental death of a child at an early age, the birth of a severely handicapped child, or a man slipping on a banana peel and dying in the resulting fall. The comfort that an irrational, religious approach provides for many individuals in many diverse situations cannot be overestimated.

In the course of the 2012 Election Campaign, Richard Mourdock aspiring U.S. Senator (Indiana) stated that a child conceived in a forcible rape was part of God's plan. I can only assume that Mourdock's defeat was also part of God's plan. Would a rape of Mourdock's granddaughter also be a mere event on some celestial calendar?

The most rational amongst us has little to offer in competition with the religious individuals dealing with horrible "storms you cannot weather" situations. Saying that "stuff happens," while an accurate statement, provides little solace to an individual dealing with a personal tragedy.

The reader is encouraged to engage in a bit of homework in regard to Chance. Unless the reader is unusually resistant to the premise of this treatise, he should be able to conjure up an abundance of personal, even game-changing examples.

A. A row of pine trees were planted by a man five years ago. Each tree is growing in accordance with its genetic background and the advantages/disadvantages of its environment. A feeding deer accidentally stumbles upon them and systematically crops off the "leaders," the central or dominant part of the young tree, or all of them except one. That one will continue to grow unimpeded with its growth determined by its genes and environment, unless another hungry deer happens upon its scene or the home-owner decides to dig it up and transport it to an inhospitable site in the shade of his home.

B. A housewife drives to school to pick up the kids. She delays her departure a few seconds in order to tie her shoe. As she is speeding along, she runs over a squirrel and kills it. The death of this rodent is clearly, yet inexplicably linked to an untied shoestring. Even though many years have passed, she still thinks about this event occasionally.

C. Let's single out a classic book, *The Bridge of San Luis Rey* by Thornton Wilder. This book told the story of several seemingly unrelated people who die as the result of being on a durable Inca rope-fiber suspension bridge in Peru when it fell into a deep chasm. The question raised: Why were these people, of all people, on that bridge at the exact moment of its collapse?

D. Consider the common sense of Tom Hanks expressed in *Forrest Gump* and *Castaway*. In the former, he saw life as a box of chocolates, each one of which had a content that was unknown until it was experienced. In the latter, alone on an island, his character was impressed by his ignorance of what the next day might provide, i.e. he never knew what might be washed upon the shore by the tide each day. If he was able to open a new package that day with some gift befallen from the FedEx plane on which he crashed in the first place, he could use objects in new ways as tools to help him survive being stranded.

E. Someone wins over $3 million in a lottery.

F. Dr. James Richards, an eminent feline expert, dies in a car crash occasioned by his desire to avoid hitting a cat who was crossing the road (August 2012).

G. (August 2012) The owner of a German shepherd dog, Missy, found abandoned and dying on a Colorado mountain, is now facing a cruelty to animals charge.

A pair of hikers found the dog tucked into a tiny nook between some rocks, but after eight days on the mountain, Missy was too weak to move and too heavy for the couple to carry. The pair posted a plea on a Facebook forum. Soon, they had volunteers who headed up the mountain in a snowstorm, found the dog, and rescued her. Without Facebook, there would have been no rescue. Twenty years ago, Missy would have become one dead dog.

Hopefully, the reader can supply many comparable personal examples. This would be something unexpected or lucky that changed the course of his life. If not, there is the possibility that the reader has led a rather restricted life. Examples could include fortuitous events which had significant impact upon the reader even though they happened to someone else.

Chance is powerful. It can often trump or override the impact of Nature and Nurturance in the life of a plant or person.

While Chance is unpredictable by definition, it's important that people understand early on that life contains within it many events and circumstances over which they have no control.

Nagasaki Atomic Bombing 1945

Compiled by Wm. Robert Johnston, Johnston's Archive
16 October 2005

Date: 9 August 1945

Chance
Chance smiled on Kokura; Nagasaki's hammering is detailed in this report. Consider any more recent catastrophe in the U.S.A. for other examples of the role of Chance in determining damnation or salvation.

Location: Nagasaki, Japan

Type of event: combat use of nuclear weapon

Description:

Following prolonged strategic bombing of Japan during World War II, the United States conducted the second combat use of a nuclear weapon (following the attack on Hiroshima 3 days earlier). A B-29 bomber dropped a single Mk-II "Fat Man" atomic bomb over Nagasaki, estimated population 240,000. The Mk-II was an implosion design nuclear gravity bomb using plutonium. The primary target city, Kokura, had been covered by clouds, as was Nagasaki (the secondary target) when the bomber arrived. The bomb was dropped through a gap in the cloud cover over a point somewhat displaced from the city center. It detonated 500 meters over Nagasaki at 11:02 AM local time with a yield estimated at 21 kilotons...

On the day of the bombing, an estimated 263,000 were in Nagasaki, including 240,000 Japanese residents, 10,000 Korean residents, 2,500 conscripted Korean workers, 9,000 Japanese soldiers, 600 conscripted Chinese workers, and 400 prisoners of war. Casualty figures are uncertain; despite many surveys (some figures presented here are extrapolated from partial surveys). Estimated fatalities are 70,000 (various published estimates range from 22,000 to 74,000), including 2,000 Koreans and at least 100 POWs. After 1950, deaths attributed to radiation include about 35 leukemia deaths, 175 other cancer deaths, and 85 non-cancer deaths. New cases of leukemia peaked in 1952.

Nature/Nurturance/Chance Patterning

I'll share a personal choice with you. In 1943, I journeyed to Milwaukee to be inducted into the military services. I passed the physical exam as did almost everyone else in those days. If one was warm, he passed.

Then, like immediately, I was given my choice of service: Navy, Army, or Marines. I was dumb as the proverbial shovel and no rational reason occurred to me. I opted for the Navy. I clearly carried within me all the ingredients of that decision although they were unidentifiable. While I hadn't thought about this matter at all, when confronted with this situation, I expressed what may have been determined by some of the following Nurturance ingredients:

> The death of my soldier uncle in WWI may have contributed to it.
>
> My realization that John Wayne's portrayal of a flag-waving Marine was hooey.
>
> It might have been a recruitment poster showing a flag-waving, smiling sailor on the prow of destroyer sailing into battle with the enemy. (Interestingly enough, I ended up as a flag waving signalman on a destroyer.)

If they'd asked me if I wanted to go to Peru or what kind of ship I wanted to serve on, I'd have had a response. My responsiveness was in place. If you were confronted with a similar decision that had to be made, what branch of service would you choose? Delve deeply for the basis of your decision—and you will come up dry.

At that same time, a fellow inductee had chosen the Army and was standing in a group of men who had expressed that choice. A man then came by. He had no special uniform or credentials that would have allowed him to hold sway over this group of men. But he said something to the effect, "The Marine quota is low today, you guys are in the Marines." An oddity, per **Chance**? What happened to these inductees? What might have happened to them if the quota for Marines had been filled on that day?

I have procrastinated for nearly three years in composing this Magnum Opus. (The reader may have decided already that this is neither "Opus" nor "Magnum." And he'd be right. It's just part of my devilish sense of humor, which was formed without choice on my part!) Such dawdling is clearly understandable to me. I quit several times. Once again, I had no real choice in this matter. If I had a different Nature/Nurturance/Chance pattern, I would have proceeded otherwise, i.e. I might have become an astronaut or a denizen of Skid Row or a writer with the stature of a Stephen King. Incidentally, this "understanding" relieves me of any of the negatives or guilts associated with the term "procrastinator" or the production of this work. "Stuff happens!" and I was just being "me."

Very little of your Nature/Nurturance/Chance configuration is known to you. Even if you had such knowledge, it wouldn't be very helpful in planning for your future. Such knowledge would become just another element in the Nurturance category. How it would influence you and the course of your life is unknown. While you can certainly make an educated guess regarding the answers, it has been said that a little knowledge is a very dangerous thing. Knowing what you don't know is a real strength.

It's been said that if you want to hand your God a good laugh, tell Him or Her just how you're going to spend the next three years. Too many people harbor the illusion that proper and conscientious planning will lead to predictable results.

Chance, a form of Nurturance, is powerful and lurks out there, ready to trump that planning.

Your future cannot be predicted and your past cannot be fully understood.

Chance has never been accorded proper recognition by personality theorists. Chance is kind of a nuisance in that it interferes with the flow of orderly/rational predictions of behavior. Chance is really a form of Nurturance, its importance and previous de-emphasis requires that it becomes part of the "Big Three" of determinants of personality.

In some of my extended dawdling episodes, I may have wasted a lot of time in attempting to justify my position, assembling and aligning bits of knowledge that would lead any reader to believe that I really knew what I was talking about. Was that really just wasted time? Or was it a series of experiential events that were necessary before I could write this current Magnum Opus, this big-time effort to explain everything about all living things and how they got to be that way? Perhaps I came to believe that the process I was addressing was too complicated for anyone to describe properly. As I close in to finish off this work, I believe this to be true. Just maybe, in developing this Magnum Opus, I have "labored mightily and brought forth a mouse," a treatise unworthy of your attention or concern. That remains a distinct possibility.

Dawdle time is now over. Consider what might have happened to this dawdling process if, <u>by Chance</u>, something of major significance had happened during the last three years, e.g. the onset of cancer, an unexpected hot love affair, an auto accident, or the outbreak of another World War. It would seem likely that this project might have stopped dead in its tracks. I'm clearly getting ahead of myself, no mean trick that.

But after dawdling, I have been able to set the reader on a path that might lead him to consider my position seriously. Some will be comfortable and accepting of this possibility; others will not. You are reminded that it's my belief that none of the members of any of these groups and those lost somewhere in between had any real choice in this matter.

CHAPTER 6

The Treatment of Mental "Illnesses": Ill-considered, Ineffective, and Unbelievably Expensive

I hope that by now you've been properly impressed by **Nature, Nurturance** and **Chance** as incredibly complicated determinants of your "being." It's my hope that these determinants have worked well for you; that you have lucked out over the course of the years. However, at some time during your life, you could develop a significant psychological problem. You might then seek treatment by contacting a member of the psychiatric establishment. You'd be impressed—and depressed—by the difficulties you'd encounter in any such attempt.

Sad to relate, it's virtually impossible for most people to avail themselves of a bona fide psychotherapist.

It's my view that responsible psychotherapy, as treatment modality for mental problems, is as dead as a dodo. I'll list some reasons in support of that belief.

1. It's common knowledge that people avoid seeking psychiatric help until the problem is so severe that it demands attention. Accordingly, the benefits of an early intervention aren't generally available. As is obvious, a well-entrenched problem will be more difficult to treat. Psychotherapy would be most effective if it was made available earlier, but the system postpones intervention. (It's a bit like the joke that has the patient going in for treatment of a cold, but they don't treat colds. He's told that he should go home and wait until he develops pneumonia, and then he can come back and be treated.)

2. Insurance companies' policies dictate that the number of psychotherapy sessions be limited, usually six or eight. However, if a personal problem is severe enough to warrant a psychiatric/psychological referral, then it will not yield in this limited amount of time. Additional sessions can be purchased, but at a high hourly rate, few can afford them.

3. At the beginning of psychotherapy, the therapist must establish rapport with the patient so as to elicit valid information about the nature of the problem and its possible origin. This requires considerable skill. Psychological testing is sometimes required to provide a fuller understanding of the problem. All of this takes time; time that will not be available but will be subtracted by the insurance companies from any psychotherapy that is to follow.

4. Now reconsider the subject matter and conclusions of the four chapters immediately preceding this one. All of the possible determinants of personality and their complex interaction would be unavailable to the provider. Remember that no one can understand himself or anyone else fully. The necessarily incomplete patient personality description would be of little help. It could be misleading.

5. The reader must be aware of the difficulties involved in such an assessment. As is the case in all learned behaviors, there's a multiplicity of specific determinants and their interactions. Some of the determinants may be forgotten or repressed. (Standard psychoanalytic treatment is based upon discovery of repressed memories, bringing these to a conscious level, and integrating them into the patient's personality may take years to accomplish. Some patients report undergoing such treatment for 10-20 years!) Some crucial determinants may have been subliminal; the patient was unaware of them at the time of their occurrence.

6. Let us revisit the jigsaw example of Chapter 1. I see a similarity between the assemblage of highly-personal information involved in understanding a patient and the completion of a jigsaw puzzle.

   It's assumed that the jigsaw puzzler has all the pieces of the puzzle he is trying to assemble. The therapist usually doesn't come close to having a complete package.

   The psychotherapist must identify significant determinants of his patient's personal problem and put these puzzle parts together in order to have a coherent picture of the problem he is to treat. Consider the problems of the therapist when crucial pieces are missing. Some may be important; some may be inconsequential. The nature of the parts may be distorted by the patient. He may have seen too many Dr. Phil shows and deliver as "facts" behaviors that have no relation to his problem.

   It's kind of like adding pieces from several different jigsaw puzzles. Some therapists have been known to create or cram extraneous pieces, those which may fit into his own theory of personality development. One extreme example of this involved a therapist who conjured up twenty or so different personalities in his patient. It was pure hokum, although it seemed to put *The Three Faces of Eve* to shame for a while.

7. Therapeutic orientation: If push comes to shove, most therapists will lay claim to being associated with a major school of personality theorists, but in practice, they proudly claim that they've picked elements from a variety of theories—and that the result is a theory of their very own, one which is superior to any of the sources for it. A skeptic, such as myself, might accuse them of "winging it," i.e. doing what they do without any clear-cut theoretical reason. I title this end result as being "**amorphously eclectic,**" a damning title. It means that therapists may select a few traditional theoretical constructs, add his or her own notions, and assemble the lot into a personality theory lacking in form and precise definition. There are probably as many different theories and approaches as there are to practitioners. Completely lacking in insight, these practitioners then proceed on the assumption that their individual expertise is greater than any of the recognized experts in this field. I beg to differ.

8. Picture then the plight of the seeker of mental health treatment. He doesn't know what he's getting into. It's not the sort of thing you can check out at the Better Business Bureau. He has little to gauge the approach, the expertise, or the success of the practitioner. Possession of an M.D. or a Ph.D. by the therapist isn't necessarily a compelling credential.

9. For a more comprehensive account of the questions about and criticisms of profession and its professionals, the reader is referred to *Sides Seldom Seen: A Novella*, 2004, Scobie, Nancy Clark and Thurston, John R.

The mental health system is slow to acknowledge its problems. It would have more patients than it could handle if psychotherapy was the preferred treatment.

Psychotropic medications are a boon to this industry. Using the medical model or mental illness model, the practitioners concentrate on the obvious complaints or behaviors. There is no need for any exhaustive search into the individual's background. "This is nice, but by no means necessary." In diagnosing, they seek similarity of a patient's complaints/behavior to those of individuals inhabiting one of the many diagnostic categories (See Chapter 4). They often rely on hearsay, psychological test results, and past behavior.

(I'm reminded of an old joke told about a patient seeking treatment of a physical illness. Doctor asks, "Have you had this before?" The patient replies, "Yes." The doctor says, "You've got it again.") While past behavior is a reasonable predictor of future behavior, it often provides little information regarding the causes of either.

Another joke that many practitioners fail to understand: A guy comes in with an incapacitating fear of heights. The psychiatrist evaluates him and diagnoses him as an ill individual, an "acrophobic," who has an incapacitating fear of heights. When asked about the cause of the fear, the psychiatrist says it's because he has acrophobia. The obvious circularity is lost upon many professionals who should know better. There's no suggestion of any understanding of the real sources of the fear.

The medical, diagnostic approach requires establishing a diagnosis of the illness which is then used as the basis for delivering treatment.

Dr. Thomas Szasz, who recently died in 2012, took issue with the need to view mental patients as suffering from an illness. The diagnostic approach is inappropriate when it comes to understanding and treating psychiatric problems. It is too simple. His reasonable approach, described in his classic volume *The Myth of Mental Illness* never came close to being accepted.

All psychiatric patients must be diagnosed. The *DSM (Diagnostic and Statistical Manual of Mental Disorders)* provides a very full range of diagnoses (See Chapter 4).

Diagnostic and Statistical Manual of Mental Disorders

The Diagnostic and Statistical Manual of Mental Disorders, 5th Edition (DSM) is based on the "medical model," an approach with demonstrated effectiveness in understanding and treating physical disorders. In implementing this approach, the DSM lumps together patients with mental symptoms in common. A name is then given to this constellation of symptoms. This is then a diagnosis, a mental disease or disorder. Some personal background information along with the results of some medical tests are examined in a search for the cause of this disease. A determination is then made to establish which of the available treatments are most effective. All of that sounds very orderly, commendable, and even scientific, but it just doesn't work with "mental disorders."

Except in instances where there is clearly a physical cause for the malady, the "medical model" is inappropriate in its application to the mental disorders. The causes of most mental disorders are complex and unique for each individual who is suffering from them. The DSM simplistically crams patients with similar symptoms into diagnostic categories, but these people are different in many ways. The resulting diagnosis tells nothing about the unique determinants of the problem and provides little information to establish individualized treatments.

The DSM has been recently revised (2012). This is the 5th edition. This revision required thirteen years and the work of 1,500 mental health experts. In my opinion, they "labored mightily and brought forth a mouse." Most importantly, they failed in their efforts to clarify and justify the logic and rationale of this approach. The basis for their adding or eliminating "diseases" remains unclear. They added or seemingly created several new illnesses, e.g. shyness, hoarding syndrome, binge eating, severe bereavement, skin picking, and autistics.

The once popular diagnosis of Asperger's Syndrome has been expunged. Asperger patients of the past are now tossed in with some other autistic diseases. In addition, they had considered a couple of new ones, "parental alienation syndrome" (the difficulty that children experience after their parents' divorce) and sexual addition (hypersexual behavior) but these potential "diseases" were not approved. Troubled people in these areas are probably not eligible for treatment because they aren't "ill" according to the DSM-5.

Incidentally, homosexuality was defined as a mental disorder until 1974. This was changed by a two-thirds vote of the APA. As is evident, one-third (or 3,810) psychiatrists continued to regard homosexuality as a treatable mental disorder.

It's been said that marriages are made in heaven, but lived on earth. I'm not sure where the DSM was conceived, but its practical application takes place on earth. What sounds so scientific in the DSM, even with its psychobabble and statistical decimal points, doesn't really contribute understanding and assistance when applied to our earth and the troubled individuals of its population.

But it will follow as that night the day that there will be a DSM diagnosis for every patient in need of psychiatric treatment. One compelling reason for this: The provider will not be paid by most insurance companies for his series of the application lacks a diagnosis.

A playful analogy may be in order that may illustrate the point I'm attempting to make. It stems from a TV program that ran from 1959 to 1965 called *Rawhide*, starring Clint Eastwood as a randy cowboy named Rowdy Yates. The theme song tells how cattle are to be treated. With a little twist, these words can describe how psychiatric patients are treated:

> "Keep them movin', movin', movin'
> Though they're disapprovin'
> Keep them dogies movin'
> **Rawhide!**
> Don't try to understand them
> Just rope and throw and brand them."

A snapping whip sound accompanied this song.

"Dogies" are patients, the "brand" the diagnosis. "Don't try to understand them": Personal understanding is nice, but not necessary. "Rope and throw"; drug therapy and/or hospitalization. "Keep them movin'": The insurance company's limits the days for hospitalization. "Though they're disapprovin'": Few psychiatric patients are content.

In the 1950s and 1960s, drugs were used primarily to make the patient treatable. If he was severely agitated or depressed, the therapist could not proceed. Drugs are now the end-all.

Drug treatment had many advantages over psychotherapy:

1. There's no need for any intense study of the patient's personality and past. As before, "This information is nice, but by no means necessary."

2. Patients prefer treatment by pills to long-term, intrusive, and personally-demanding psychotherapy.

3. It's more cost-effective than psychotherapy.

4. Pills are more acceptable in a medical setting.

5. The representatives of drug companies—the real "pushers"—readily provide alleged research findings that identify the drug and dosage appropriate to the different diagnostic categories. Their approach might be described as a hard sell. They also hold out hope that some "silver bullet" drug will be found that will eradicate any need for alternative therapies.

Oft times, a drug treatment program requires only minimal contact between the patient and a psychiatrist. Any psychological treatment is farmed out to psychologists, psychiatric social workers, and/or alcohol counselors, who typically charge less. After establishing the appropriate diagnosis, psychiatrists may confine themselves to periodic "med checks" to assess the results to the drug treatment they provide. These topics are touched upon in Chapter 4 and in the aforementioned book, *Sides Seldom Seen*. At best, a drug treatment program quells or squashes problems. It needs little or no understanding of the causes of the problem.

Do I deplore the current approach? As is obvious, I certainly do. Can it be changed? Yes, but the problems are enormous! Some have likened the problems in effecting change to those encountered if one were to move a cemetery across town.

Suggestions

1. I support the therapeutic approaches advocated by Dr. Albert Ellis and Dr. Carl Rogers. Their current popularity is unknown to me.

2. I support Dr. Ellis' approach because of its simplicity, its common sense, and its concentration upon the Now. No need to dwell on the past unduly.

   In essence, he conceptualizes personal problems in terms of A, B, and C.

   "A" is the outside world and all its stimuli raining down on the patient.

   "B" involves the perception of the patient, what he sees or experiences with the material delivered by "A."

   "C" is the resulting stress or psychological comfort from the perceptions undertaken in "B."

   One can do little or nothing about "A." One should concentrate a therapy program on the patient's "B" perceptions. Suggestions can be supplied by the therapist as to changes in "B" which might improve the patient's' psychological state in "C."

   This approach can be understood more easily than the other therapeutic programs. It's as easy as A, B, C!

3. Dr. Rogers emphasizes, among many things, **a concentration upon the Now, the patient's determining the course of treatment, and the need for the patient to explore personal issues by talking about them.**

4. **I feel that personally-troubled patients can improve if they talk about their problems.** Indeed, their inability to talk to others might be an important part of the problems they present. Obviously, the patient must be highly selective in whom he shares his views about life and his problems.

I've explored the topic of **self-therapy** fully in a book, *Sharpening Shadows* (Scobie, Nancy Clark and Thurston, John. R.). In it, we contend that there is no need for a professional. Informal and unsupervised group therapy supports this view. Indeed, I support the position that a patient can be helped if he talks out loud about his problems to himself. The cathartic value of such an approach is obvious. It couldn't be cheaper. Alcoholics Anonymous (AA) is successful as it implements this approach.

I'll close with an old joke. All my jokes are old. A psychiatrist is asked, "How can you sit there for eight hours a day, week in and week out, listening to these horrifying personal problems of your patient?" The psychiatrist replies, "Who listens?"

Closing Comments

1. Could it be that it's really the patient's talking that is an agent of improvement? The presence of another, even a psychiatrist, may be irrelevant.

   I've been a critic of chiropractors because there is no scientific evidence for the therapy they provide, but I do know of people who seem to be helped by visits to a chiropractor. It could be that simply touching is helpful. The body is made warm and relaxed. The patient is encouraged to talk during the treatment by many practitioners.

   I know of one chiropractic case where a psychological "prop" seemed to work. An older lady was told that she was a "91." That made sense to her. She knew she wasn't a "100," but "91" wasn't all that bad. After years, she graduated to a "92" and then a "93." She felt better knowing that she was improving. As far as I know, there was never any basis for any of the numbers provided her by the chiropractor.

2. I've been in and around the psychiatric establishment for maybe 40 years. Psychotherapy requires an active and intense involvement on the part of the therapist; a 24/7 kind of involvement, for a conscientious therapist probably takes the problems home with him, and this would make intolerable emotional and intellectual demands upon him. The number of such individuals will always remain limited. Therefore, psychotherapy is becoming increasingly unavailable to patients. Drugs will continue to be the preferred treatment.

3. Be forever skeptical of psychologists and psychiatrists who are wedded to the DSM and its medical model approach to understanding troubled individuals. If, in answer to what's the matter with a troubled patient, the professional says, "He's a schizophrenic," feel free to challenge him. He knows precious little about the patient and about his role as a professional.

Afterthoughts

Barack Obama was elected to serve a second term as President of the United States of America.

Two Senatorial candidates were defeated: Todd Akin (Missouri) and Richard Mourdock (Indiana).

Todd Akin had stated that "Women's bodies would automatically prevent pregnancy in cases of **legitimate rape**.'" This ignorant view suggests that those raped women who become pregnant were not really raped, but that they were unjustly accusing the man of this crime, that it was an "illegitimate rape."

Richard Mourdock said that if a woman was raped and became pregnant, "It was something that God had intended to happen." This conjures up a picture of a benevolent God viewing—and perhaps applauding—an act of rape from start to finish.

The ignorance of these remarks is monumental. Rape is rape. The victim should be encouraged to do whatever she feels is necessary in dealing with her problems (or his, if the victim is male).

One might ask Todd Akin and Richard Mourdock what each would do if a granddaughter claimed that she had been raped.

According to the theory elaborated in this book, a rapist has no choice in the matter. He was impelled to rape a woman. But this does not portray rape as an innocent exercise. Behavior has consequences. He did the crime, so he must do the time. There is no need to plumb the depths of his psyche to determine whether or not some "mental illness" "justifies" his crime. Now, there's no need for the presence of hired guns—psychiatrists or psychologists serving as expert witnesses. Too often, the proceeding requires the jury of laymen to make sense out of their conflicting and confusing testimonies.

I am sad to relate that the testimony too often supports the position of the defendant or prosecutor who is paying the expert. The matter is now simplified. The jury has only to determine whether or not a rape took place. If so, a prescribed sentence is imposed. Both the victim and society have been accorded justice. (See *Anatomy of a Rape*, the second part of this book.)

Gun Control Controversy, February 3, 2013: <u>An Important and Unaddressable Mental Health Issue</u>

After the slaughter of the young schoolchildren and their teachers at Sandy Hook Elementary School in New Jersey, there has been a great deal of talk about the need for gun control. In relatively short order, both talk and need will die down. The likelihood of anything constructive materializing is slight.

Fear rules in the long haul. The NRA and the neocon right of the Republican Party provide a clear-cut, albeit wrong, solution. Arm everyone! "The only way to deal with a gun-toting bad guy is to have a gun-toting good guy confronting him," is their slogan. The Wild, Wild West is its template. The Second Amendment of the Right to Bear Arms allegedly supplies a great deal of constitutional cover for those proposing this dangerous idea.

Three possible laws have been under consideration with only the first given a second look.

1. Maintain a register of felons and mental patients who would be prohibited from purchasing firearms.

   Felons can be readily defined as law breakers—those who have committed felonies or crimes. Hopefully, there would be some attempt to restrict the restriction to those crimes that involve the use of firearms.

   "Mental patients" are included in a very mixed bag. Most mental patients are non-aggressive. Picking the potential shooters would require more precise criteria than are currently available. Those implementing this approach would cast a very wide net that would permit perhaps 1 accurate designation and 100 or 1,000 or 1,000,000 mistakes. This "false positive" problem is well known to social scientists.

   Substantial civil rights issues would need to be resolved. This approach could probably be adopted in some watered-down, irrational form. This will create the illusion that something is being done. Post-diction or "Monday morning quarterbacking" is easily accomplished. Identification of a mass murderer in advance of his crimes is next to impossible.

   The mental health establishment individually or collectively cannot be accounted on to provide anything of substance to the resolution of the problems of citizen guns and their killing fields.

2. Establish restrictions on production, purchase, and possession of guns with large-capacity magazines or clips of cartridges. Currently, it is thought that seven is the magic number; clips with eight or more would be prohibited. Common sense would argue that this is more than reasonable; that there is no need for any more cartridges if one uses guns for recreation or protection of the home.

   However, fear dominates the initial debate. For example, would such a restriction handicap a young woman confronted by between three to seven criminals that were intent on raping and pillaging her, her children, and her home? Patently silly, such arguments are offered seriously and accepted, particularly by the NRA.

3. Establish restrictions on production, purchase, and possession of AKAs and other battlefield firearms. The same sort of arguments cited in the previous paragraphs pertain to this contentious area as well, but there seems to be a special justification for the possession of the weapons with great killing power. It is said that they are necessary if there is a time when the U.S. Government might swoop down upon the individual gun owner—in Blackhawk helicopters, no less—to take his weapons away from him. The argument is that he needs heavy

> artillery to defend himself, his weaponry, and his possessions. Is it not obvious that in this unlikely, ludicrous "survivalist" scenario, the all-powerful U.S. Government would blow the weapon owner (and his Second Amendment card) to smithereens in a matter of milliseconds?

But braying about Second Amendment rights fits right in with the absurd braggadocio of the survivalists, especially when he has had a second beer in a neighborhood tavern. They portray themselves as heroes in an imaginary conflict, fighting the good fight against overwhelming odds—without really risking anything other than the tired ears of listeners who have nothing better to do. Some might refer to all this as delusional behavior.

All of the concerns and need for action died out very quickly as the memories of Aurora, Sandy Hook, Columbine, and other comparable killings faded.

There is some precedent for the fate of gun control legislation and mass killings. A very long time ago, car accidents were both rare and the subject of a community's conversation. Now, they are commonplace and generally ignored unless very large numbers of people are killed. Because of modern technology and instant access, we hear of mass destruction and natural disasters right when they're happening, videos streaming of tragic events on YouTube and going viral on the Internet. When hundreds of people die, nobody bats an eye anymore.

Sad to say, even today, murders of two to four people at one time occur regularly and are ignored or accorded only minimal newspaper coverage. Up the road a very short bit, it might take ten or more victims to raise a ripple in the public consciousness. The recent theater shooting in 2012 in Aurora during the latest Batman movie seemed more influential for the movie industry than the 12 people who died, their families, and the over 70 injured at the event.

We then extend to mass murderers the same level of attention and concern that we accord automobile accidents.

Is this the America we really want?

CHAPTER 7

A Religious Reconnaissance

In my early years, my sainted grandmother taught me many things, although I didn't notice it at the time. Now, I would clearly categorize them as important, early-on forms of Nurturance. The reader is reminded that Nurturance refers to circumstances promoting the learning of new responses and losing or extinguishing old responses. Her admonitions included avoidance of any serious discussion of politics and religion with anyone.

She indicated clearly that if I were to violate these admonitions, friendships might disappear, personal dislike would flourish, and my life would not be an easy one. This didn't stop her from referring to Catholics as "Catlickers" or "mackerel snappers" (this latter refers to eating fish on Friday because "The Church" then prohibited eating meat on that day) or saying that the Pope's nose was the last part to be seen of a chicken as it flew over the fence.

Although married to a Catholic, she observed none of the practices of that religion. Maybe to be on the safe side, she did occasionally donate money to a small Presbyterian church on Birch Street in Eau Claire, Wisconsin. But when the minister of that church visited her home, all of us would remain silent and motionless until he had departed.

The minister would have had to be very dumb not to notice this deception. To me, a developing youngster, this was not at all unusual.

Although Mormons were "as scarce as hen's teeth" in our area, she and her friends found some jokes about them.

> Always take at least two Mormons with you on a fishing trip. *If you just take one, he'll drink up all your beer.* (This is a reference to Mormon abstinence from drink).
>
> If a Christian doesn't recognize Buddha and a Jew doesn't recognize Jesus, who doesn't a Mormon recognize? *Another Mormon in a liquor store.*
>
> Why does a Mormon woman stop having children at 35? *She feels she just can't handle 36 kids.*

Were those Mormon and Catholic jokes cruel? It didn't seem so at the time.

I've fudged a bit by recording two major violations of my grandmother's admonitions. I've recorded the religious jokes for your edification and amusement. I've already identified myself as a dyed-in-the-wool Democrat. Perhaps I'm simply living up to a developing reputation as one who is consistently inconsistent. And of course, I side-step any responsibility for any of this. "I am what I am and that's all I am!"

Religious beliefs do have a lot going for them. While I offer only the most complex, difficult to understand explanation regarding people and events, religions suggest that there's some Chess Master or something up there that knows what is going on. Religion offers heaven and salvation, and inasmuch as your religion provides many answers, you have no need to think or engage in what you consider to be choices. These are big-time advantages. But bear in mind the role of Chance in determining whatever religion that embraces you. You didn't embrace the religion. You never had any serious choice regarding this or any other matter.

My stated position touches upon another biblical statement: "There, but for the grace of God, go I." I substitute "mindless Chance" for the "God." For the devout, that change is blasphemy. The biblical statement supplies a reason for a person's unacceptable behavior. This does run only a bit counter to the facetious, "The devil made me do it."

Another biblical statement provides for an acceptance of the unacceptable, the maddening "Personal storms that can't be weathered," "And the peace of God, which transcends all understanding, will guard your hearts and minds in Christ Jesus," (Philippians 4:7). In other words, there is some meaning or method in this madness. Perfectly horrible things are to be accepted as a part of some divine plan that, by definition, cannot be understood, e.g. one child dies in an explosion while another does not. The scientist within me cannot accept this belief.

JNDs and JNNDs
(Just Noticeable Differences and Just Not Noticeable Differences)

At this time, it seems mandatory to revisit Chapter 4 and to interject some concepts which have deep roots in experimental psychology.

During the early days of psychology as a science, an incredible amount of psychological research was devoted to investigations of our senses, i.e. what was scientifically happening when we would smell something or if we were touched? For example, how far apart on the skin must two simultaneous tactile stimulations (touches) be before they were realized as such—a Just Noticeable Difference between two points rather as one stimulation? Did this JND vary when different bodily areas were stimulated?

The reader can, without guilt, disregard these studies. While conducted in accordance with the Scientific Method, they failed to generate much of anything that would be helpful in understanding and assisting people. Can you think of anything duller?

However, the concepts of JND and JNND *per se* are very useful in understanding beliefs and how they are learned.

But first, we can use an example involving physical change to illustrate the concepts of JND and JNND. After a year, it can be ascertained that a person has grown taller, that change has taken place. If one measures the height of an adolescent annually, it will be clearly noticed that there has been a difference. How about every month? How about every day? As the frequency of measuring is increased, so is the likelihood of first determining JNDs (emphasize the "just") and then maybe JNNDs. (There's no doubt that change has taken place; it's just that it isn't discernable or noticed.)

These concepts can be applied to human learning. The end product of learning can be identified, but the steps/changes taken to accomplish this end cannot. When they are identifiable, they are referred to as JNDs in change. When they are not, they are referred to as JNNDs. An awful lot of changes/learning takes place without the learner being aware that he is learning.

No one is born with religious beliefs and biases. These are learned over the course of one's life, often without any awareness that such learning is taking place.

Can you understand a bit of my religious biases by reading a few jokes and stories? Maybe yes, maybe no, but the reader is reminded of the many thousands upon thousands of other nurturing/learning experiences related to my biases that no one will ever know. The number and variety of JNNDs may approach infinity.

Let's concentrate on religion and a few other beliefs to illustrate the point being made in the previous section. When you were first aware (JND) that you were a believer and under what circumstances? You'll have a real problem in coming up with a scientifically-defensible answer to that one. Consider if you will the huge number of JND and JNND learning that took place as you developed your religious belief. By definition, you were denied any knowledge of the latter.

It's with some trepidation that I devote this chapter to my "take" on religious beliefs. It's my basic belief of that such beliefs are learned early on in circumstances devoid of choice or control on the part of the learner. Accordingly, I think that it would be instructive if believers would challenge the validity of their beliefs.

For illustrative purposes, I have chosen to critique Christianity and the Ten Commandments which are regarded as the Word of God. Of course, you know by now that I never had any choice as I developed opinions about them. For the "being" that I am at this point in my life and at this stage of this writing, my "decision" to comment on Christianity was inevitable. Some readers might say that my writings are hostile and incredibly ignorant. And of course, they had no real choice in coming to those conclusions.

It might be of interest to have someone attempt a comparable critique about other faiths. If anyone is interested, it should be pointed out that the followers of some faiths would not only frown upon such inquiry, but might single out the critic for execution. In 2012, a 14-year-old Pakistani girl, Malala Yousafzai, was shot on a school bus because her attacker believed that she had violated some Moslem beliefs related to girls and their education.

One isn't born a Christian, a Methodist, a Hindu, or a Moslem. As Bloody Mary sings in the musical *South Pacific* about prejudice, "You're taught to believe." Most of us are born into a presumably friendly land: the family. One then learns the customs of that family. Religion or lack thereof happens to be one of these customs. It may be difficult to identify the first religious learning experience or the flood of them (JNNDs) that take place in childhood, adolescence, and early adulthood.

The earliest religious learning experience might take the form of a baptism and attendance at a church, catechisms, social events, etc. A lot of such religion-related "stuff happens." As a collateral event in this learning process, one might also learn that the other religious beliefs are suspect, downright inferior, or just plain wrong.

Benefits and Down Sides

Many simple rewards for the belief learner accrue early on. Some form of heaven and the security of associating with other believers are two important benefits. These continue on and are supplemented with more complex rewards as the individual matures. The roots of one's religious beliefs are deep and strong. Deviations from these are frowned upon by the believer's associates and may be actively punished.

This belief acquisition process fits neatly into classic psychological learning theory: Habits which are reinforced or rewarded are retained; habits that are punished or unrewarded vanish. This learning or indoctrination produces strong habits or religious beliefs that are highly resistant to change.

An individual becomes very set in his religious beliefs early on.

Religious beliefs provide a way of life that can be rich and rewarding. If the learner adheres to these, he's provided with a format for living. The family looms large in this process. Reasonably regular prayer to a deity is an important part of this. As long as the learner prays and lives his life according to the religious tenets of his belief, he will prosper. As he encounters the inevitable problems and challenges of life, he has been furnished with an understanding of these and appropriate responses to them. If he strays from his beliefs, he knows that redemption can restore him to the straight and narrow. He is also promised something of an ultimate reward; when he dies, he will go to a heaven where he will live "high on the hog" eternally. All will be beer and skittles. He is in a win-win situation. Non-believers are on their own as they live their lives.

Behavior dictated by religious beliefs has incredibly important consequences. Killing is sanctioned in certain circumstances. As I write, this an 11-year-old Pakistani retarded girl may be executed because she, perhaps unknowingly, was observed burning some pages of the Koran. Suicide bombers, following the dictates of their faith, believe that the death of infidels is justified. Perhaps such killing may even provide a passport to their heaven.

Dying for one's religion or martyrdom ranks high in some religions. If a choice between death and faith is presented to the learner, the decision is clear as a bell.

It's not my purpose to castigate Christianity or any other religious beliefs. I lack the credentials and/or interest to do so. I'll leave this to others. I'll just state some of my opinions that I believe have a rational basis. Bear in mind that I believe that I, bring brought up as I was, really had no choice in the acquisition of any of these ideas.

I do have a pet peeve. On the rarest of occasions, I've shared with churchgoers that I envy of them for the reasons cited in previous paragraphs. After all, a belief has no end of advantages: Security, companionship, clear-cut rules to live by, prayers that can provide control over many things, the ultimate reward in the form of eventual acceptance into heaven and sitting next to the Lord on His throne. However, when I share this feeling of envy, I find myself annoyed with its reception. The listeners usually smile knowingly; they're convinced that I have a problem that could be solved immediately if I would just adopt their belief. This cuts across many Christian denominations. I'm adjudged as "wrong" as they bask in the glow derived from the belief that they, and perhaps they alone, are absolutely "right." My disbelief can be viewed as valid as their beliefs. I believe the sanctimonious smiles are those of smug, ignorant, and un-Christian individuals. I don't point this out to them. I don't say to them that, "Christianity sounds like a real good idea; someone should try it out sometime."

I have beliefs which many would regard as irreligious. As I say endlessly, I really have no real choice in the formation of those beliefs. As the cartoon character Barnacle Bill was fond of saying, "I am what I am and that's all I am." People who need labels might call me a "free thinker" or a "humanist." Others might zero in with "agnostic" or "atheist." This labeling is acceptable to me. I've absolutely no control over others and their opinions. "Sticks and stones may break my bones, but names will never hurt me." I believe that my belief system is truly unique unto me; that

I'm unclassifiable.

Nevertheless, my belief system allows me considerable freedom in commenting on belief systems generally. I'm not "married" to a belief. After many second and third thoughts, I have chosen to include an article (next chapter) that I wrote ten years ago regarding the Ten Commandments. I wouldn't change a word of it. Many readers would consider it a critique; I would think that a "chiding" would be a more appropriate term.

I find myself supported by the statement of Albert Einstein: "The Bible is a collection of honorable but still primitive legends which are nonetheless pretty childish." The letter containing this quotation has just been offered for sale on eBay with a starting price of 3 million dollars.

To paraphrase comedian Bill Maher, a disbeliever, "Prayer is an extrasensory effort to communicate with an imaginary companion."

For those Christians and others who are easily offended by similar irreligious commentary, you might skip Chapter 8 and find something better to do.

The Need to Challenge Belief Systems: A Controversial Area

As we deal with this life of constant growth and change, useful resources would be invaluable. Some seek and often find guidance and advice in churches, mosques, and synagogues. Some regularly consult a horoscope. Others may rely on the likes of "experts" such as Dr. Phil, his "Philosophy" and the coterie of experts he has assembled. In various forms, "Advice to the Lovelorn" columns pepper newspapers and magazines. Some people may unknowingly rely upon echoes of the words they thought they heard while sitting on their mother's knee. The list of such potential, other resources is a very long one.

These many resources vary considerably in the practical and significant assistance they provide. Some are useful. Others may be outdated and counter-productive. The latter are often heavy on the don'ts—the things we are not to do. There is an absence of the do's, the assertive actions that we must initiate to improve ourselves and our situations.

There is no question that Shakespeare got it right in one of the soliloquies in Hamlet: "There are more things in Heaven and Earth than are dreamt of in your philosophies." I'd go one step more and say that there are many undreamt of unknowns out there that are absolutely beyond our abilities to identify, understand, and control. The "assistance" that many belief systems provide is a country mile away from the help that many people need to adjust more effectively in this day and age.

First and foremost, we must define a "Changeling." A Changeling is made of change. He or she must first identify and challenge their basic beliefs. The purpose of this is to determine what is working for the individual and what is not, and the intention is not to demolish an entire important belief system. The objective is to identify the what and why of those elements in a belief system that aren't working.

Many people simply can't do it. There are strong taboos against challenging strong belief systems such as religions.

As you consider it, you have no choice in the matter. The person you are at this moment has their opinion at the ready, awaiting the stimulus for expression.

But a belief system must be vigorously challenged if there is to be change. If one fails to do this, progress is unlikely—indeed, impossible.

I decided to attempt to lead by example. I chose to challenge the most basic of beliefs of the Christian faith, The Ten Commandments. My critique is hidden away in this document under the authorship of a fictitious St. Jay, an Apostate. As I indicate in the preface to this challenge, I'm sure that most Christians would reject my contentions and some would be able to provide good evidence for this rejection.

But it should be pointed out that well over half of the population of this planet would reject The Ten Commandments out of hand. In turn, each of these competing religions could profit from some scrutiny and questioning as well. Any such effort would be viewed by some believers as blasphemy, a crime that should result in the death of the unbelievers.

I also believe that many people want and need a strong religious belief system. In America, it's their right to believe whatever they choose to believe. I have trouble with religions only when they assume that their belief system is the only one. Atheists, agnostics, and people who have no interest in religion have rights that should be observed.

No less a philosopher than *All in the Family*'s Archie Bunker displayed his disbelief in religions when he proclaimed that "Religion is where people believe in something that no one in their right mind would believe."

My only point in all this doesn't involve making choices as to which religion got it right. Religions should invite challenges. If they have defensible reasons for a given belief system, there is no need to be offended by questions or alternate views.

"Changelings" must feel free to challenge all of their belief systems, including religion. In doing so, they can determine what works for them and what doesn't. If they fail to do so, then the interference from counter-productive beliefs can be like the proverbial elephant in the living room; very important, unseen, and unattended.

An Afterthought

Vague condemnations of my positions are not helpful. Specific arguments are welcomed.

This results from the incredible complexity of the subject matter, my inability to get my mind around it, and my shortcomings as a writer. Some writers are content to write and then symbolically throw it all at a wall to see how much will stick. They then print what has stuck. This hasn't been my style, but as I have proofread this, I can easily see where a reader might get that impression. I go with what I've got. I don't believe that I really had much choice in the manner of my presentation.

But Changelings, those in search of an improvement in their personal lot, might find this discussion in Chapter 8 necessary, interesting, and even provocative. All beliefs can profit from challenge. What is the useful "wheat"? What, pray tell, is "chaff"?

A lot of religious advice and counsel may have been appropriate at another time and in another place. The Ten Commandments may not pass current muster on all counts. Sometimes their interpretation may lead to unnecessary frustrations and restraints as they constrict the number of options available to those who wish to deal more effectively with the present and what the future may hold. A challenge to this basic Christian belief is often a necessary prelude to constructive change. The number of Christians who would take issue with this paragraph is legion.

CHAPTER 8

A Religious Renegade

The Renegade: In the guise of a fictitious renegade, St. Jay, the Apostate, I have chosen to single out The Ten Commandments as a prime example of an established part of the Christian faith that is rarely questioned by its practitioners.

The Christian basic belief is that these Commandments are God-given. I have chosen them in order to set something of an example; if these Christian Commandments can and should be challenged, then all beliefs can and should be challenged by everyone. If you accept the need to challenge a belief, you are well on the way to shake loose from some of the shackles imposed upon you in the past. In a way, I'm attempting to lead by example. If I advocate the challenge of a most basic belief, then all beliefs can be challenged.

Virtually all other religions have different, similarly unquestionable and unquestioned credos. It's my belief that if one is to grow, he or she should occasionally challenge the basis of their lifestyle and their beliefs—religious and personal—retain that which works, and supplement what remains with an attempt to develop new ideas and approaches. One need not cast aspersions on the beliefs of others to accomplish this purpose. Followers should be able—and even eager—to defend their religious beliefs if called upon to do so.

Most religions seem antagonistic to change. It's almost as though the followers of each had decided that their religion got it right the first time around. Recently there has been a controversy between believers in the traditional Bible and those who wish to introduce gender-neutral language into it. The 2011 translation of the New International Version Bible (or NIV) doesn't change pronouns referring to God, who remains "He" or "The Father," but "brother" or "sister" replaces "brother" in the statement of John, the Evangelist: "If anyone says, 'I love God,' yet hates his brother, he is a liar." "Sister" now joins "brother." These and other similar changes are opposed by such groups as the Council on Biblical Manhood and Womanhood. This organization holds that women should submit to their husbands in the home and that only men can hold a position of leadership within their church. What do you think of this and other comparable controversies?

Do you object to thinking about such matters? Or are you one who is comfortable in challenging all beliefs, including your own?

Maybe a trial run is in order. The reader is encouraged to study and challenge the beliefs of a Wichita, Kansas Baptist group. Its members hold that God is causing the death of members of our military forces. He is doing this because of our society's acceptance of homosexuals and their lifestyle. If the logic in this escapes you, you are not alone. A leading member of the group, Margie Phelps, says that President Obama "is most likely the Beast spoken of in the Revelation"

(*Time*, March 21, 2011). The U.S. Supreme Court has recently sanctioned this group's desecration of veterans' funerals as a form of "free speech." Isn't it obvious that this far out belief system should be challenged at every opportunity? If they weren't so bothersome, they might not warrant much more than a second glance from outsiders. What is your take on this matter?

In March 2011, a strange Florida clergyman named Terry Burns finally burned a copy of the Koran even though he has been made aware of the dire consequences of such an act. It was part of a mock trial that accused Moslems of promoting terrorist activities. This destruction of the Moslem's Holy Book was potentially offensive to well over a billion Moslems. Some sought to retaliate by killing a dozen or so UN workers in Afghanistan. Burns' beliefs led directly to these deaths. He is unrepentant, indicating he is a Christian acting on the basis of his Christian beliefs.

Potential Limitations

As I singled out The Ten Commandments for consideration and commentary, I considered them from my own highly personal view: That of a critical, scientifically-trained non-believer. Some of my colleagues, most of them Christians, have expressed concerns that some others might regard this approach as profane, sacrilegious, and/or offensive. I could be viewed as a great White Satan or anti-Christ. While this wasn't my intention, I accept that possibility. I understand why some would question my qualifications for undertaking such an endeavor. I would suggest to them, facetiously, that they might be in the position of extending forgiveness or praying for my redemption. I'm certainly no saint in any sense of the word I have no theological background, experience, nor serious interest/involvement in formal religion in any form. I remain open to arguments that if I were to be properly back-grounded and educated, I would "see the light."

I go one step further. I adopt a semi-facetious approach that many would consider anathema when it comes to discussing such serious, scriptural matters. While this comes easily to me, I believe a light-hearted approach is essential in such discussions. Sour seriousness would inhibit or even prohibit the atmosphere necessary for free and open discussions. Have you ever noticed the change in informal conversation when the clergyman walks up and becomes a participant?

The reader is reminded that I regard myself as "irresponsible" as a critic of religion. I had no choice or control over the circumstances/factors that caused me to develop these and all other views.

My acknowledged lack of credentials should ease the concerns of some who might worry that my critique could ever be considered a serious challenge to the basic tents of Christian faith. Anyone who might become unsettled by this possibility can disregard my commentary completely or murmur smugly, "It can't be much. Just consider the source." I find this position most understandable, but persons in search of improving their personal lot might find this addendum to be both interesting and even provocative. All beliefs can profit from challenge.

A lot of traditional advice and counsel may have been appropriate at another time and in another place. But The Ten Commandments may now fail to pass muster. They may lead only to frustration and restraints as they inhibit the range of our efforts to deal more effectively with the present and what the future might hold. The challenge of basic beliefs is a necessary prelude to the constructive change of a person. The number of Christians who would take issue with this paragraph is again legion.

An Alternative Belief

For a variety of reasons, I recommend that you consider "The Twenty Suggestions" (in Part III to follow) as a current, practical, and effective source of useful counsel and advice. These suggestions are just that; faint hints or indications that may be accepted or rejected with ease and impunity. They are the product of my 30-plus years of experience as a clinical psychologist and professor of psychology. They are brief and to the point, mercifully free from the pretentious "psycho-babble" that too often clutters this area of psychology. My clients and students have found them useful in a variety of highly-individualized ways, and such individualization is important. It must be pointed out that the goals of "The Twenty Suggestions" (Part III) are noble. There's nothing in them that is antagonistic to the positive attributes of any other belief.

Biographies are a rich source of information regarding the personal utility of beliefs and their utility. Without needing to experience the pain occasioned by a poor fit, one can sift and winnow and cast out from consideration that which is obviously inappropriate for you. Famous actress Ellyn Burstyn, for example, came from a dysfunctional family headed by a distant, demanding, and uncaring mother. Despite winning an Oscar in 1974 for her performance in *Alice Doesn't Live Here Anymore*, she spent a lifetime trying to prove to that mother that she measured up.

Replicating the problems of her family in many ways, she sought out many therapists and mystics to better understand herself. She rejected her Catholic faith and tested out a multitude of others in her unsuccessful search. On one occasion, she was told by a therapist that she should confront an ex-husband who carried a diagnosis of paranoid schizophrenia, apologize to him, and exact a promise from him to stop stalking her. A get-together was arranged and what seemed to be a truce was established. Eight days later, he committed suicide by jumping out a ninth floor window.

Her guilt for this was immeasurable and prolonged. Along the way, she had embraced the teachings of the Sufi sect of the Moslem faith. This helped her for many years, but she never seemed to develop and employ a set of beliefs that would comfort and sustain her. Eighty or so years old now, she is still searching.

No less an authority than Suze Orman, financial expert, has suggested that Americans, now despairing of becoming very wealthy because of the sea change in their economic futures, have turned inward to assess their worth. The pursuit of personal importance now may involve more of who one is rather than how much one has. I have doubts about this. But if so, this will require Americans to engage in a new and strange venture that they are ill-equipped to handle. As they need help and direction as they engage in this search, some new guideposts might prove useful for them.

Such guideposts are now offered freely to those who seek a better life. These pithy pronouncements of "The Twenty Suggestions" may be helpful. Some people may use these suggestions as a checklist, simply reading through them for ideas as to how they might improve. Some may have their interest piqued by one or two suggestions to the point where they wish to explore them fully. Therapists might encourage periodic readings as part of an ongoing treatment program.

Parents might find "The Twenty Suggestions" a starting point for a personal dialogue with their adolescent children. Their use as focal points of group discussions appears promising.

People dealing with complex change find personality theories to be of little use. They want concrete suggestions or directions that will encourage them to think deeply and productively as they continue to fashion a tailor-made strategy for living their own lives. As a stimulant to engage in new and constructive thought, I believe that "The Twenty Suggestions" does just that.

One, two or all 20 of the suggestions could have a significant effect upon one's life. The reader is encouraged to try them on for size. If the shoes fit, wear them. There's no downside to this practice. While one can "break" a Commandment, one can't "break" a suggestion! There isn't any hellfire awaiting the Changeling who chooses to reject any or all of them. If a suggestion doesn't work out, one's life will simply go on as before, but if one or more of these suggestions click, a person's life may be altered and enriched to a significant degree; problems can be avoided or dealt with more effectively; the ideas they suggest may open up new worlds to explore, experience, and enjoy.

The Ten Commandments*
As Reviewed by St. Jay, the Apostate**

It is my belief that this treatise has a decidedly positive, progressive, and useful flare about them that is in sharp contrast with the negative/authoritarian quality of "The Ten Commandments." Accordingly, I feel under some obligation to explore the basis for that assertion.

I began to look at each of "The Ten Commandments" through the eyes of an innocent, untutored, and disinterested observer. As I warmed to the enterprise, I came up with some valid wonderment about some of them. I chose to phrase these challenges in a light-hearted, even facetious manner. I'd like to think that the questions I raised and the concerns I've expressed could be easily addressed, answered, and dismissed by any competent authority.

That remains to be seen. If I've treaded upon anyone's delicate sensibilities, I offer my sincere apologies in advance. I realize that people do take their religion seriously. I have no real choice as I feel compelled to write and publish my views. I believe that I'm balancing the need to avoid offending with my need to pursue enlightened inquiry.

My purpose is to stimulate, explore, and illuminate thought in myself and in others. The bedrock of this basic belief of mine can be found in an early childhood spent in the company of a wonderful and politically-incorrect grandmother who always told it like it is and encouraged me to do the same. Much later on, I became guided by what is known as "The Wisconsin Idea," the "fearless sifting and winnowing so that Truth shall become known." While formal religion is certainly a far cry from my personal experience, professional expertise, or serious personal interest, I feel quite comfortable in raising and expressing some questions and concerns about this basic Christian document.

I should not have to remind the reader that the bases of my belief and that of the reader were established through learning under circumstances that were devoid of choice and control.

1. **THOU SHALT HAVE NO OTHER GODS BEFORE ME.**

   For some, this might seem like a demand for a monopoly without any need to earn this exalted status. It would seem proper for people to be accorded the opportunity to pick and choose. If HE (ME) is truly as great as HE says He is, then HE should and would be the overwhelming choice in any competition. But HIS absolute statement doesn't provide for any such test. Then, one must consider the possibility that "HE" could be a "SHE." As is, any competition does seem to be ruled out and sexism might run rampant.

   Maybe a strong position such as this is required because of false gods that prevail so easily. Mammon and Mammonism clearly dominate Wall Street and other financial quarters. And when push comes to shove regarding big-time athletics, other "gods" are easily in the ascendancy.

Sunday church services are rearranged to accommodate parishioners who must observe every movement of every Green Bay Packer. A Roman Catholic priest even gets a sitting ovation, replete with some tittering, if he concludes a service with, "Go Packers."

Some seemingly unsaintly Packers, such as Brett Favre, are treated with greater deference and devotion than would be accorded the holiest of the Holies. If the dearly departed Reggie White, both a minister and a Packer, couldn't cross the Bay without the benefit of bridge or boat, it might have come to a surprise to his following. Fervent fans came close to believing that the very deceased Vince Lombardi had really appeared at a Superbowl celebration. The $10.00 piece of Tundra Turf removed from the field at Lambeau Field could very easily fall within the definition of a form of religious relic.

2. **THOU SHALT NOT MAKE UNTO THEE ANY GRAVEN IMAGE OR ANY LIKENESS OR ANYTHING THAT IS IN HEAVEN ABOVE, OR ON THE EARTH BENEATH, OR THAT IS IN THE WATER BENEATH THE EARTH.**

"Graven" is the key word here, i.e. an idol made of wood, stone, plastic, etc. Any site for its construction is clearly ruled out. No "idol" thoughts or constructions are to be tolerated anywhere. But there is evidence that doesn't really rule out representations that come awfully close to being graven.

The Sistine Chapel at the Vatican has a full share of these with its creating being the most touching. Statues and artworks of Jesus Christ, along with assorted representations of angels and saints, are found wherever there are Christians. There are many artistic religious works that aren't really art forms. It's often difficult to tell whether the faces on many statues and paintings represent religious ecstasy or severe mental retardation.

This would seem to be an easy Commandment to observe. How many Christians on a given afternoon would turn to making graven images if there was an opportunity to watch the Packers or view the growing of their grass or the drying of paint?

3. **THOU SHALT NOT TAKE THE NAME OF THE LORD, THY GOD, IN VAIN.**

This seems to mean that you aren't supposed to invoke the name of the Deity unless you really mean it and that the expression is vitally important to you. You don't waste it on the inconsequential. Christians are to save mention of the Deity for truly important occasions. Deathbed situations would be clearly appropriate. How about basketball players crossing themselves while mumbling a prayer before attempting a free throw? On the face of it, this and similar, trivial invocations would seem to be grossly unfair. The player's opponent must now contend both with him and his God. And what if he misses? Does this rejection send a special message to the shooter?

This Commandment seems to be a clear injunction against any swearing or blasphemy, and this prohibition makes a lot of sense. Saying, "God damn it!" after hitting your finger with a hammer seems both trivial and irreligious. One should save this ultimate destructive empowerment for important occasions. There are special times in life when one's situation may require the invocation of heaven-sized power and damnation. It might be instructional, albeit unsettling, when a person utters an ultimate God-rousing curse and nothing happens to his target, but that is another matter.

4. **REMEMBER THE SABBATH DAY TO KEEP IT HOLY, SIX DAYS SHALL THOU LABOR, AND DO ALL THE WORK, BUT THE SEVENTH DAY IS THE SABBATH OF THE LORD, THY GOD.**

This seems to be a real good idea in principle. If formal religion is as important as some Christians allege it to be, then certainly one day, perhaps even more, should be fully denoted to its observance. In practice, it would seem that many people embrace the work-free element of Sunday without the immersion in the faith that is required. To many, Sunday provides an opportunity for unbridled recreation and self-indulgence. Clergymen who feel that they must make their sermons entertaining or work them in around football games seem awfully close to breaking this Commandment.

5. **HONOR THY FATHER AND THY MOTHER.**

Even though she comes in second, the mother's act of giving birth would seem to make her worthy of being accorded some honor. But otherwise, the Commandment appears too automatic. The father's contribution to the production of a child is usually non-demanding, momentary, and pleasure-laden. Absent from this Commandment is any suggestion that parents must earn the honor, esteem, and high regard of their progeny. Earning this honor should require an incredibly demanding lifelong commitment on the part of the parents.

Why should this honor be automatically accorded to the likes of a Susan Smith (who rolled her car into a lake with her two kids strapped inside), O.J. Simpson, a child abuser, or a parent who creates a chaotic, fear-laden atmosphere within the home?

6. **THOU SHALT NOT KILL.**

Formal religion and our society allow all manner of exceptions to this great idea. In time of war, chaplains on one side support the killing of the enemy, which in turn has chaplains of their own who condone this practice. Even when both sides are primarily Christian, each side declares their cause to be the "right" one, a position that sanctions the killing of those on the other side—the "wrong" one.

Various holy wars remain with us with "death to the infidel" not far from the lips of the combatants.

Exceptions appear to abound. It's generally agreed that killing is permissible in the name of self-defense if the killer must contend with a life-threatening situation.

The conservative anti-abortion Christian constituency routinely invokes this Commandment to deny women choice regarding what they may choose to do with their bodies. In what appears to be a contradiction, some support capital punishment or feel that it's justifiable homicide to kill an abortionist.

Our psychiatric establishment provides a means by which those said to be acting at the mercy of an irresistible impulse or labeled as "mentally ill" can kill with impunity.

The Holy Bible seems to be chock full of incidents where killing is condoned, and even encouraged:

(II Samuel 4:12) "And David commanded his young men, and they slew them, and cut off their hands and hanged them up over the pool in Hebron."

If we look at Matthew 10:34 and Deuteronomy 13:6-9, Numbers 31:17-18, we find:

"Do not suppose that I have come to bring peace on earth. I did not come to bring peace, but the sword," and "If your very own brother, or your son, or your daughter, or the wife you love, or your closest friend, secretly entices you, saying 'Let us go and worship other gods,' do not yield to him or listen to him. Show him no pity. Do not spare him or shield him. You must certainly put him to death." Or, "Now kill all the boys. And kill every woman who has slept with a man, but save for yourself every girl who has never slept with a man."

7. **THOU SHALT NOT COMMIT ADULTERY.**

While this Commandment has a simplistic sound to it, Christians accepting it should insist that their churches provide more sex education, more effective prenuptial counseling, much longer engagement, and later marriages. Alternatives to marriage should be given serious consideration.

8. **THOU SHALT NOT STEAL.**

This seems straightforward, although some might view the tax-exempt status of churches as a form of grand theft of sanctimonious larceny. In addition, the televangelists of the 1980s to present day continue to fleece the sheep and profit unduly.

9. **THOU SHALT NOT BEAR FALSE WITNESS AGAINST THY NEIGHBOR.**

There would seem to be no problem accepting this Commandment until one remembers the Salem Witch Trials and the Spanish Inquisition. In those circumstances, false accusation and perjurious testimony were solicited and accepted by the churchmen involved as long as the "evidence" supported church dogma.

10. **THOU SHALT NOT COVET THY NEIGHBOR'S HOUSE; THOU SHALT NOT COVET THY NEIGHBOR'S WIFE, OR HIS MAIDSERVANT, OR HIS OX, OR HIS ASS, OR ANYTHING THAT IS THE NEIGHBOR'S.**

One might think that the last-mentioned prohibition is so all-inclusive that those that precede it are unnecessary. It's interesting to note the priorities with the home first and the wife second. God surely knew how to use the possessive case.

This Commandment is in special need of updating. Maybe "washer and dryer" should be substituted for "maidservant"; "pickup truck" for "ox," "auto" for "ass"...unless they had something other than a dumb beast in mind.

However, there should be some additional prohibitions provided in regard to this "anything that is the neighbor's" statement to make this principle clear and free from gender bias. As phrased, it comes from a man's point of view. One can be reasonably sure that most Christians might support the prohibition of a woman coveting a neighbor man—or a neighbor woman. They might not want to contemplate the possibility that any man might covet a neighbor man! A few additional words should cover this covetousness.

Some question might be raised about a man coveting his neighbor's wife. If this didn't lead to any overt action, an occasional semi-licentious daydream to that effect would seem harmless. After all, such an activity would be complimentary to this woman as well as to the man who has wedded and presumably bedded her. In this regard, consider former President Jimmy Carter. No one, except maybe the Pope, Jerry Falwell, and Oral Roberts, would be regarded as more devoutly Christian than this man. But on one occasion, before a spin control operation was contrived to the public what Carter "really" meant, he openly owned up to an innocent "lusting in my heart" for a woman who was not his wife. His honesty and openness were refreshing, if only for a moment.

Final Commentary

In general, "The Ten Commandments" have a decidedly negative or inhibitory quality about them. They tell Christians what they are not to do with little attention paid to what they should do. Their applicability to many facets of modern life is problematic.

I should point out to Christians that I am not a finished "being" and that a charismatic proselyte might yet point out the error of my ways. I wouldn't bet the farm on it, but he could tap some compelling learning experiences that I have forgotten, repressed, or failed to give proper emphasis in my personality formation.

*Source: *The Holy Book in the King James Version.*

**A.K.A. John R. Thurston, Ph.D.

CHAPTER 9

Summary, Conclusions, and Suggestions

As I write this chapter, I must admit that this treatise of mine has been overly-ambitious from the get-go. It has taken an unusual effort to explain and summarize the basic explanatory principles that allow an understanding of what happens to people, including you, the reader, as they live their lives from the moment of their conception until they shuffle off this mortal coil.

At the very beginning, the ovum and the sperm get together for a great moment: your conception.

At that time, **Nature** defines you. In part, you are governed by the genes that were bestowed upon you. **You had no choice or control in this matter and many others.** This comment will recur throughout this writing.

No attempt will be made to attempt any detailed definition of genetic contribution to your personality. Needless to say, if any one of the relevant couplings of the many thousands of your ancestors hadn't taken place, you wouldn't be here today. (You certainly had no choice or control in these matters.)

Genetic research is now an exciting, dynamic, and productive field. They've gone far beyond "It runs in your family." But if you like, you can still blame your failure to fit into your jeans on those genes provided by a maternal grandmother.

Dr. Phil remains in hot pursuit of a "Warrior Gene" that will account for aggressive behavior on the part of an adolescent or adult. I believe that this is another example of overstatement on the part of people who should know better. At best, the "Warrior Gene" is merely one of many significant factors, interacting with one another in a complex environment that results in aggression, variously defined.

Be prepared form time to time to see announcements with headlines such as "Alzheimer's Studies See Genetic Links." In light of the high incidence of this malady, many scientists, patients, and family members are very interested in research associated with it. Newspaper reports of results are often misleading, overly optimistic, and provide little useful information.

The genetic components of **Nature** set limits on what could happen to the individual. Just a few years ago, it was thought that these couldn't be changed. This is no longer true. Genetic research is an exciting and very promising field.

Nurturance beings to move in immediately on the fertilized ovum. You are nourished by the blood of your mother. Her uterus provides you with warmth and protection. Some say that the developing embryo is experiencing a period of "intrauterine bliss," but there are exceptions to this. You have no choice regarding the adverse effects if your mother was carrying the HIV virus or if she remains zapped with drugs during this crucial time. By Chance, your umbilical cord could wrap around your neck and deny you oxygen. A lot of other harmful things could happen. **You have no choice or control in this matter.**

You are now within the beginning of a developmental process in which you change in a slow, not readily apparent manner. I'll go one step further. This dynamic process and its components cannot be discerned and identified in advance nor when it's occurring nor after it has happened. To know yourself, you'd need to have knowledge of the process and all its components. That's not possible!

You are now born, thrust out into the light of day. **Nurturance** now moves into high gear. If you're lucky, you become a welcomed member of a good family, the heir to all manner of good things that can happen to and for you. There are many negative possibilities as well. I'll leave the identification of these to your limited recollection and unfettered imagination.

All sorts of people appear in your world. Generally, your mother is the centerpiece in this operation. **You have no choice or control in any of these matters.** Each and every one of these people and other circumstances has impact of varying significance upon the development of your personality. Each is at a stage of his or her own personal development.

You'll grow and develop in a physical environment that you didn't choose. In varying degrees, it will impact your personal development over the course of your life. As is obvious, your personality would be affected differently if you were born in the Sahara Desert, Baffin Island; Altoona, Wisconsin, or some other place.

Let us advance until the time when you begin making decisions. **Or, more realistically, think that you are making decisions.** In reality, all of the ingredients of what you believe to be "choice" are already in place **awaiting the stimulation which will bring them forth**. The stimulation will come from anything in your external physical environment, the people included. It also can take the form of the internal self-stimulation of your thoughts or your "stream of consciousness." Your awakened moments are never free from this self-stimulating process and are being changed by whatever you've learned from each stimulation, and moving on to the next stimulation and on and on and on throughout the entire course of your life. You shift back and forth between the external and internal stimulations. You learn and change constantly as you react in this fashion. You are both a part and a product of this process. You never escape from it. **You never have any real choice or control over this process and its ingredients.**

The reader is reminded that there are no free passes, although the person has no responsibility for the process that is constantly producing him, his behavior, or his misbehavior does have consequences. This becomes part and parcel of the learning process. If his reactions are well-received by members of his society, they or similar ones are likely to be repeated when he is confronted with another situation requiring a reaction. If they are not well-received—prison, shunning, fisticuffs, etc.—they may be supplanted by more acceptable reactions or retained for a variety of reasons in spite of the negative reaction.

I choose to emphasize the role of beliefs in this summary. But I really have no alternative. Personal beliefs are incredibly important. Over the course of your life, you will develop many strong belief systems. These guide your life in the many useful, important ways. But on the negative side, by the same process, you may have become a deeply-prejudiced individual, e.g. you hate Methodists or persons practicing some other religious faith, Democrats are deserving of anathema, you dislike hippies with a vengeance, you just don't like your neighbors even though you can't say why. As is obvious, the list is a very long one. The developmental process is the same for all of your beliefs. They can be incidental or consequential. You can merely dislike your neighbor or enthusiastically applaud the Holocaust.

Some might say that you acquired many prejudices when you were too young to know better. You're blameless! **You had no choice or control.**

Are your belief systems serving you well? If challenged, do they really make sense? Have you ever challenged any of them? If not, why not? Do you take umbrage when someone else suggests that a belief of yours is flawed or outrageous? What was your reaction to my semi-serious critique of the Ten Commandments chapter that preceded this one?

Any worthwhile belief system should be able to withstand criticism. The two preceding chapters on religious beliefs might be an acid test of that.

If some of your systems are not working for you, just maybe they should be changed. Change requires strong motivation. Change often occurs slowly in steps that are indiscernible from one another. Bear in mind that you really don't have within you the determinants which will impel you to change. They must be external and will probably appear as a Chance event; perhaps the reading of this treatise.

I urge you to dwell upon this topic and develop an understanding for or questioning of all that's involved. At the same time, you must realize that I believe that you have no choice or control in the response you make to this suggestion. You have no choice or control over any of your important learning experiences.

That's my position, starkly stated. It follows, then, that the causes of behavior are so complicated that there is no chance of anyone ever fully understanding any other individual.

Hopefully, you're now aware of the complexities that I've introduced, and with that comes the realization that you or anyone else can never really identify the determinants of your personality, the "you" that you are.

I'll not stop there. Chance events inevitably complicate this incredible complexity that's your personality determination.

Chance, really a sub-category of **Nurturance**, is so powerful and important that it deserves equal billing with **Nature** and **Nurturance** as a determinant of your personality.

Chance events can range from those that are easily and readily identifiable as significant and life-changing to those that are so subliminal that you are denied awareness of them. All of these can change the process called "personality development" without awareness on your part.

How does one escape from following the path laid down by one's past? One must change. However, great forces are in place which make this unlikely. The tethers to your past are formidable and very resistant to change.

Chance is a powerful but an undependable and predictable resource for change. Something or someone may come to your attention by **Chance** and provide you with the need and the means to seek out viable alternatives to the set pattern that has been your life. Something about the resource inspires you to act on what has been given you. **Chance**, by definition, is beyond your control.

Let's toss the ball into your court a while. Think band and identify Chance events that clearly impacted (both positively or negatively) the course of your life your belief systems. I'll provide a few examples to get you started.

1. Let's say that you're a steadfast, set-in-your-ways Catholic man. A red-hot, free-thinking young Lutheran woman may vault onto your scene by **Chance**. As you and she interact, you might entertain a few doubts, problems, and opportunities that would never have occurred to you as options a few months, days, or even minutes ago.

2. You have a heart attack. In your recuperation, you have an unexpected abundance of time to think about yourself and your life. You take advantage of this.

3. Your wife unexpectedly tells you that she has found a lover and wants a divorce. You hadn't even realized that she was not happy.

4. Someone tells you that you're growing old. You hadn't really considered this matter before.

5. As I blush modestly, I suggest that this treatise, "There, but for the mindless whims of Chance, go I," might provide an impetus to modify your rigid beliefs. **Living is a Chance-laden undertaking.** The reading of my works was probably occasioned by **Chance**; it had absolutely nothing to do with any pre-ordained rendezvous with destiny. Nothing in it could compete with some agents of change, like the young woman of the previous paragraph. Challenging and changing personal beliefs is an awesome task.

6. Similarly, "The Twenty Suggestions" of Part III may be helpful.

Chance may provide an impetus to change. Some may believe that the lack of control/choice dooms the individual to a set pattern, but this pattern can be useful and rewarding. It need not be a life of quiet desperation. As has been suggested previously, a person may be jolted into change by some dramatic or significant stimuli. The result isn't necessarily a good, trouble-free one.

Any person attempting to engage in a significant personal metamorphosis might be one of the last to notice any evidence of change; change that is perhaps obvious to very close friends and relatives. Seeking out such observations from time to time may allay the discouragement that is part and parcel of the process of change. But the "being" you are at these moments just might not choose to reach out for such assistance.

Change isn't a smooth process. There are many bumps in the road. The person engaged in this journey must fight against the well-entrenched support systems of a previous style of life. Important personal beliefs are highly resistant to change. Discouragement must be anticipated and accepted as part of the cost of proceeding into some new and more fulfilling "Promised Land."

Our **Nature** and **Nurturance** reach out to find expression in every facet of our learning and living. A capricious Dame Chance is always there to unpredictably interfere, to trump "the best laid plans of bugs and men—and women."

"There, But for the Mindless Whims of Nature, Nurturance, and Chance, Go I."

A Suggestion:

The reader is invited to turn to the next section, *The Anatomy of a Rape: It Took Two to Tangle* for an opportunity to test his or her understanding of a man and woman involved in a vicious crime. Do your previous beliefs help or hinder you as you proceed? Hopefully, your newly-acquired knowledge of **Thurstonian Theory** will be useful.

John R. Thurston, Ph.D.
Clinical Psychologist
2014

Part II

The Anatomy of a Rape
"It Took Two to Tangle"

This portion of the book provides the reader with an opportunity to evaluate and improve his or her empathic skills. The question is why a particular man and woman became involved in a vicious crime—a rape.

Does your belief system and knowledge of human behavior help or hinder you as you proceed? Hopefully, you will find the Thurstonian Theory to be useful.

John R. Thurston, Ph.D.
Clinical Psychologist
2014

It Took Two To Tangle:
A Rape Explored

John R. Thurston, Ph.D.

An Invitation to Inquiry, Innovation, and Involvement
2014

PROLOGUE

Throughout our lives, our personas are constantly bombarded and shaped by powerful forces and circumstances. While some are clearly identifiable, the most profound may be provided indirectly by people we have never met and will never come to know.

Chance events are far more important determinants of ourselves and our lives than most people realize.

So it was and will be with a man called Curtis and a woman named Kay. Their story will now be told.

So it was and will be with you, the reader. You are currently in the midst of your own personal story. Someday it, too, may be told.

TABLE OF CONTENTS - PART II

INTRODUCTION

Part A

The Rape

(From a newspaper article in the Eau Claire, Wisconsin *Telegram Observer*, January 15, 2005)

"An Eau Claire County jury last month convicted a Chippewa Falls, Wisconsin man of battery and sexual assault felonies. The assaults against a then twenty-one-year-old University of Wisconsin-Eau Claire coed occurred more than a year ago.

Curtis Thompson, 24, count face a maximum prison sentence of 42 years.

A self-styled landscape architect, Thompson was convicted of beating and raping his girlfriend after 11:00 p.m. on November 7, 2003. The attack began near the south end of the UWEC footbridge over the Chippewa River. In the course of the assault, the victim was dragged across the footbridge and along the pathway under the Water Street Bridge until they reached a secluded area in nearby Owen Park.

The Eau Claire County District Attorney, Harold Harms, expressed his horror over the nature and the brutality of the crime. Inasmuch as the woman had not reported the assaults until months after they had taken place, he had to take special pains to enable the jury to understand just how the "Battered Women's Syndrome," fit into the picture. The victim had initially denied that the attacks had ever taken place.

In the "Battered Women's Syndrome," the woman remains emotionally attached to the offender despite the abuse. Through the offender's domination, threats, and infliction of isolation, she is made to feel guilty for her part in the assault. She often comes to believe that she is totally responsible for being physically abused and battered, that if she had behaved differently all would have been well. In effect, she had become "brain washed" into these beliefs.

The day when the assault took place, Thompson had been drinking with the victim and some of her girlfriends since 5:00 p.m. at the Bellow Inn on Water Street. He had become enraged when his girlfriend had talked with some male UW-EC students. As a result, at about 9:30 p.m., Thompson stormed out of the bar. The woman and her female friends returned to their dormitory, Horan Hall.

Later, Thompson phoned her and demanded that she meet him near the footbridge. She complied. When she met him, he proceeded to punch and slap her repeatedly in the breasts and face, shove her into the bridge railing twice as they crossed the Chippewa River, and eventually push her down the steps at the north end of the bridge. She did not cry out although she was in great pain. She was bleeding profusely from her nose and mouth.

After he dragged her into the darkness of nearby Owen Park, he demanded that she strip. Despite a wind chill temperature of 10 degrees, she proceeded to do so. He then forced her to have vaginal, anal, and oral sex with him. Then as she lay on a brush pile, he urinated on her face. Throughout all of this, he kept calling her a "bitch" and a "whore." Then, while stomping on her with his boots, he threatened to kill her. After several minutes, he broke away and staggered back toward the footbridge.

Worried that he might harm himself, the woman ran after him.

She tripped him on the steps of the bridge. In the resulting fall, he claimed that he had hurt his leg. After this, she half carried him back over the footbridge to nearby Horan Hall where the two of them went to sleep.

Despite massive bruises and two black eyes, she attended her university classes early the following morning. When asked by a professor about her injuries, she told her that she has fallen down in the shower.

Later that morning, one of her friends went to the Campus Police to register a domestic assault complaint against Thompson on behalf of the woman.

However, when approached by the campus cops, she refused to cooperate and denied that she had been assaulted. She repeated her excuse. When the Eau Claire Police Department became involved, she insisted that Thompson had done nothing wrong.

Even after the assault, the woman continued to live with Thompson for several months, bearing him a child sometime in early fall of 2004.

In October 2004, the woman changed her mind and swore out a criminal complaint against Thompson.

In the opinion of the district attorney, the woman's credibility was the deciding factor in the jury's determination. She was at all times firm and forthright in her statements regarding details of the attack and her initial lies regarding the assault.

While continuing on as a student, the woman has since transferred to the University of Wisconsin-Platteville.

Eau Claire Circuit Court Judge Betsy Belknap will sentence Thompson in March 2005.

Part B

Why?

Now, what do you make out of that?

What might a reader's "take" on the article, the circumstances that it describes, and the central characters who played a part in it?

While there would be a natural tendency to focus on the attacker, the role of the woman is obviously in need of considerable attention. For simplicity's sake, the word "he" will be used in that which is to follow, but "she" could and should often be replaced in a rereading. This serious of events in this attack clearly involves the unique interaction between two extremely dysfunctional people.

Why, tell me why—?

He did not have God in his life! Either he had never gone to church or he had gone to the wrong one.

He was "genetically predisposed," programmed before birth to commit sexually violent acts.

He had gone to church too much. His religion may have been so replete with sexual taboos that it impacted his life in a distorted sexual perspective. Maybe he had a mother like "Momma White" in Stephen King's novel *Carrie*.

He came from a dysfunctional family.

His hormones were out of alignment. His testosterone level was out of sight.

He was evil incarnate.

He was "wired" wrong. His underlying neurology, with its axons, dendrites, synapses, tumors, et al, determined his actions.

He was "chemically imbalanced." Maybe he was suffering from some "bipolar disorder."

He was born under the wrong Zodiac sign.

He had not "successfully negotiated the Freudian psychosexual phase" of his development, whatever that might mean.

He was possessed by demons, i.e. the devil done made him do it.

Maybe he just wanted to be loved.

He was zonked out of his mind with alcohol or other drugs.

He was "emotionally disturbed."

He was flat-out "goofy." He should have been in some "goony bin."

The above "explanations" and undoubtedly others of the reader's own devising are very probably based on overly-simplistic generalities. But one or several in combination are probably satisfactory for the purposes of most people, and there is some substance to most generalities. After contemplating the article for a minute or two, most readers might think "Ain't it awful?" for a millisecond before they nod their heads in agreement with themselves as to cause. The reader thinks that he knows or that he knows enough, but what he doesn't know is that he doesn't really know much of anything about the event. Then, without a second thought, he will move on to the sports page or the entertainment section.

However, if anyone really wanted to know the truth of the matter, the required work and personal involvement would be formidable.

Part C

Commentary

Inasmuch as this book contains a story about rape, it might be useful to begin with a definition of this act. *The New World Dictionary of the American Language, Second College Edition* (1980) tells us that rape is "the crime of having sexual intercourse with a woman or girl forcibly and without her consent or with a girl below the age of consent (statutory rape)." That seems simple and straightforward until one attempts to apply it to events occurring in the real world of our experience.

Volumes have been written and are being written about just exactly what constitutes "consent" or "withholding consent." And current usage of the term does not restrict it to women. Young boys are raped by pedophiles. The Catholic Church is reeling from charges of rape of young boys by members of the priesthood. Men can be raped as well; this practice in prison constitutes a significant, growing, and largely ignored problem.

This dictionary definition is so dispassionate, devoid of any description of the rapist's motivation or the agony, fear, and despair of the victim. And the public might like it that way. Few, save the victim and her family, spend much time considering these deeply personal issues. People in the community may make jokes. "If you're about to be raped, just lay back and enjoy it," "Confucius say 'Rape is impossible. Woman without pants can run faster than man with pants halfway down.'" All too readily, many believe that the rape incidence figures are much too high, that "she was really asking for it."

In Bosnia, Kosovo, Afghanistan, Iraq, and many other countries, family members of the victim compound the problems of the individual who has been subjected to ritualized rape by enemy forces. They believe that there is always some compliance or consent. The woman must be subjected to ostracism for the rest of her life. In Afghanistan, multiple rape has been doled out as a proper legal sentence for a woman who committed some minor transgression involving local customs.

Knowledge about these crimes and their determinants is either non-existent or superficial in character. Each rape is a unique event. To understand what was involved would require very serious study of the lives and personalities of both the criminal and his victim. As has been mentioned previously, such in-depth personal explorations are hard to accomplish. One might think that "sex offender treatment programs" would routinely amass such information about background and motivations of this criminal. One would be wrong.

It would be easy for the reader to dismiss the explicit sexual history of Curtis and Kay as flat out "filth." This characterization is merely an easy way out. Simple condemnation is simple-minded. To understand fully the part that these two play in the rape, it is necessary to know how their pasts factor into it, and that requires detailed accounts of the ingredients or determinants involved in this crime.

With this highly personalized approach, the reader can begin to come closer to developing a full understanding of what really went on in the lives of these two people. Only then would it be possible to realize that in this instance that both Curtis and Kay were truly victims. One can invoke words such as "fate," "They were forced to play the cards that were dealt them," or "Shit just happened."

Even in a family newspaper, the rape was described in fairly explicit detail. Accordingly, it is believed necessary to use explicit details in describing any and all events that may have preceded it. Most of these may be foreign to the reader. They may have never have experienced, or even have known about what happens to persons such as Curtis and Kay during the course of their lives. This represents a naiveté that prevents people from developing a full understanding of the incident and why it—or something else equally offensive—was bound to take place.

There is nothing of *Ozzie and Harriet* in the background of either Curtis or Kay. Knowledge of an ostensibly "normal" family situation is insufficient to understand what is involved in all this. The reader is urged to tarry over these unsavory moments in the lives of these two individuals.

What if he or she had experienced these? Consider the impact they would have had. And these many moments in the lives of Curtis and Kay did have devastatingly effects in determining these two distinct and highly dysfunctional personalities. Without full and lingering consideration of these moments, the reader is denied the ability to empathize and to understand them fully.

While it may sound downright sacrilegious, the motivation and behavior of either Curtis or Kay are as difficult to understand as those of Mother Teresa. Most readers are denied the requisite empathy to understand all that is involved with almost anyone, their problems, and their accomplishments. Complete knowledge of another is impossible. Humility regarding such understanding of others exists in short supply. Most people are unduly impressed with their ability to understand those around them. People can come closer to accomplishing this if they recognize their inadequacies as they continuously search for the truth.

Part D

Guideposts

Old Russian Proverb

"Up to the age of five, the individual can be shaped,
From five to ten, he/she must be bent,
From ten until fifteen, he/she must be broken
And after that, the only solution is the grave."

In the Beginning

Nurturance begins to have important impact on determining one's destiny the moment of conception.

Pure Illusion

The notion that an adult has a full measure of independence, thus enabling him to exercise great control over the course of their life and their ultimate destiny.

Born Free*

A Modern American Pithogram

At birth, some say that an individual's options and opportunities are virtually unlimited.
Immediately, a process begins which diminishes this fount of freedom.
The individual is devoid of choice and control over the diverse forces and factors that are determining the kind of person he is becoming.
The loss of options is not optional.
One loses personal freedom by tiny, subliminal amounts.
This progressive diminution of freedom and consequent elimination of choice is both sad—and inevitable.
People like to think that they have choices and can make them freely.
This does not appear to be true.
People are thus not as responsible as they've been led to believe.
Irresponsible people commit irresponsible acts.

*As always, the proponents of the doctrine of "free will" and choice are invited to state just when and how any individual escapes the fetters of their past so as to make decisions or choices in accordance with or defiance of some mysteriously-created ideals or moral outlooks.

Part E

A Warning

The early chapters contain strong material that some readers might find offensive. Many of the passages contain graphic and explicit descriptions of sexual actions and experiences. Some might feel that these descriptions are downright pornographic in character, written by the author to titillate the prurient interests of readers who seek such stimulation. While that is always a possibility, Curtis Thompson's and Kay Nelson's experiences (Nurturance) are detailed in an effort to allow the reader to come just a bit closer to understanding them as two troubled individuals.

It is assumed that each was not born (Nature/heredity) a loose cannon, the dangerous male sadist or the spineless woman who must submit to just about anything. A process of development must be considered. What happened? While the reader might fervently wish that all children are raised in a family atmosphere comparable to that of *The Waltons* of TV fame, this did not take place with either Curtis or Kay. He was sexually savaged en route to his becoming a sexual savage. She had been savaged as she developed into a submissive "Rosie Roundheels."

Generally speaking, Chaos Theory provides some level of understanding. Chaos Theory suggests that will be there is a rhyme and reason for everything that a person might do; the rationale becomes available only retrospectively. Chance factors play a large part as determinants. Once the event has occurred, it is possible to tie it to other circumstances in its history. An oft-cited example involves the fluttering of a butterfly's wings in the Amazon sets in motion a series of events culminating ultimately in a Florida hurricane. In principal, this makes sense. But Chaos Theory does not provide any basis for forecasting events. One would be hard pressed, for example, to identify the single butterfly whose flapping wings set in motion a process culminating in an event far up the road, the Florida hurricane.

Similarly, Chaos Theory is of no use in predicting specific events in an individual's life. While sexual abuse as a child increases the likelihood of that person becoming a sexual abuser in later life, exceptions abound to this general rule. If nothing else, Chaos Theory emphasizes life's complexities and our inability to predict or control behavior.

"Shit happens!" That crude observation may cut to the heart of the matter. It may convey a sense of our futility in understanding, predicting, and controlling events. Once "whatever" happens, we may only be able to deal with it without much in the form of understanding.

In a way, while recognizing the validity of Chaos Theory, an attempt will be made to override this paucity of understanding. The lives of the two, Curtis Thompson and Kay Nelson, will be explored in an effort to establish something of a causal connection between their pasts and their involvement in this crime. From this book, the reader will come to know quite a bit about each of them. With this partial knowledge, readers might develop a smidgen of awareness, the most tentative of ideas, as to why this particular crime took place at a particular time in their lives. Curtis was not born a sexual savage, nor was Kay born a victim. Few will disagree with these statements. It is not enough to say that Curtis had been "raped and sodomized repeatedly as a child"—and "as an adolescent, he tried to reverse roles, becoming the perpetrator rather than the victim." While these statements are true, they do not convey to the reader the dreadful impact of these experiences upon him. Knowledge of specific sexual encounters makes it more likely that the reader can begin to empathize with this man. If this happens, it is usually said that the reader can begin to "walk in the shoes" of the other individual. In this book, it would be more appropriate to say "lie in the bed" of Curtis or Kay. To take full advantage of this opportunity, it would be helpful to dwell on these experiences, to appreciate fully the pain and fear of Curtis and Kay as they are regularly sexually assaulted early on, and the persistent fear and anxiety they experienced for days as they awaited the next onslaught.

Had they been unknowingly and mindlessly programmed over the course of their lifetimes for such a violent interaction in and near Eau Claire's Owen Park on that night in November 2003? If their lives had been fashioned by earlier circumstances over which they really had no control, was either truly responsible in any way for that event? That is a provocative question! Wouldn't it be a lot easier just to characterize him as a bad guy and her as a submissive bubble-head who was probably getting what she deserved? We could then pack him off to prison and her to counseling. And in a hardball, real world, that is what is very likely to happen.

But to proceed in that fashion is to proceed in ignorance and it is unlikely that even the participants have a clue as to what are the determinants of their behavior on that night or any other time. None of the newspaper readers would know.

It is truly difficult to understand virtually any event in the fullest sense of the word, e.g. a newly-ordained Cardinal kissing the ring of the Pope, a baseball player stepping up to the plate in the World Series, a wife kissing her husband as he goes off to work, etc. The list of such examples would be endless.

Our "off the cuff" level of superficial understanding of other people works reasonably well. People surely don't want nor need to plumb the depths of every incident that is witnessed. This would be an all-consuming task. The individual would have no time for a life of his own. But this efficiency should be tempered by a realization that one really knows from nothing about the people who surround him.

The incident involving Curtis and Kay is a case in point. "Judge not, that ye be not judged" comes to mind immediately because any judgment about them is likely to be inaccurate. This realization lends itself to the need for a more compassionated and constructive understanding of others. This then extends to others who assume a judgmental posture regarding people such as the readers. It is not that these often "self-appointed, self-ANOINTED" are simply evil, cruel, or vindictive. They are merely ignorant of that which you have come to realize. In the words of the old song, they're "more to be pitied than censured."

Readers might be inclined to believe that the fictionalized histories of the two principals are born of fantasy, that they are so far-fetched as to be unbelievable. However, all of the personal experiences on which this book is based are known to have taken place in the lives of real sexual perpetrators and their victims.

It is not this book's purpose to ruffle your feathers or make you insecure and depressed. This might happen if one truly understands his limitations in understanding other people. If you seek a challenge, the extended accounts of Curtis and Kay will provide it. Such a realization might require change. If you haven't the desire to learn or to change, you may wish to avoid the rest of this book.

If you are prepared to get "down and dirty" in an effort to enhance your understanding of this rape, read on. If not, you may have better things to do.

Section A

Curtis Thompson, as seen by Curtis Thompson

CHAPTER 1

Early Childhood

My name is Curtis Thompson. As of late, I guess that I've wondered more than most about how I got to be who I am and the sources of all the problems I've put upon myself and others. I'm certainly in deep trouble with the law at this time. In trying to figure things out, I've thought a lot, read a bit, and watched a slug of TV talk shows. All of this hasn't helped me at all. I've pretty much come up blank.

I haven't got a clue as to what happened in my early years. I talked to a counselor once and he said that I was "repressing" things that were crucial during those times. And I guess that could be. But it is not at all helpful to me to know that there are things I should know about that I will never know about. The counselor said that maybe some formal psychoanalysis might uncover that which I was repressing. He also informed me that there was no possibility that I would ever be able to avail myself of such treatment.

I remember virtually nothing of my father, Brian. As near as I can figure out, he walked out on my mother, Cindy, when I was about one year old. I don't know why. My mother has never talked to me about him and I guess she never will. The closest I came to getting some information was when I overheard some of my relatives talking about him with my mother. My mother's two sisters, Cecilia and Grace, would occasionally visit our home to drink coffee, eat a roll, and gossip. I can remember them telling me to go to the other room while they talked. They said at that time that "little pitchers have big ears." I had no idea of what that meant.

If I really strained those big ears while remaining out of sight, I could hear bits and pieces of things that were well beyond my understanding. One time, they went into gales of laughter when one told a story about a man reading poetry. He was supposed to say, "I leaned over and snatched a kiss." Instead, he said, "I leaned over and kissed her snatch," and while I remembered this, it wasn't until years later that I finally caught on as to why they were laughing so hard. At another of the gatherings, Cecilia said to my mother that she had seen "Bad News" over in the next county. I assumed that this referred to my father. My mother made no comment. Needless to say, I had never asked about him. My mother and I never talked about anything personal. Things were rough for us during that time. My mother's wages at Ernie's Supermarket barely paid our bills. We never went anywhere. We watched TV. My mother would drink a lot and then go to sleep.

CHAPTER 2

Later Childhood: An Initiation

Out of the blue one day, when I was about seven, my mother announced that she was getting married. His name was Ken Schneider. He was recently widowed, a welder, and had a son, Lloyd, who was about 13 years old. I had never seen either of them until they walked in the door shortly after the announcement. I never knew how she met him or why they had decided to get married. If I had been a bit older, I'd have put two and two together when my new sister, Myrtle, arrived some six months after the wedding ceremony. We had moved into his tiny trailer south of town. It was plopped down amidst many other trailers. I found most residents of these to be unfriendly, distant, loud, and rude. There were many angry shouting matches at virtually any hour of the day or night. Loud country music blared incessantly.

In the early years, I found myself sharing a bed with Lloyd. As I had always slept alone before, I found this uncomfortable. But as I had no choice, I made the best of it. Lloyd and I got along fairly well at first. He had a hobby of building model airplanes. He gave me one of his old ones that I flew around the house until its wing was broken. We watched a lot of TV. On rare occasions, the four of us would go out to eat at McDonald's. They let me play in the kiddy area. Lloyd never joined me. I guess that at his age, he considered himself too old for that sort of stuff.

In the main, I guess things were going all right. My mother didn't appear happy, but then, she never did. She looked as though she were beaten and defeated. I guess that she was. My stepfather worked long hours on occasion. There were many times when weeks would go by without his working. I guess he made good money. He spent a lot of it on booze. In the beginning, no one seemed to mind if he came home drunk. Drunk or sober, he barely acknowledged me from the very beginning. He'd nod in my direction and say, "Hello, Curtis" when he arrived home. His own son was treated in the same manner.

While I had gotten along in school reasonably well through the first two grades, I started to get into some serious trouble shortly thereafter. My problems emerged at about the same time that we moved in with my stepfather. I was adjudged as "behaviorally maladjusted" because I wouldn't study, skipped class, and beat up some little kids. They had me see a psychiatrist. As I scored high on the Wechsler Intelligence Scale for Children-R, lack of intelligence wasn't an issue. Ritalin was prescribed. I was pretty well zonked from that point on. I kind of wandered around my home and classroom in a daze most of the time. I wasn't learning anything and my grades showed this, but at least I wasn't doing anything that got people in an uproar.

When I was about eight, something happened that was extremely significant in light of my later problems. Lloyd and I were now sleeping in small but separate beds. We never had much to do with one another. A six-year age difference is a lot when you're a little kid. Our time around the house was spent watching TV. We often saw each other naked. We just wore our shorts to bed.

I was impressed by the size of his apparatus and the amount of his pubic hair. On one occasion, I even saw an erection of his. But we never talked about anything; certainly not any "dirty stuff." We had our share of wrestling and bedtime roughhousing with pillow-throwing and the like.

Then on this one fateful evening, after he'd turned out the lights, he had his arm around my neck as he wrestled with me. He wouldn't let go. He tossed me onto my bed, bellied up to my backside, and held me really tight. I could feel his hardness on my bottom as he rubbed up and down on me. Neither of us said a word. While this was certainly unusual, I wasn't frightened or even embarrassed. He certainly wasn't hurting me. He started to breathe heavily as he rubbed rhythmically against me. In very short order, I heard something of a gasp from him as I felt a pulsation from his penis. After a few seconds, he abruptly shoved me away from him as he headed toward the bathroom. He emerged a few minutes later and went to his bed without a word. Something different and significant had happened, but I didn't have a clue as to what it was all about. I was to find out shortly.

Maybe three nights later, after he'd turned out the lights and gone to bed, he got up and joined me. Again, neither of us said a word. He had taken his shorts off. It was immediately apparent that he had an erection as he forced it against me. But this time there was no neck hold. His hands went directly to my crotch where they began to massage my balls and penis. I liked this closeness that I was experiencing; I can't ever recall being held before. After a bit, he shifted his hand just a little and unsnapped my shorts. They were then slowly lowered to my knees as he thrust his penis repeatedly into the crevice of my butt. After several minutes, I heard the gasp as before and this time felt a rush of some fluid into my crevice. After a bit, he loosened his hold on me and returned to his bed. Not one word had been uttered by either of us throughout this entire episode.

He was back at me the next night. The experience then developed into something of a ritual which was repeated virtually every night. I came to expect it and even looked forward to it during the early stages. We never talked about it. I began experiencing something of an erection myself. I still didn't know what was going on, but it seemed that Lloyd was doing some older, manly things and I was getting closer to him by helping him. This was good for me even though I knew we were doing something wrong. The fact that we were doing something together was very important to me. Nobody else was spending any attention on me or time with me, as my mother worked a lot and was very busy with Myrtle.

After a couple of weeks, a change was introduced into our ritual that was anything but enjoyable for me. On this night, he apparently was no longer content with the superficial rubbing. He wanted more. It was evident that he wanted penetration. And it was equally evident that I was too small to accommodate him. It hurt. At first, I squirmed to avoid this thrust. Violating the rules of our silent conspiracy, I quietly muttered something like "Don't," and "Please," but he was intent on completing his mission. No longer content with gentle massage, he grasped my hips tightly as he entered me fully and repeatedly. I cried out in pain. He slapped my head hard as he whispered harshly, "Keep quiet, you little son of a bitch. They'll hear you." It hurt terribly, but I stifled any outcry. His gasp was great this night. He shook me and shuddered as he came inside me. As always, after a bit, he relaxed, withdrew slowly, released me, and went to his bed.

I was still in great pain. A trip to the bathroom revealed that I was bleeding. This experience was horrendous...and unfortunately, it became the standard. After a bit, he no longer turned off the lights. He seemed to enjoy watching me in my pain and humiliation. It happened almost every night. I felt that I had no alternative but to accommodate him. After enduring this agony repeatedly, I attempted to use some Vaseline to ease my pain. But in as much as he knew that this would minimize the friction and delay his satisfaction, he took the tube from me and shook his head slowly and emphatically. Lloyd would have none of it. And it was crystal clear to me that more than his sexual enjoyment was involved. An important part of his pleasure was inflicting pain on me. He began to pinch and punch my nipples and privates while he was doing me. My tortured movements added to his satisfaction. I would have cried out, but I knew that I would be harshly punished if I were to do so. I had become a sexual slave. He could do anything he wanted with me. I had nowhere to turn.

I find it interesting that I can remember these early events in such graphic detail. Many years have passed. Far worse things have happened to me with some regularity. Yet, what Lloyd did to me early on is as clear as if it happened yesterday. I can remember watching TV with my mother, Myrtle, and Lloyd. We sat quietly without speaking. Myrtle sat close to our mother, who cradled her in her arms. I truly envied Myrtle at those times. My mother was anything but demonstrative, but her cuddling expressed an affection that I had never known or certainly could not remember being on the receiving end of. When there was some particularly good comedy in a sitcom, my mother would look at Myrtle. They were smiling at each other. They were sharing. There were many such special moments. At such times, I tried to join them by laughing outrageously. I was either ignored or frowned upon as an interloper who was spoiling a special moment for them.

After the 10:00 p.m. news on WATU-TV, we always went to bed. I spent each and every evening in absolute dread of what was to happen after the TV was shut off. In a strange way, I tried to hold back that moment with repeated glances at the clock. But eventually, the TV news would end, and I would get ready for bed and lie down, awaiting Lloyd's arrival and onslaught. It happened with relentless regularity almost every night. On those rare occasions when he would not join me, I remained tense and awake until the very early hours. I was terrified that I would wake up with him next to me. My Ritalin gained me no respite during those long and anxious hours.

One morning when I was about nine years old, I was awakened by my mother's scream. Myrtle was dead! My stepfather called 911 and medics were on the scene shortly. Lloyd and I were told to stay in our rooms as they did their work. She could not be revived. The cause of her death was determined to be SIDS (Sudden Infant Death Syndrome), although they said that she was too old to qualify for that diagnosis. She had just died in her small bed in the parental bedroom from no ascertainable cause.

My mother was inconsolable. I tried to put my arm around her, but she brushed me off. The funeral was a nightmare. As we belonged to no church, a minister had to be hired to say proper things. We went through the required ritual. And eventually, it was over. Afterwards, my aunts, Cecelia and Grace, joined the rest of us in our trailer. The trailer court neighbors had provided some food and drink. The cramped quarters were extremely crowded initially. My aunts unsuccessfully tried to promote some conversation. People exited at the earliest opportunity.

Auntie Grace had taken me aside shortly after her arrival. It seemed that she and Cecilia were concerned because I hadn't cried at any time during the entire proceeding. She put her arm around me and asked me how I felt. I didn't like this physical contact. Although I really felt nothing for Myrtle at the time, I told Grace the things she wanted to hear. Eventually, she rejoined Cecilia and they left. My mother had retired to her bedroom and could not be coaxed out. My stepfather became falling-down drunk and soon passed out on the couch.

Lloyd had gone into our bedroom at the earliest opportunity. I was left alone in the company of my unconscious stepfather. I turned on the TV. I had no recollection of what I watched. My mother remained in her bed for weeks. As she stared at the ceiling, she would neither move nor speak. It was obvious to me that something was very wrong, but I could do nothing.

CHAPTER 3

The Mother's Departure

In the year that followed, the only time my mother would get up was when she had to go to the bathroom. And then, she stopped doing that. She was unconcerned with the basics of personal hygiene. Things had really gone to hell between my mother and her husband. The relationship had never really been good in the first place. They had never really talked to one another. There was never any display of affection on either of their parts.

They had always argued a lot. Initially, communication took the form of shouting matches, but my mother would be silenced quickly. He would often throw things on the floor and demand that she pick them up. Then, after she had done this, he'd throw them down there again and demand that she retrieve them. He taught her compliance. If she didn't comply, he'd hit her hard and repeatedly. Lloyd and I would just stand around, ignoring these beatings as much as possible in the crowded quarters of the trailer.

One time I'd read a "dirty book" that was being passed around. In the stories, there were people who made their partners wear dog collars as they kept them on leashes. I hadn't believed it at the time, but what was happening to my mother came pretty close to this.

With paper-thin walls, both Lloyd and I knew a lot about what went on in their bed. My stepfather Ken would often come home very drunk. He would flop into bed with my mother. Sometimes, he's sing wildly, "I'm back in the saddle again." When he got to the "Yippee, ki-yi-o" part, he'd slap her alongside the head to hurt her and to cause increased action on her part. He'd quiet down after a bit. After much squeaking of bedsprings, there would then be dead silence. She was always silent as she accommodated him. She knew that eventually, he would finish and leave her alone.

Perhaps Myrtle's death was something of a final straw for both of them. After all, the child was the only reason that they were together. On one night two months after the funeral, my stepfather came home drunk as a skunk. He went into the bedroom and he began shouting at my mother. Things like, "Why don't you move?" "It was a sorry day that I met you." "What in the hell is wrong with you?" "You stink." "You've always been a sorry piece of ass." Then he began to slap her, and he was slapping her hard. She didn't cry out. As always, she remained silent. After the usual squeaking bedsprings, we heard him staggering out of the bedroom and out our front door, shouting, "I'm going out and get me a real woman." Dead silence then prevailed.

Then one day, she didn't get up. In fact, she didn't move at all. Ken came home drunk as usual. He ranted and raved at her for a while, and then got frightened when she continued to lie motionless on the bed with her eyes staring at the ceiling. She had been behaving oddly a lot of the time, but this was different. None of us had a clue as to what to do. Finally, Ken walked up the street to get Ms. Slavic to come take a look. She ran the grocery store concession at the trailer park. She came back, took one look at my mother, and said, "Call 9-1-1," and Ken proceeded to do just that.

The ambulance arrived in about fifteen minutes. The crew peppered my mother with a lot of questions. That proved to be unproductive. The attendants then turned to us. We had no answers. We didn't know what to say. I remember feeling ashamed that my mother was causing all this fuss. Ms. Slavic volunteered that as she thought that the poor woman had had a stroke. Her vital signs were checked. She passed on all of these. The ambulance crew then drove off to the hospital with her.

Ms. Slavic left after assuring us that my mother and all of us would be in her prayers. About an hour later, after fortifying himself with a couple of beers, Ken left for the hospital. Neither Lloyd nor I made any effort to go with him. He returned about three hours later, stopping at a gin mill for a considerable time on the way back. He said that they were keeping her for observation. As he was in one of his ugly moods, Lloyd and I did our best to steer clear of him. In a small trailer, that took a lot of doing.

They could find nothing physically wrong with her. A psychiatrist was called in. Almost immediately, she was taken up to the psych ward. None of us had visited her. When Ms. Slavic got on his case, Ken would call in to find out what was going on. And in truth, nothing much was happening. She remained motionless and mute. I had never been around anything like this.

After about a week on the psych ward, she was transferred to a nearby state psychiatric hospital. We had no insurance, had already run up quite a tab, and the meter continued to run. Ken had been called in for a consultation with her doctors. Most of the conversation apparently was about how Ken was going to finance her care. They informed him that she was a "catatonic schizophrenic" and that her prognosis was poor. They were trying out various combinations of drugs on her, but without any success.

As far as I know, Ken never saw her again. I went up to visit her after about four months. She didn't know me. She and the other patients on her ward just sat in their chairs, rocking back and forth, like a bunch of zombies. They staff seemed to think that this motion was a sign for hope. I tried to talk to her, but she just stared off into the distance. I left after about 15 minutes. Among other things, I wondered who would ever work in such a nut farm.

I haven't been back since. For all I know, she is still there.

CHAPTER 4

"Sex Uber Alles" Stage 1

It became apparent that Lloyd was extremely diverse and virtually insatiable in his sexual interests and appetites. Sex was his whole life. It became a large part of my life as well. I haven't mentioned school or classmates much at all. I had endured the first few years in something of a Ritalin fog. While I had gotten off the stuff a year ago, I no longer caused the kinds of problems that occasioned the prescription in the first place. Maybe they thought that I was a successful treatment case. I was able to go with the flow. I did what was required of me. I didn't do well, but I was doing better than the teachers expected of a "Ritalin kid." I'd be passed on to the next teacher who was also uncaring and insensitive. Most other kids shied away from me because of my reputation as a classroom troublemaker.

The last few years, I had begun to look at some of the girls, but I was timid and shy in their presence. And who wouldn't be? I was weird. I got through the school day in kind of a daze and then went home to spend anxious hours waiting to be "poged" by Lloyd. I can't tell you how much tension I endured every day waiting for Lloyd to have at me. And if he didn't sexually conquer me, this was even worse in a way. I'd still be waiting for him to show up beside me. If he balled me, I'd have a few hours of peace and quiet, but then I'd wake up the next morning and it would start all over again. I thought I could get used to it, but I couldn't. Who would ever want to know a thing like me?

While Lloyd had previously concentrated his attentions on me, neighborhood girls were now becoming involved in his activities. A lot of neighbor kids would be hanging out around the trailer court when suddenly Lloyd, one or two of his buddies, and an adolescent girl would disappear from the scene. They would be inside our trailer. What were they up to? I had a pretty good idea. Lloyd told me to stay outside and to beat on the door if his father showed up.

If nothing else, I had become devious in my ways. I lurked around, made myself unobtrusive, and then quietly sneaked inside. I found a nook near the door where I could observe everyone and everything without detection. They were playing a child's version of strip poker. They did this for days on end with different girls as participants. The girl would always lose and the boys would get the glimpse that they sought. Surprisingly, in the early days, things never went further. I think that Lloyd was a bit fearful and wanted to check things out thoroughly to see what he could get away with. He didn't want to be found out. All the boys and some of the girls found this card game to be enjoyable.

On occasion, if a girl became uneasy, balked, or said that she wanted to leave, Lloyd would become unhappy. When cajoling didn't work, he quickly got very angry and demanding. This was a side of him that I knew very well. He twisted the girl's arm as he said, "Now, you don't really mean that, do you?" and she was then quick to assent because she know that he would do more.

She many never have gone into our trailer willingly again, but she had served his purpose. He seemed to want the girls to resist. He enjoyed hurting people. I know that the pain he was inflicting on me with regularity was more satisfying for him than his orgasms.

Later on, he refined his neighborhood techniques so that he could do whatever he wanted with whomever he wanted. His threats insured the return and continued participation of the girls and few of the younger boys. They were afraid of him, and he used that fear. He would often threaten to hurt their younger brothers and sisters. A threat to poison a pet of theirs invariably worked for him. He was as much in charge of the neighbor kids as he was of me.

Later on, it became apparent that when alone with a girl, he was far from content with a mere glimpse. He would grope to his satisfaction. He gained special pleasure if he could make them cry. He liked to slap them around. In very short order, as he developed both sophistication and confidence, he would insist upon going all the way with them. Infliction of pain remained the crucial ingredient in his satisfaction. I watched most all of these developments from my vantage point. He did whatever he could get by with. And that covered a lot of things. His interest would vary from time to time. He explored all of them completely.

When I became eleven years old, he chose to involve me in these primarily heterosexual escapades. I had been somewhat thankful for his interest in girls and younger boys because as it did take the pressure off of me. While he still had sex with me occasionally, it was not the same. It was almost as though he just wanted to show me that he was still in charge and that he could always "do me" if he wanted to, more to reinforce the principle of the thing than to get satisfaction from the act itself.

His need to control me took a different way. He would corral a neighborhood girl in our trailer and tell her to strip. The charade of the poker parties was a thing of the past. If she resisted or was slow, he'd grab her arm and the twist would insure compliance. Then, he might bring me in for a look-see from beginning to end. He would say something like, "Look and learn." By this time, he had incorporated the pain and humiliation into the heterosexual act as well. He was inventive and imaginative in devising different ways of doing this. As instructed, I watched and I learned.

After a bit, he wanted more form me than my performance as an observer and admirer. He insisted that I attempt intercourse with one of his partners. Sometimes he demanded my participation after he had achieved satisfaction with the girl. I didn't know what he meant when he said, "You'll enjoy a wet deck." Or he would find someone, oft times ugly, retarded, or intellectually slow, who he felt was beneath him. He would then insist that I see that she was undressed and eventually mounted by me. This was humiliating for the girls and for me. And with my immaturity and insecurity, I was both clumsy and impotent. The resulting debacle was a source of great and continuing glee for him. After I had failed, he would often require that I masturbate in front of him and the girl. He was in charge and could do what he wanted with us. No one ever challenged his authority.

So here I was, my mother locked up on the psyche ward, which left me alone with Lloyd and his father. Ken was whacked out of shape with booze and drugs most of the time. Despite this, he managed to hold down a full-time job as a welder. He often worked overtime. He ignored me just as he had before. He felt that I was a completely unjustifiable drain on him. He said that he'd gotten suckered into taking care of me.

Ken spent a lot of his "off-time" in a drunken stupor in the company of the many floozies that he would bring over to the trailer. Lloyd, on the other hand, was moving on. He was rarely at home. He had discovered Selma, an older woman of about thirty-five years who was more than a match for him. Selma had just received a considerable settlement from the divorce of her third husband. She had a huge, luxurious house that Lloyd came to admire greatly. He overnighted there with such regularity that others in the trailer court thought that he no longer lived with us.

According to conversations I overheard between Ken and Lloyd, the sexual appetites of Selma were virtually insatiable. And surprise, surprise, she was able to teach him a thing or two. Apparently, her strong needs to derive satisfaction on rare occasions from being hurt and humiliated played right into Lloyd's sadistic drives. Her occasional tendency to hurt him was not so well received. His father hung on his every word. As they moved out of earshot, Lloyd said that she was into threesomes. I thought that he asked Ken if he'd be interested but I am not sure of that. And I never heard Ken's response.

CHAPTER 5

"Sex Uber Alles" Stage 2

After considerable thought, I decided to emulate Lloyd. He had told me to watch and learn. Aside from the sex, he had taught me deviousness, the absolute need to avoid detection and punishment for anything I elected to do. I was insecure around girls. It was with that in mind that I set out to find a young boy to see if that was the way I really wanted to go. Just maybe, that was doable. And there were a lot of unsupervised young boys, aged seven to ten, hanging around the trailer court.

Who, how, when, and where? I decided that my trailer was safe, that the time would be determined by the considerable absences of Lloyd and his father. While I had never been the aggressor before, I certainly knew how. The "who" thus because the crucial question. I then explored my motivations in a way that probably never occurred to Lloyd. Was I as dominated by needs to hurt and humiliate as he was? I thought about this a great deal. I had been painfully punished by Lloyd. Did I really want to apply a distortion of the Golden Rule in my situation, i.e. do unto others as you have been done by them? Did I want any partner to endure such experiences? Was it necessary for my satisfaction?

And how about "love," that which I had seen at the movies and on TV? In the old dramas, I'd seen, there was no touchy-feely at all. I watched some of these in disbelief. One that I remember was *It Happened One Night* starring Clark Gable and Claudette Colbert. This comedy was made in the 1930s or early 1940s. I forget which. For reasons that escape me, the plot required that the two of them spend a night together in what passed for a motel in those days. Now this would have been a great opportunity for them to get it on. Instead, they hooked up a blanket on a rope which divided the motel room and insured privacy for each of them. They referred to this as their "Wall of Jericho," and they remained apart through that night. At the end, it was suggested that this wall would "come tumbling down" and the two would eventually join. Granted that this was a comedy, but it reflected the customs of the time. Sex was sacred in some way or other and to be undertaken only after marriage. Note that I say "undertaken" as opposed to "enjoyed." There was also a scene in this wherein Ms. Colbert drew her skirt up over her knee at a roadside so as to entice a truck driver into stopping and providing a ride for the two of them. This was considered very risqué at the time.

I watched *Gone with the Wind* and many others of that time period. In these, people just held one another and were gratified by that experience. When there was a kiss, it, in and of itself, was a gratifying experience. I was more familiar with the "suck face" format, ram your tongue down her throat, a transitory prelude to an immediate—if not sooner—tumble in the sack.

Now, were those old-timers completely out of step with a reality as we know it today? Or maybe, just maybe, did a caring holding of one another and gentle kiss have something going for it? As you may gather, I thought about all of this a lot.

It would seem that I'd have been the last person in the world who would raise such questions. I've been programmed in the tradition of "quickies," "Slam bam, thank you, Ma'am." I'd been nailed routinely in this fashion by Lloyd's hammer. And that was not great.

I've never been held, hugged, or kissed by anyone in a warm and loving manner. Lloyd's early holding didn't count. Accordingly, and warm expression of affection would have been very foreign to me. Auntie Grace came close as she held me at Myrtle's funeral, but I couldn't accept it. She was my aunt, it was at a funeral, and she was basically trying to corral me for questioning.

I think that I wanted to be hugged and kissed. I can remember clearly how warmly and closely my mother had held Myrtle while we all watched TV. I had wanted that experience, but I had no way of obtaining it. Had I ever been hugged and kissed? I couldn't remember. Maybe mother had hugged and kissed me early on, but she stopped when my father took off.

Did she feel that I was responsible for his departure? What else might I have done which would have cast me out of her circle of love, warmth, hugs, and kisses? And she was the only one I knew who could have loved me in the special way that mothers can. Perhaps she was nutty and unresponsive even way back then. Maybe my father held and hugged me. I'll never know. It would never have been appropriate for Lloyd or his father to hug me. Lloyd's wrestling holds, his crude clutching when he had sex with me and others was anything but what I was thinking about.

I even remembered how I had enjoyed holding newborn Myrtle when she and mother returned from the hospital. And I had been shut out of that experience when my mother caught me checking on what made Myrtle a baby girl.

Maybe my concerns about these matters reflected an effeminacy, thereby reinforcing developmental anxieties of mine regarding my sexual identity. Maybe I should abandon these wonderments and get onto the business of being a man. Maybe I should take up hunting, belch and fart a lot, scratch my balls, and humiliate women as I used them for my own purposes. My stepfather was a great example of how to do this. Sad to relate, Lloyd was the major role model in my life, but as he taught by example rather than words, the many questions that I might have posed were never asked. As I thought about this, I wondered where Lloyd had gained all his moxie.

I had now become a "big pitcher who had two very big ears." No one talked to me, but I had learned how and where to listen. One day, I overheard Lloyd and Ken talking about someone called Fred, the brother of Lloyd's mother. Ken said that Fred had died in a car accident. He went on to reminisce about Fred. He said to Lloyd, "You two were really tight for a while. I was so busy that I couldn't take you on those camping trips. I think that he was really fond of you when you were younger." Lloyd didn't say anything for a few minutes. Then he exploded, as he said, "I'm glad the motherfucker is dead." His father was surprised and taken aback by this. But in accordance with the family tradition, he made no further comment about Fred. He began to talk of other things. I wondered about what went on during those camping trips. I didn't understand Lloyd, but just maybe I was beginning to.

CHAPTER 6

"Sex Uber Alles" Stage 3

As odd man out and the isolate of our household, I had a lot of time on my hands. What to do? I'm sure that the idea of retaliation or revenge, whether or not my mind at the time, might have been the driving force behind my activities from this point on. I was a very angry 14-year-old by this time. My lusts and sexual drives were substantial. Masturbation did the trick for a time, but I decided to branch out.

I was dreadfully insecure regarding sex with a partner. Indeed, I had considerable doubts regarding my sexual identity. I had been involved in a homosexual relationship with Lloyd for many years. Was I a queer? As I've indicated before, the earliest parts of this involvement had been pleasurable. I had enjoyed being held, having my genitalia gently massaged, and found pleasure in the minimal arousal I experienced at that early age.

The pain of the anal penetration was a frightening turnoff for many years. I had come to fear Lloyd en route to his complete enslavement to me. But even so, in the latter years, I found myself getting an erection as part of the sex. Lloyd was so intent on getting off that he never even noticed. If he had, I don't really know what form our relationship might have taken. At the end, I had fantasized hurting him through anal penetration, or having him provide oral sex for me, or our engaging in a "69" with both of us performing oral sex on one another. My sexual thoughts centered about Lloyd and about other males. These never went beyond fantasy. My fear precluded this. Needless to say, I never discussed any of this with anyone. The nature of Lloyd's sex with me didn't even provide any opportunity to lay hands on him. And as strange as it may seem, in these dreams, I did want to hold and be held by someone.

My relationship with females was strange and disconcerting. I knew all about the anatomy and the way things were done. I had observed or read about the near-infinite number of possible interactions between men and women, but my actual experiences were such as to foster fear and wonder about whether or not I was a queer. As a 14-year-old, I thought a lot about this. This rumination on my part led only to an increase in my insecurity and anxiety regarding having sex with others, either male or female. Lloyd had been my only homosexual partner, with him as the pain-inflicting aggressor and me as the recipient. My sexual experiences involving women had included only "seconds" from Lloyd's partners, or "unacceptable partners" that Lloyd had dredged up for his own amusement.

I have never been alone with a girl or woman. Lloyd was always there to observe my shortcomings and to laugh about my pitiful efforts. So here I was with an erect penis and a desire to do something about it, and I didn't know what to do.

CHAPTER 7

A Potential Predator

And, after endless thought, I came to a most tentative conclusion. I'd have to try some things out and see how they went. Maybe there is more than sex involved in important personal relationships for me. Maybe I can hug, kiss, and talk with the person with whom I'm having sex. While that seems unlikely to me, it couldn't be ruled out.

For openers, did I really want a male as a sexual partner? I considered myself reasonably attractive and in good physical shape. A few girls have been eyeing me before I looked away, and I had been hit on by some older guys until Lloyd scared them off.

Boys of my own age of fourteen or fifteen were possibilities. I don't know too many, and my experiences have been limited and unrewarding. A year ago, when Lloyd was busy elsewhere, I ran across this former classmate of mine. He invited me over to his place to reminisce. We got to horsing around and wrestling. At any rate, we got into crotch hand-holds in very short order, and we masturbated one another—with the lights on, no less. While the orgasm was great, the aftermath was not. We looked kind of sheepishly at one another, conversation lagged, and I made up some excuse that I had to go somewhere. As I departed, we each said that we should get together sometime. Of course, we never did. As adolescents, we probably had special anxieties which were only momentarily allayed by "pounding each other's pud."

Now, younger boys were a real possibility. As a "victim" at the tender age of seven, I should have the special know-how as to how to proceed.

It was amazing to me how quickly I found a potential partner. I met him at Ms. Slavic's. He was nine years old, a bit on the pudgy side, and nobody liked him. Kelly lived with his mother in the third trailer down from ours. He was alone almost all of the time. His mother worked full-time at Harper Technology. It was common knowledge that she was heavily involved with a married man. The two of them met very frequently in a room they rented at Ramada Inn or Holiday Inn. They kept shifting around so as to avoid detection. Both drank heavily. And while she had no recollection of doing it, she had confided her motel-hopping strategy to a fellow woman trailerite. From that time on, everyone sort of knew where she was when she wasn't with Kelly. She was absent from his scene a great deal of the time.

The day after I met him, just as my stepfather had left for work, I heard a knock at my door. It was Kelly and his mother. He had brought her over to meet me. She had been a very beautiful woman not too many years ago. She was now pushing forty. Her heavy work load, excessive drinking, and turmoil in her life were beginning to take a toll. I must admit that I did wonder how she might be in the sack. She was grateful for my interest in Kelly. And I was charming. I had the feeling that I had alleviated a bit of guilt she was experiencing because of her neglect of her child.

She was smiling and responsive when I suggested that Kelly and I would have to get together again. So Kelly became my target. Maybe even a "your place or mine" kind of deal. He was alone a lot. I had seen him before I began my quest. I had said hello to him on several occasions, although I didn't know his name. He always wore a Vikings t-shirt. I wandered by his trailer several times before I encountered him. I greeted him and told him that I was a Vikings fan, too. I asked him about the chances of the Vikings in the next game on Sunday. He went on and on about how bad their quarterback was. I thought that he'd never stop talking.

By the time I left him a half-hour later, we were on a buddy-buddy "Kelly-Curt" level. According to plan, I bided my time and didn't wander out of doors very much until three days later. As I passed his trailer in late afternoon, I found him sitting on the steps. I thought that he might even have been waiting for me. Certainly, as a lonely little boy, he was waiting for someone. I greeted him warmly. We talked a bit. Then I invited him back to my trailer for a "cream cone." He accepted the invitation willingly, even enthusiastically. I kept the door open. I got out a couple of cones. I sat in a chair while he lounged on the sofa. As he talked and he talked and he talked, I pretended to listen.

According to play, I didn't get anywhere near close to him this time. Eventually I said something like, "Well, it's getting late. I suppose that your mother will be looking for you." He replied, "No. She won't be back until tomorrow afternoon." Bingo! He had said that she always supplied him with a refrigerator full of goodies when she was going to be away for a while. I then asked if this happened often. He said yes. I complimented him on being able to stay alone in a big trailer. He kind of beamed in response to this compliment. I patted him on the shoulder as he left.

According to plan, I talked about Kelly with a next-door neighbor, Ms. Slavic, the neighborhood gossip. I didn't seek her out. She happened to be cleaning up a flowerbed near the access road. She ran the convenience store. I said that I had just met Kelly and the he seemed to be a nice kid. She gave me an extended chapter and verse account of Kelly, his mother, her distant and current past, and even the name of the married male friend. On her own, she volunteered her concern about what she called Kelly's "abandonment." I told her that he and I were fellow Vikings fans. She said that she was glad that we had met. "Maybe the two of you can watch Sunday's game together."

In what seemed to be an effort to encourage me to do just that, she volunteered some Fritos and pop. It was clear that she saw me as a potentially constructive influence. The thought that I could be a predator was far from her mind. She was genuinely concerned about Kelly. I saw her as an invaluable ally. She added an aura of respectability to my acquisition of Kelly as a potential partner. I phoned Kelly and told him that Ms. Slavic had come up with a great idea. I then invited him over to watch the Vikings game on TV. Lloyd and his lady friend would be attending the game. My stepfather would be working. I had a clear field. I told Kelly to clear Ms. Slavic's idea with his mother. He said that there would be no problem. He accepted my invitation on the spot.

Sunday rolled around. Kelly stopped at Ms. Slavic's to pick up some goodies. He arrived a full hour before the game time. I had changed the furniture around a bit so that both Kelly and I would be sitting on the sofa to watch the game.

And that is what we did. We munched Fritos, drank the soda, made with the high-fives when the Vikings scored, and talked about manly things. I came to like him. He was just a neat kid. Aside from the high-five physical contact, we touched one another as we jostled on the sofa during some of the tense moments near the end of the game. The Vikings' win made it all the more of a great day for him. Just before he left, he lay back on the couch as he rested from all the excitement provided by the game. I had anticipated this and had my left arm on the back of the sofa. It seemed natural as I brought my hand forward to tousle his hair and straighten his cap. I thought that he leaned, ever so slightly, toward the crook in my arm.

He didn't want to leave, but according to plan, I made no further moves. I had watched him more than the game and found him to be appealing. My building erection during the game led me to do more, but I stuck to my plan and ushered him out the door. I instructed him to stop by Ms. Slavic's to thank her for the refreshments she'd provided, and he did just that. He stayed there a full 20 minutes. As the trailer court's resident gossip, I'm sure that she was pumping him for information. And of course, it was all good. Things couldn't have gone much better for me.

We met in my trailer the next afternoon. His mother would be out for that night and most of the next day. He seemed somewhat awkward at the outset. I made every effort to put him at ease. He was going to turn on the lights. I told him to wait for a bit. "Darkness is our friend," I said. I then put my arms around him and he did the same for me. I told him about how much I had thought of him, our special friendship. As he was quiet at first, I encouraged him to talk. I whispered how I like touching him and being touched in return. I then lowered my hand to his crotch and began to stroke him. In short order, I lowered my pants as well as his down to his knees.

At that moment, the door to my trailer swung open and a figure entered. The lights were then switched on. It was Lloyd. Although clearly surprised by the scene before him, he began to laugh uncontrollably. As he gasped for air, he said, "Just wait until Dad hears about this!"

CHAPTER 8

Run Rabbit, Run

The moments after Lloyd's unexpected entrance are blurred in my memory. Kelly began to cry as he ran for the door. Lloyd blocked his exit for a while and then let him go. I went into the bathroom, emerging from it moments later.

Lloyd was sitting on the sofa with a bottle of beer in his hand. Sneering and laughing at the same time, he said, "Well, come on now, little brother. Tell me all about this." I was speechless, absolutely devastated by what had happened. In the midst of this, I wondered about Kelly, whether he had gotten home all right, and how he was feeling. And what was I to do? I couldn't stand Lloyd's mockery, and it would never stop. I would always be reminded of this night. I was sure that he'd tell his father as well. What would he do? Would they kick me out? My mind checked out one possible course of action on my part after another. Each was worse than the one that had preceded it. I felt anger. I felt like screaming. I felt like killing Lloyd. What did I do? I ran to our bedroom, packed up as many clothes as I could into a duffle bag, and ran wildly into that night. It was cold. The trailer court was about five miles outside of town. I started walking in that direction. I had no idea what I was going to do.

Many cars passed me as I slogged along the highway. Some slowed down as though they might stop. I became fearful when that happened. Lloyd might be tailing me for all sorts of God-awful reasons. Eventually, one car stopped. The driver was a portly man in his forties or fifties. He asked if I needed a lift. "Here we go again," I said to myself; an older man in search of some action.

He asked me my name and where I was going. He identified himself as Lyle Mentor and said that he was heading for a hunting shack north of Minong. I was surprised when he didn't invite me along. Instead, he said that he was stopping in town for a bite to eat. He asked me if I wanted to join him. We ended up that Burnie's Buffet where I pigged out to the max. I really didn't know when or where I might eat again. I cooked up a story for him to the effect that I had been kicked out of my house by my father. He didn't ask why. Instead, he asked where I was going. When I told him the Twin Cities, he pulled out a couple of twenties and handed them to me, and then drove me over to what passed for a bus depot. He had already paid for the meal. After wishing me luck, he said goodbye and drove off on Highway 53, heading north to Minong country. I never saw him again. He had been a real strange stranger in my world. He had not used me in any way. He had generously helped me at a time in my life when I desperately needed assistance.

I got on the first bus to Minneapolis. I slept most of the way, although I was jarred awake at each of the many stops. I stumbled off the bus finally, deep in the heart of Minneapolis near midnight on a cold fall night. I started walking and ended up on Hennepin Avenue. I ventured up a few of the side streets from time to time. I encountered many drunks and flashy women. None of them were remotely interested in me.

I walked, and kept walking. Then, at about 2:00 a.m., I came across a group of scroungy kids who were hanging out on some steps. They were smoking, playing grab-ass, and laughing a lot as I passed. They invited me over and asked if I'd like to sit down. They didn't give their names nor did they ask me for mine. I was a bit leery of them, but I sat down anyway. There was something comforting about being in the company of other people. An hour passed and they seemed ready to go inside. One of them asked me where I was going to crash. Did I have any money? I said that I had five dollars. One said that he'd take that and I could sack in with them. I agreed to this as I had no place to go. They took my five as we walked toward their room. Little did I know, but that room was to be my room for the next two years. These kids—or young men, shall we say—became close friends and confidants. They became very special in my life.

CHAPTER 9

Loring Park, Minneapolis, Minnesota

It turned out that my new friends were hustlers. On most evenings, they'd hang out around Loring Park along with many other young men. They'd wait to be picked up by men in the many cars that cruised the area. My friends, and many others in our neighborhood, provided sex for these cruisers; sex of all different kinds for prices that were negotiated on the spot. Eventually, I joined in.

A book could be written about this three-year time period. Perhaps I shall write one someday. Suffice it to say, it was a dangerous, demanding, and degrading period in my life. Now, Lloyd had been both demanding and degrading, but he never posed a threat to my health or my life. I came to realize shortly after I became one of the boys that this lifestyle virtually guaranteed daily encounters which could kill me. Murders were not all that unusual. The shadow of AIDS and other sexually-transmitted disease were always there. I signed on with a pimp for a while because he seemed to provide safety. I went back to freelancing when I caught him short-changing me.

I dealt with these major problems as I have dealt with virtually anything bad in my life. I was into denial and minimization. Other people could be killed or become diseased, but not me. Similarly, I was not a degraded boy-whore, but rather one who was using other men for my own purpose. I was not associating with the scum of the earth. Rather, my good friends and I lived free, unfettered, and fulfilling lives.

I really believed all that B.S. Time passed quickly. Three years seemed to be an inconsequential amount of time. While I really hadn't changed or grown psychologically, I told myself that my flashy clothes and offbeat hairdo represented substantial accomplishments. My days were all the same. I'd get up late, eat whatever was available, watch TV with the other boys, smoke a little pot, dress up a bit, grab a pizza, and head for Loring Park. We'd walk or stand around as we were ogled by the customers driving by. One would eventually stop and signal me over. We'd haggle over the price of doing what he wanted.

I would do anything a customer wanted. I'd get $40, $80, or even $100. As a freelancer, I didn't have to split it with any pimp—nor with the IRS for that matter. It was all clear cash in my pocket. After a customer had done his thing, he'd drive me back to the park. My availability would start all over again. Things didn't taper off until one or two in the morning. Then I'd head for home and sleep. Some of these nights were slow, but on others, I made as much as $400.00. Then I'd get up late, watch TV with the boys, and on and on and on.

Same scenario, same routine, for nearly three years. I did have special low points, like the time I was picked up by a customer who then picked up three of his buddies. They beat me up, used me every which way, and dumped me out at 4:00 a.m. ten miles from home after taking all my money. But luckily, that was the exception. My life became a dull, sex-dominated, monotonous routine.

CHAPTER 10

Seriously Propositioned

Then, a very big even occurred in my life. A guy in a Porsche drove by several times before stopping and calling out to me. I hot-footed over in anticipation of a big fee. He asked me to get in the car and talk a bit. So far, this was routine. Then he asked me if I were hungry? Would I have dinner with him? I went along with that.

We were seated at a supper club's table when different things began to happen. He put a hundred-dollar bill in my hand, saying that this will pay for my time. He said in so many words, "My name is George. We'll be here for about an hour. Order what you want. I want to know all about you. You've got a great body and I'm attracted to you. After an hour or so, if I like what I hear, I may make you a proposition. If you go for it, we'll have to talk a bit more. If not, I'll take you back to the park." Now, that sounded good to me. It sure beat standing out in the cold, haggling and sex and the end result.

But who was this joker? He was large, in his forties, well-dressed, sort of regal in his bearing. He sure talked funny. He looked and talked a lot like Charlton Heston.

He wanted to know, so I told him about me. To say that I strayed from the truth is the understatement of the century. I fashioned a story that was both creative and consistent. I made it up as I sat there. I looked dead in the eyes of the man as I told him my tale. I had become orphaned at an early age in Mauston, Wisconsin. I was never told how my parents died. I was shuttled into the system with an endless series of foster parents, changes in school, and psychological evaluations. I was smart although my grades never showed it. I was healthy except that my teeth were a mess. I got along well with other people. I had gotten along so well in Madison with my last foster father that we had developed a hot sexual relationship. His wife caught us in the act and blew the whistle on us. This man was about to have large boom lowered on him. As the violated youth, I'd have to participate in unending court proceedings dealing with his crimes. I couldn't take that, so I cut and ran at the age of 16. I knew a kid in the Twin Cities. I ran to him. He was one of "the boys." I roomed and worked with him. To add a touch of authenticity to my story, I asked this George if he might have seen my friend out at the park. He'd been wearing a blue bandanna, I said. More hooey.

George had watched me intently as I ate and told my story. At the end of a little over an hour, he held up his hand to stop me.

He then began to speak. "I'm not sure that I believe you, but your story does have a ring of truth to it. I've seen you before at Loring Park. I asked a friend of mine to pick you up last week and then tell me about how you handle sex. He said that you were a bit moody, but that he was well satisfied. Does any of this surprise you? I would think that it would. Once I take an interest in someone, I go all out. I could have had you checked out by a P.O., but I have great faith and confidence in my personal intuition. You've got a lot of potential but you come short in several important ways. Your language is atrocious. You can't seem to put a sentence together. You use far too many 'aint's' and you say 'You know what I'm saying,' when you run out of words. I'm certain that you don't understand some of the words I've been using. Your table manners are terrible. And your teeth clearly need fixing."

As he talked about all of this, he sounded like a real dormal, pain-in-the-ass teacher that I once had. That one had a slogan that he was forever saying, "Articulate and you may become articulate." I had no idea what he had meant.

"George" went on to say, "My name is Andre Beshar. I came here from Pakistan a long time ago. I am thoroughly Americanized. I am an architect and have a highly successful practice in Chippewa Falls, Wisconsin. I like young men. I like what I see in you right now. I like what I think I see in your potential. With proper guidance and opportunity, you can go far. I want you as my sexual partner."

That's really the way he talked. I was amazed at what he was saying.

He went on. "I'll tell you what you'll get if you accept my offer. You'll have your own room in a large house in Chippewa. You can furnish it as you like. A brand new TV and a computer seem like some things that you'd want right away. But anything goes. I'll make sure that your teeth are fixed by a fine orthodontist I know in Eau Claire. As we'll be eating together, I'll have ample time to point out the errors of your dining etiquette. I'll buy you a new wardrobe so that you can get rid of the clothes you're wearing. You'll have an allowance of $300.00 a month and more if you need it. You'll be enrolled in a special school. On second thought, I'll hire a tutor and you can be home-schooled.

Either of us can drop out of this arrangement at any time. If you feel like leaving, simply go. If I ever feel that you should leave, I'll provide you with $3,000.00 to ease the pain of your departure. Does any of this sound like *My Fair Lady* or *Pygmalion* to you? Have you never heard of them?"

I hadn't.

He continued on, "If you haven't, your tutor will see that you do." He went on, "You can have all the friends you like, but you are not to have sex with them or bring them into our home. My sexual needs are simple and straightforward. When I want you in my bed, I'll tell you. That will probably be two or three times a week. You will do what I ask of you. I prefer anal sex, although oral sex may be required on occasion. You will be silent throughout unless I tell you to speak. When I am finished, you will return to your room. Do you have any questions about any of this? I want our mutual understanding to be clear."

I knew that I had to respond in some way or other. I asked, "Won't people think that there is something fishy about this arrangement?"

He replied, "Don't worry about that. You are a guest in my house. People can think what they like, but I'm sure they'll never question or investigate your presence. You may even choose to adapt a new name, although that may cause too many problems."

I asked, "How would I get around? Where is your place located?"

He said, "I'm located on a 40-acre tract of land on Lake Wissota, about ten miles out of Chippewa Falls. Incidentally, Chippewa Falls has a population of around 12,000. It is about 12 miles from Eau Claire, a more cosmopolitan and interesting city. I have three cars: the Porsche, and older Cadillac, and a 1998 Chevrolet. Either of the last two would be available for you. Do you have a license? If you get into any trouble with the law, I've got the DA in my pocket."

He certainly didn't mince words. And he did talk funny. As I was interested in predecessors, I asked straightforwardly, "Have you done this before? If so, what went right and what went wrong? Why are you making this offer at this time?"

He replied, "You'd be the third young man in the ten years I've been sponsoring this arrangement. The first, Eduardo, stayed for three years. He had been an exchange student and finally felt that he had to return to Ecuador. The second, William, left a month ago. He had fallen in love with a college student in Eau Claire and could no longer keep up his end of the bargain. He left two weeks ago. Each departed on the best of terms with me. I had farewell dinners for each with hugs, kisses, and the aforementioned check as a token of my affection. They had done well and were sad about leaving. And it had worked out very well from my standpoint; I had been well-satisfied with each in this somewhat unusual arrangement. I'll never see either of them again."

He paused, "I think it worked out well with them because I was so up-front and clear about the details. There was no room for misunderstanding. I've attempted to do the same with you. You certainly should know by now what you'd be getting into."

He then said, "I'll ask you a question, and I won't expect an answer now. What do you want to become when you grow up? You probably don't know. If things work out between us, I can be very helpful to you once you decide."

He paused again. "So what do you think? Or do you want to take some time? If so, I'll take you back to the park now and we can have breakfast tomorrow. You could let me know then. I'm staying at the Marriott out by the airport if you have any further questions."

He certainly had a straightforward way of looking at things. He was formally contracting for my sexual services. He did so in the same way that he probably hired his cleaning lady or the man who provided lawn care. He simply wanted to have sex with a willing and non-demanding partner on his own terms. The impersonality of his proposed arrangement had a special appeal for me. Compared to what I had been doing, he was describing a kind of paradise.

Although I had already made up my mind, I told him that he'd have his answer at breakfast in the morning.

He said, "Fine, let's make it the Holiday Inn, downtown that is, at 7:00." He then drove me back to Loring Park. I started for home as soon as I got out of the car. I began packing my bag.

CHAPTER 11

Kept and Keeping Up

I'll pause in my narrative at this time to review what took place during the three years of my arrangement with Andre Beshar. He surely kept me on a short leash. It was six months before he allowed me to call him Andy, and that was about as personal as it got. He lived up to his end of the bargain in every way.

My teeth were attended to almost immediately. After some expensive capping, crowning, whitening, straightening and whatever, I had a glorious smile, and I smiled frequently. I felt that I had really lucked out.

My responsibilities in bed were fulfilled with ease, and even a modicum of pleasure. Sex with him was smooth and pleasurable. He felt no need to humiliate or hurt me. He liked to have the room lighted with many small candles. Strange instruments, presumably Pakistani, provided the background music that I took to be exotic. He took his time as he leisurely sought and achieved his pleasure. I chose to exact great enjoyment from our intercourse even though I played an extremely passive and submissive role in it. While oral sex had been cited as a possibility in our initial discussions, he never requested it.

He seemed more than content with a routine that never varied. Once we'd silently finish disrobing, we'd enter his spacious bed from opposite sides. I would lie on my side to await his entry. He appropriately applied a gel initially, but within a matter of a few weeks, I became so relaxed that this was not necessary. He made no effort to insert himself manually. He placed his hands gently on my shoulders as he allowed his penis to find and penetrate my opening. He would then push his penis deep within me, allow it to rest there for a while, and then withdraw it as a prelude to more active participation. He then varied the rhythm of his thrusts for reasons that were known only to him. In this regard, he seemed uninfluenced by the throbbing beat of the music. He took his time. Sometimes our sex took 20 minutes or more. I came to be able to anticipate his orgasm as he strained his body, held my shoulders tightly, and thrust deep inside of me prior to his explosion. He would then shudder before relaxing in the extended afterglow. He would continue to hold me. After a considerable and pleasant time, I quietly departed, shutting his door as I left. He appeared to be very satisfied. I knew that I was. I was proud of myself. I was doing some things very right for a change.

Initially, I had a lot of idle time on my hands. This was nothing new. I'd had a lot of day-long leisure time in Minneapolis before I went out for a night of hustling.

But this time, things were different. I became a very different person because of my new situation. I didn't realize it at first. I had experienced an epiphany! My life had undergone a "sea change." My use of these terms exemplifies how much I had changed. Before my contact with

Andy, I was as ignorant as a board and as dumb as a shovel. I had always known that I was smart, but I had never given any evidence of it. School had never challenged me in any special way.

Now things were unbelievably different. Andy hired Mike Noonan, a Chippewa Falls High School English teacher, to provide me with homeschooling. He showed up every night for two months at the very beginning before disappearing from the scene. And he really didn't teach me anything *per se*, but he was incredibly stimulating. He opened up new horizons for me. He convinced me that I could—and most importantly should—learn. It was in my own special interest to learn as much as I could. And while I didn't believe him at first, he said that I would enjoy learning. He sort of skipped over mathematics and science, emphasizing reading and the development of a vocabulary. He provided me with no end of materials and techniques to increase my word power and improve my reading skills. He relied heavily upon the computer in the beginning.

The Internet was a bonanza. Mike bought an enormous amount of software. I followed through on all of his suggestions. My vocabulary blossomed. At the same time, I began to read. And surprise, surprise, I was a speed-reader. I would devour books at a single sitting. This played in well with my increasing vocabulary. Not only was I learning the meaning of words, but I was learning how to use them properly. When I wasn't reading, I was writing. While no world class literature was issuing forth from my pen, I enjoyed the creativity that was involved in my self-expression.

Anyone who reads this should be surprised as well. But consider if you will the chapters that you have read so far. Would you have expected that degree of scholarly expression from a fatherless pederast and boy prostitute who had a catatonic schizophrenic for a mother and a pathetic, Ritalin-ridden education well into his freshman year in high school? The answer is obviously no.

But I had caught fire. For example, for a time I developed an interest in mystery books. I read all that were available at the Chippewa Falls Library. I ordered the newer ones from Amazon. I found others with similar interests on the Internet and chatted with them at length. I joined the Bouchercon Society, an organization of mystery writers and readers. I even attended a Bouchercon get-together in Atlantic City, New Jersey. I met and talked with Stephen White and other famous mystery authors.

Andy supported me in all of this. I had found out what *My Fair Lady* and *Pygmalion* meant and how these expressions pertained to my circumstance. I think that he was a bit smug and self-satisfied when he thought about how right he had been about me. But I had exceeded his expectations. While he kept Mike on a retainer, it soon became obvious that I was a self-starter from the get-go. Mike had only to sow the seeds of motivation, provide me with resources, and then get out of the way.

After my mystery period, I checked out the classics. While I didn't warm up to Shakespeare, I read everything written by Chaucer, Dickens, and Jane Austen. At another time, I emphasized history, i.e. the history of man, English history, American history. I had never before considered let alone appreciated how interesting an important this subject was. Mr. Pebbles, my history teacher, had been uninspired and uninspiring. He doted on dates. As an independent reader, I learned more in a day than I had ever learned from Mr. Pebbles.

I became very proud of my accomplishments. I began to develop a sense of confidence and personal identity that would have been impossible to even dream about before I moved in with Andy. I was Curtis Thompson, and Curtis Thompson was very special.

I enrolled at the nearby University of Wisconsin-Eau Claire (UWEC as it was called). Surprisingly, or perhaps not so surprisingly, I found the experience to be a turnoff. I felt superior to my fellow students and to most of my professors. After my independent home study, I found the UWEC experience to be tedious and uninspiring. I had enrolled in the most elementary courses in Psychology, Biology, English, Sociology, and Mathematics. I didn't care for math at all. In the other courses, I read the required textbooks in their entireties during the first week. Then, sitting in classes three times a day became boring beyond belief. The professors droned on as they spoke about the material that was already available from the textbook.

And then I saw her—"across a crowded room," no less—in the Bellow Bar.

Although I didn't realize it at the time, I was about to experience yet another sea change in my life. But this one, in contrast with the one involving Andre, would set in motion incredibly unsettling self-doubts and problems. The resulting feelings of unworthiness and inferiority would impel me into a series of acts which would end in tragedy.

CHAPTER 12

Rent-A-Boy Reflections

I had lots of time to think. I thought a lot about Andre, how he came to select and train me. In my search for understanding, I came up with some pretty weird scenarios. But I knew that "Truth is stranger than fiction." Who would ever believe the true story of my life?

I had been a voracious reader. With my new vocabulary and speed-reading skills, I knocked off books at an amazing rate. At the time, there was little direction or purpose to this reading. If a book came within range of me, it was read.

I remembered an enormous amount of the contents I had read, which surprised me. When I was at UWEC, I'd occasionally come join others in a little "Trivial Pursuit." I was a phenom at that game. Fellow players were amazed. And I didn't know where all that came from. For example, where had I learned that the word "trivia" had a Latin origin related to crossroads or the intersection of three roads where people would leave inconsequential messages for fellow travelers? I had no idea.

I retained a treasure trove of information. Was any of it truly relevant to what was going on in my life? I didn't know, but that didn't stop me from incorporating a lot of it into my many scenarios or plots that might explain my current situation.

A lot had been written about the Mafia or the Cosa Nostra. For years, people were skeptical about such the existence of such an organization, operating effectively and purposefully, just out of public view. And it turned out that there were real Godfathers, consigliores, and a Cosa Nostra.

I had read a great deal about homosexual and pedophile groups. It seemed nonsensical at the time. Sex was such an individual activity, dictated by the people and the circumstances in which they found themselves. It strained credibility to think that there might be an informal, secret organization dedicated to protect its members and provide for their perverse sexual predilections, but there were stories that supported this possibility.

Was there a loosely-knit underground homosexual conspiracy amongst university administrations that provided a safe haven for gays? Some campuses were well-known as being very accepting and permissive while others were not. There was an oft-repeated, albeit apocryphal, tale of a male college professor who got caught in a college dorm having sex with two of his male students. Was he summarily fired? No. The story has that his superior supplied him with glorious recommendations and references with the understanding that he seek employment elsewhere. He did that and landed a job as a Dean of Boys at a vocational school in Northern Illinois.

There were also endless stories about the Catholic clergy. Some of the Seminaries were said to be so gay-laden that the "straights" felt impelled to leave. Vivid descriptions of homosexual orgies at these institutions were forthcoming. The Catholic hierarchy was said to be most protective of homosexual or pedophilic priests after they had been ordained. If an irate father reported that his son had been desecrated by the parish priest, a quiet transfer was arranged. With the parent mollified by the disappearance of the miscreant and a substantial payoff, there was no problem. Priests who could not keep their peckers in their cassocks or their hands off of young boys may have set records in the numbers of different assignments that were made for them.

All the stories and rumors were said to originate from the anti-Christ or anti-Catholic element in our society. Then a huge scandal erupted. Indeed, where there was smoke, there was fire.

How about man/boy clubs comprised of the elite of the hidden pedophilic community? Stuff and nonsense once more, right? Well, the more I thought about it—and I thought about it a great deal—this possibility became more and more reasonable. I had known for a long time that travel agents provided homosexuals with cruises and resorts where they could be very comfortable. Although the advertisements were properly phrased so as to be published in straight newspapers, there was no question about the nature of the service they were providing. "Singles" were welcomed. Implicitly, they would not be alone for very long on one of these trips. All members of the homosexual community knew exactly what they were offering. Some of them suggested that there could be some bonding (not as in "bondage") if men would bring their "sons" along. Several guys had offered me such excursions, and I was more than willing to take them up on it, but they wanted off before they followed through on the plans. Some companies were offering special trips to Amsterdam and Bangkok. The code word seemed to be "affinity." You could join an "affinity group," i.e. go with people sharing a common interest. And according to some travel agents I talked with, these excursions were very popular. In Bangkok, the tourist could select his own boy, kind of a "Rent-A-Boy," from a large group for an entire week, or even longer. And rest assured, the boy would show him more than the temples and the klongs.

In a real way, I had been Andre's "Rent-A-Boy" for nearly seven years. How and why had I been selected in the first place? I no longer believed the cock-and-bull story that he had concocted long ago. I truly believed that part of this game he played with me required deception. He simply had to know many things about me that I didn't know he knew, and I couldn't find anything about any of this. He simply sat back and pulled strings. He probably had done the same thing with my predecessors, Eduardo and William. He had had each for about three years. Each had aged and may have become progressively less appealing to him. When he tired of them, he unloaded them. It was as simple as that. Andre didn't need to justify his actions, but he had probably compiled a laundry list of reasons for his dissatisfactions. Then he played along with the boy, having fun as he manipulated the life of his hired counterpart. Control was very important to him; it could have been his middle name. Bear in mind that Andre's sexual needs were simple and readily satisfied.

Presumably any clean youngster willing to present his bare behind would have sufficed for Andre's sexual purposes. Then when Andre opted to terminate the arrangement, he very probably chose the reason that was likely to occasion guilt and regret for the other party. I don't know how it worked with Eduardo, but for William, it was undoubtedly the girlfriend. William's thinking was probably similar to my own. "I had it so good and now I screwed up. If I hadn't met Sadie…"

In his own devilish way, Andre was sure that this would cause further problems up the road a piece for the person who had been kicked out. In the case of William, would he not remember the idyllic life with Andre when he encountered some inevitable problem with his girlfriend? The hand that had long controlled William continued to do so long after he was no longer on the scene. And his $3,000.00 payoff was a nice touch. This was part of the original agreement. It cut down on the likelihood of any fuss when "the boy" had to leave; only fond recollections, along with some regret and guilt.

In very short order, my thinking had transformed his remote possibility in a virtual certainty. There were man/boy groups. If there were such referral sources, this could account for Andre's selection of me.

Section B

Kay Nelson: A Personal Reprise

CHAPTER 13

The Last and the Least

My advent unto this earth was not a welcome event. Apparently, my parents had had a haphazard program of birth control. While they agreed at the outset that three children were enough, they had already produced eight before I arrived on the scene. My mother, Sharon, clinging vaguely to her version of Catholic beliefs, was against "the pill" but went along with her husband's use of condoms. Steve, a long haul trucker, would often get very drunk on his occasional return to his home, and on these occasions, caught up by testosterone and booze, he would forget to take proper precautions from time to time. These lapses were all that was necessary to produce a very large family. I was now the last in line, an unwanted tagalong. I believed that I was so viewed by my parents. Over the years, I came to accept that perception as well.

I was simply lost in the crowd during the early years of my life. The older children were wise to the ways of the world of our parents. They were better equipped to compete for the scraps of attention and affection that they would occasionally scatter amongst us. My father was simply not there—physically nor psychologically—a great deal of the time. Mother was overwhelmed by the demands laid in her lap. She had begun to drink a great deal.

It is difficult, if not impossible to describe the impact of all of this upon who I believed I really was. I became starved for attention and affection. I hadn't a clue to identify ways by which I could satisfy these important needs.

My older siblings, armed with superior strength and experience, would often use me to accomplish their own ends. Early on, they could push me down and make me cry. Later, they would punch me, call me names, or do other things in order to accomplish this. As the youngest, I became something of the family punching bag, a sitting duck. If things ever got dull, and they often did, my brothers and sisters singly or collectively could then turn to me and get a rise out of me. In a small house completely lacking in parental supervision, there was no escaping them.

This then became the pattern of the first five or six years of my life. It was hell. I became very silent. No one seemed to notice because no one ever talked about anything in our household. My silence came to be a frightening prison populated by all manner of ghosts and goblins. I was tense all the time. I spent a lot of time feeling sorry for myself, and there was good reason.

Repression entered into my adjustment pattern early on, although I knew of no such term at the time. I couldn't remember much of what my sibs had done to me. If I thought of something that might remind me of an especially disturbing incident, I would distract myself and thus never remember it, and this usually worked. But occasionally, circumstances conspired so that I was constantly reminded some of what bothered me most. Upon each such recollection, I would become unsettled again.

An example of this took place when I was about two or three. Aunt Anise had taken pity on me at Christmas time and had given me a large toy dog that I named Elmer. Elmer and I became inseparable. He was my friend. I talked to him about things that bothered me. As I learned later on, Elmer was the equivalent of an imaginary companion for me. Then one day, an epiphany took place, a dreadful moment of truth; an event that provided me with proof positive as to where I fit into the scheme of things.

One day, my oldest brother, Steve, Jr. became bored. He had tired of watching TV. He looked around for something to do. As he had often done in the past, he picked on me to make his life interesting.

He walked up and wrenched Elmer out of my arms and called to the rest of his brothers and sisters. "Come on, let's have some fun!" I was crying wildly by this time. He held Elmer high above his head as he walked around and around the living room. The other kids joined in and soon they were in a line, stomping and shouting as they went along.

Steve set the tone for this parade by the words for their marching song:

"Kay is ca-ca. Ca-ca is Kay.
The only difference 'tween them
Is that ca-ca goes away.

Elmer is ca-ca. Ca-ca is Kay.
Let's take Elmer
And make him go away."

They chanted this over and over again.

The kids really got into this, soon stomping their feet hard and shouting out these awful words as they marched around the room. I was running alongside Steve, trying to wrest Elmer from his arms. Still singly loudly, Steve then led the march into the bathroom. He tossed Elmer into the bowl and tried to flush him down the toilet. But he couldn't do it. Elmer was simply too big. Even with repeated flushings and poking with a stick, Elmer just wouldn't go down the drain. After a bit of this, the interest of the group faded. Tiring of the game, all returned to the living room to watch TV. All except me. I fished Elmer out, and I cried and cried.

Elmer had been damaged in all the soaking and poking. He was never the same. And in a very real sense, neither was I. Repression was no use to me in this instance. Every time that I used the bathroom, I was reminded of what had happened and how upset I had been. I came to believe deeply that I would be flushed down the toilet if ever my brothers and sisters had such an opportunity. Shortly thereafter, my mother had dealt with the situation by throwing Elmer out with the trash one day when I was not looking. I, too, could disappear. No one would care. No one would notice.

Kay was ca-ca.

Ca-ca was Kay.

While this event stood out in my recollection, such personal put-downs occurred with relentless regularity throughout my childhood. I got the message. It was loud and clear.

CHAPTER 14

Some Seeds are Sown

School became something of a godsend for me. Not only was I able to escape my disturbing family life, but I discovered that I had something going for me. I was astonished when the kindergarten teacher told me that I had a nice smile. No one had ever said anything like that before. And I was smart. I did well in my school work. People noticed this. They frequently complemented me on my accomplishments. I became happier than I had ever been before. However, it wasn't all beer and skittles. Fellow students can be hurtful toward one another as they deal with their own personal problems. They found, as had my siblings, that I was timid and vulnerable, much like a deer caught in the headlights. Some of my classmates delighted in saying things that would upset me and make me cry. This worked every time. It didn't take much, and I had no one to go to for help.

So I turned to myself for solace and solutions. I didn't sit down one day and come up with this. It sort of developed over the course of time. I came up with something that worked. I had found over the course of time that if I ignored the taunts of others, these tormentors would eventually go away and leave me alone. Capitalizing on this bit of knowledge, I made myself inconspicuous. I stayed by myself as much as possible.

This tact had advantage. With so much time by myself, I would bury myself in school work. As a consequence, I did extremely well in school. I became educated; maybe even bookish. I was rewarded with high grades in class work and deportment. My teachers frequently described me as a quiet and studious child. Little did they know what was really going on.

But at the end of the school day, I always had to come home, and things never seemed to change there. My father was rarely there. Mother was frazzled and drunk a lot of the time. My siblings continued to use and abuse me, albeit less frequently and in more subtle ways. No one in my family, but no one, ever said anything nice about me or my accomplishments in school. Neither parent ever talked to me about anything personal.

As the brothers grew older, their tormenting took on markedly sexual overtones. When I was about eight, one or two of the older boys would take me off to a corner where they would "play doctor." As they had been too young earlier, they had not done this with my older sisters. At least, I didn't think that they had. This "play" would have me undress so they could look me over and paw at me a bit. Over the years, this progressed into more intense touching and ultimately into some clumsy attempts at sex. The boys would threaten to beat me up if I wouldn't cooperate, and they told me that even worse was in store for me if I ever told anyone about any of this. Of course, I never did.

In truth, this was not all that bad. Although I was embarrassed initially, I found that this was kind of neat. In fact, I chose to think of myself as being special. As long as I cooperated, no one ever hurt me. Indeed, I got excited when they felt me up. They touched me and I began touching them. All of them, especially the older boys, were really learning about sex on their own. It was, quite literally, a "hands on" project. And I became a most willing partner. I came to look forward to these sexual encounters.

My brothers were clever and streetwise kids, so they did an about-face. They started treating me nicely. Although I was surprised and leery at first, I came to like this new treatment. They'd often say nice things about me and even buy little gifts for me. They'd even give me gentle hugs every now and then. I was being treated like a little princess. The bad times were fading in my memory. I liked to be hugged and they knew it. Over the course of time, the brotherly hugging became more prolonged, and that was too nice.

One day, George brought home a Mars bar for me, suggested that we share it while I was seated on his lap. This was fine with me. I really had a sweet tooth. I was cooperative. I didn't want to do anything that might interfere with the wonderful new relationship I had with my brothers. Deep down inside, I was still frightened as to what might happen if I didn't cooperate. George sat holding me for a while as we shared the Mars bar, first with each other and then later with Samuel, who just happened to arrive on the scene. It was nice to be held and to be loved. George then began rubbing my knee in gentle, friendly fashion. That, too, felt nice.

After he had done that for a while, he inched up my leg a bit as he continued to whisper nice things about me in my ear. "Isn't this fun?" he would murmur. And it was nice to sit there being held and stroked as I took bites out of the Mars bar. Soon, his hand had disappeared completely below my skirt as he began to touch me wherever he wanted. And I liked this as well. It felt good. I shuddered a bit as he slowly inserted his finger, but in as much as it didn't really hurt and it pleased him to do this, I just smiled and looked down. Samuel came closer and began to hug both of us. Very soon, both brothers were getting pretty excited as their hands and fingers went everywhere.

And they restrained themselves. As they did this for what seemed to be a long time, both eventually stiffened and moaned softly. Breathless at the end, they even thanked me and said that I was the greatest sister in the world. I really believed them. I did so because I desperately wanted to believe them. It had been nice to hold and be held. And what had pleased them had begun to please me. Both brothers had taken the first tiny steps toward goals that clearly involved their testosterone. Their hormones were beginning to rage. This was surely better than all the force, threats, and fears of discovery. The brothers had a good thing going for them, and it had promised to get even better.

A pattern was then thus established that grew and grew over the years. I became more than willing to participate. You might even say that I was eager. I liked what I was able to do to please my brothers. By word, gestures, and presents, they expressed a love and acceptance to me that I had never experienced before. They and what we together did became very important to me, and I could maintain this wonderful state of affairs merely by being compliant, by doing the little things that pleased them.

And was this all going on under the wary eye of mother Sharon? Of course. This was partially due to the fact that she really didn't want to know what was going on. Things were bad in this family and she didn't want to make them worse. None are so blind as those that don't want to see. In addition, the boys became clever in inventing short trips which allowed our threesome to get their business done. Of course, there were many nights when "watchful" Sharon spent the entire evening at the bar and the kids had the whole house to themselves.

When I was about ten or eleven years old, our dreamboat arrangement rocked and then seemed to sink. The boys now looked for fresher, greener pastures, and they found them loaded with girls of their own age. They were still very nice to me not only because we had a good thing going, but because of vague fears that I might get angry and blow the whistle on them. I wouldn't, but they didn't know that. Over the course of time, they sought me out less frequently, and then rarely. I missed them and the activities. I began to feel lonely and depressed. I had nothing to look forward to anymore.

My parents were not getting along any better than they had in the past. Their marriage was in shambles, but neither of them had the financial or psychological wherewithal to end their farce. They seemed to do nothing but drink. After drinking, they would fight. This went on for years.

CHAPTER 15

Hot Hot Hot

When I was about twelve or thirteen, I began to take on what a sociologist would call "sexual initiative." I was "hot to trot" as we used to say in those days. After some concerns about pregnancy, I soon reveled in full adult sex, complete with penetration. I insisted on condoms. I had been sort of programmed for this. My brothers had occasionally invited friends over to join in the fun. We would shoo our sisters out of the back room and then we would have at it.

After a bit, I came to believe that I was the one who was really in control. If I didn't like one of the boys, he was out. If I liked him, he was invited back. I really liked being the center of attention. My brothers liked to watch as their friends had sex with me. But that made me uncomfortable, especially one time when I caught one snickering. From there on, I insisted on privacy. The boys went along with this because they had a very good thing going for them. In general, they were awkward and ignorant. It really didn't take much to please them. I taught them a thing or two. These little in-house orgies went on about two or three times a week for almost two years.

As I look back on it, I find it strange that no one ever blew the whistle on us. I preferred to think that my sisters were jealous of all the attention I was getting. I thought they'd tell, but they'd never did. Much later on, I found that they were having difficulties dealing with problems of their own. They couldn't have cared less what was happening to me. My father was rarely home. If Mom wasn't passed out, we'd have to wait until she did, and that usually didn't take very long.

I continued to do well in school, but this wasn't as important to me anymore. By the time I had reached high school, I knew far more about boys and sex than did any of my classmates.

To the high school boys, I was considered hot and available. They would gather around me in droves. This drove my female classmates up the wall. Some wouldn't talk to me. I kept telling myself that I didn't care about what they thought. And at the time, I really didn't. My popularity with the boys became all that really mattered to me. Popularity was more readily accomplished than academic success. It was more fun. It was only years later that I discovered that the boys had just been using me. Not only that, but they were laughing at me behind my back. I learned that I was called "Rosie Roundheels" because I could be tipped over on my back so easily. But I must have turned the blindest of eyes on any of this negative stuff. I was the belle of the ball and that was all that counted.

When I was about fifteen, in rare quiet moments, I began to wonder seriously about my reputation and many other matters. Some girls had talked to me about what some of the boys had said. They were exaggerating what was really going on. No boy would admit that he had failed in his effort to screw me. If as many had had me as they said, I'd have had to be three girls.

As I matured into adolescence, I maintained my liaisons with my brothers, but I had become fearful of discovery. I started to worry about pregnancy. When I insisted that they use condoms, their interest decreased markedly. I could have gone on birth control pills, but that might involve my mother, and I wanted to avoid any problems with her as much as possible.

Over the years, boys at school came to disrespect me in a variety of ways, some subtle and some anything but. Many made no pretense of fondness or love. Often there were no words of affection. There was little foreplay. The boys would cut to the chase, driving quickly to some secluded spot where they could get it on quickly and return home as soon as the deed was done. They would leave me standing on a corner. Often times, someone else would pick me up there and the pattern would be repeated. One time, three boys picked me up in a beat-up van. They drove to a lakefront where each in turn had at me. And then, each returned for seconds. While I didn't enjoy this at all, I really didn't know what to do. They laughed loudly amongst themselves and made crude jokes as they did virtually anything they wanted with me. While using my body, they seemed to ignore me as though I wasn't really there.

I couldn't and didn't break out of this pattern. I was a bright girl. I was learning a lot at school despite my many sexual involvements. I was making serious plans to go to college. I told myself that I had great potential and a lot to offer, but I didn't really believe this, even when I repeatedly made the honor roll. And no one else believed it either. My self-concept was in a shambles. It was close to zero. If this continued, I knew that in my search for love and affection, I would rely upon my body. I wanted to be loved for myself rather than as a vessel to provide someone momentary gratification, but that didn't seem to be in the cards. I continued to be passed from one boy to another. As soon as a boy lost interest in me, he would leave me without a backward glance. This foretold a dismal future. I became very despondent. Then I met Rob.

He was Rob Newton, a popular guy and the quarterback on our football team. As I look back on it now, my self-confidence and assurance must have been at an all-time low. If Rob smiled on me, I was in seventh heaven! If he were just a little stand-offish, my day was ruined. I'd get angry if he as much mentioned another girl's name. I became hopelessly dependent on him. But that was all right; I loved him and he loved me. I would do anything for him.

CHAPTER 16

"That Night," A Betrayal

And then there came a night that I would never forget. I was fifteen. It all started out innocently enough. Rob had become my life, and he said that he loved me. He picked me up as he had on previous occasions. We usually drove out to a nearby county park, drank some beer, made out a few times, and then headed on home. This time, however, he suggested that we go to his parents' cabin on a nearby lake. They were away for a weekend in Chicago. As I had never been there before, I thought this was a great idea. It was a wonderful place with a beautiful view of the lake—and a well-stocked liquor cabinet. Rob made a big thing out of the booze.

It was as great as he'd said it would be. As we began to cozy into the place, he asked me if I'd like to try some of his father's imported vodka. I was more than a little hesitant at first. I had seen enough of the effects of vodka on my parents to shy away from it in the past. I would have been satisfied to stick with beer. But then, tonight was special. I thought, "What the hell?" I was with Rob. We were in love, and we'd soon make love. So I said, "Sure, why not?" He produced his version of a martini: a little ice in a large tumbler, a hint of vermouth, and a lot of vodka. He took a large swallow and egged me on to do the same. I tried, but the harsh mixture caused me to choke. He laughed at me and said, "Come on, right to the last drop." Although it tasted terrible, I managed to get it down. And he was right there, ready to fill the empty tumbler. I wanted to take my time, but he was insistent.

"Now together," he said, "under the lips, over the gums, look out liver, here it comes."

I went along with this and finished the second drink well within five minutes. I was beginning to feel really good as we kissed and cuddled on the couch. We started the prelims. We'd been there many times before.

Then we heard the honk of a car horn.

Rob likely thought to himself, "Right on time."

Soon there was a pounding on the door. Rob opened the door to find Ralph and Hank standing there. They were his two best friends.

Rob said, "What's up?" Ralph replied, "We were driving around and thought we'd come up and take a look at the lake." I had never met these two before, although I'd seen them around school. Rob bid them welcome and asked if they'd like to have a drink. Of course, they would. They had several rounds.

In my naiveté and trust, I never dreamed that this was a set-up. I found out much later that Rob and his friends had talked it over a week beforehand. He had told them, "I'm getting just a shade tired of her. Let's get her loaded and all have a go at her. I'm sure she won't mind. It'll be fun to see what happens."

In my developing vodka haze, I didn't see the exchange of winks and knowing glances amongst the young men, nor did I notice that my drinks were twice as strong as any of the others. I was just enjoying myself, chatting and singing, and feeling very good. Once again, I was the belle of the ball.

After a short time, things went blank. I didn't remember much of anything after that. A lot later, I found myself on the doorstep of my house with my mother giving me holy hell for being drunk. She said over and over again in a variety of ways, "What did I ever do to deserve such a daughter? A whore? A drunken slut?" She was three sheets to the wind herself. Eventually, I was allowed inside where I stumbled to my bed. I awoke the next morning with absolutely no recollection of what had gone on that night before I had experienced my first blackout.

I felt terrible. I wondered what had gone on. In as much as I didn't have even a foggy notion of what had happened, I began to conjure up all sorts of dreadful things. It turned out that I had been involved in something so awful that I couldn't have even imagined it.

I dragged myself to school after enduring another go-round with my mother. We finally had something in common: We were both really hung over.

I saw Rob and waved at him. Not only did he fail to wave back; he started walking quickly away from me. The other two, Hank and Ralph, walked right by me as though I didn't exist. They said something to one another as they passed, but I couldn't make out what it was. They were kind of grinning at one another as they went by.

Several girls were laughing wildly, especially when one of them pointed her finger in my direction.

Suddenly woozy, I sat down by myself at a cafeteria table and tried to figure out what was really going on.

Jim, a boy I knew from the previous semester, finally joined me. He and I had seen a lot of each other a year ago until he found someone else. He smiled knowingly as he said, "I hear tell that you really had quite a time last night."

Hoping to find out what happened during my blackout, I had to ask him, "What do you mean?"

Jim replied, "Well, you and Rob, and Hank, and Ralph…and the drinking and the cabin. The story is all over school."

I was glad I was sitting down. I felt weak and frightened. Evidently, something terrible had happened, and I didn't know what, but everyone else did. "What are they saying?" I asked. "Jim, please tell me what they're saying."

Jim looked somewhat puzzled. He said, "You mean that you really don't remember what you and the guys did last night? You must have been really bombed."

He then went on to tell me the story that was making the rounds. "Well, the way I heard it was that you were kind of set up. Rob had been screwing you for quite a while and started to get bored. At least, that is what he says. He was talking about that with his friends and they came up with a plan they thought would be fun. Rob would take you up to his folks' cabin and get you started on some of the hard stuff. He knew how you were with beer and wanted to see how you were different when you were really loaded. Then, Ralph and Hank were to drop in as if by accident. Then the party really began. They kept feeding you vodka while they went through the motions of drinking as they watched you get smashed.

After a bit, you passed out. At first, they were afraid that you might get sick on them, but that never happened. Eventually, you were unconscious on the couch. While they hadn't been drinking as much as you, they themselves were pretty well snockered. At first they just sat around and laughed at the trick that they had played on you. According to the original plan, they wanted to see how funny you'd talk and what you might say, but you were so out of it that you just lay there.

They wanted something to happen. They party got really rough after a bit. They stripped you down. They got out Rob's camera and began to take pictures. Incidentally some of these have been floating around here this morning. Two of them would hold you and the other would take the pictures. You were dead to the world and didn't resist at all. They took pictures of every nook and cranny you have, front-side and backside. And then they took turns having sex with you every which way, sometimes two at a time with the other guy taking the pictures.

After they spent about an hour doing this, they sat around and waited for you to come to. You moaned every once in a while so they knew that you weren't dead. They wanted to show you the pictures and listen to what you would have to say, but you just lay there. They decided to call it a night. They put your clothes back on you, and you still didn't wake up. They thought it would be a good joke to put your panties on backwards. Did you notice that? Then they carried you to Rob's car, and he drove you home and dumped you on the doorstep. Evidently, your mom heard something and came out. Rob said that she was really yelling after she found you."

I was speechless and in shock. I could only nod at Jim as I gathered myself together and departed the school. What was I to do now? I couldn't stay in school. They all knew. I couldn't go home. I was just out of it.

So I just started walking. There had been many lows in my life, but this was the worst. I didn't know where to turn. I had absolutely no idea what I could or should do. I started running down the street.

CHAPTER 17

A Voice in My Wilderness

As I started to run down the street, I heard a voice calling my name. I stopped and turned around to see Mr. Douglas, the school psychologist. He said, "Kay, could I talk with you a minute?" I really had no choice, but I still managed to ask, "What about?"

He said, "I saw you leaving school in such a hurry and I have come to get you. We can talk here or in my office. All things considered, let's go back in the building." I went along.

After I was in his office, he got right to the point. "As I'm in with kids, I know what's going on. I've heard lots of stories and seen some of the pictures. You are in trouble and so are the boys. At this moment, though, I'm really concerned about you. I want to help. How can I do that?"

The bell for class had rung so they encountered no one in the halls. He pointed to a chair for me as he sat down behind his desk. I just said, "I don't really know what to say."

"Maybe you can just start talking. Sometimes that helps. What happened?"

"I'm so embarrassed. I don't know where to begin. I went on what I thought was a date with Rob and it didn't turn out that way. He really didn't care for me at all. And I was too dumb to realize that. Maybe I should have known. Things between us seemed so good."

"In what way?"

"Rob and I could talk about things that were important to me. I thought that he really cared for me, maybe even loved me. We had a lot of good times together."

"What sorts of things did you talk about?"

"About his plans to become a mechanical engineer. His previous girlfriends and how they really didn't measure up to me. School things. News. Gossip. Regular teenage stuff, I guess."

"You thought things were going well?"

"Yes. We were very close, if you know what I mean. But if I start to look back on things, I'll probably see all sorts of things that would have told me different."

"How do you know how he felt about you?"

"He told me. And I believed him. He said I was pretty and smart. But apparently, I'm not smart enough. I really trusted that son of a bitch."

"You shouldn't be too hard on yourself. Maybe you should just roll with the punches for the time being and not try too hard to figure things out."

"I can't even try to figure things out now. I'll go right up the wall."

"Well then, don't. Maybe we can come up with a plan to deal with your current problems and postpone attention to other matters until some later time."

I was miserable. "I wish I could die."

Mr. Douglas nodded and murmured, "I understand that."

"What in the hell can I possibly do to get out of this?"

Mr. Douglas said, "I'd suggest that we just try to get through the day…and it will be a rough one. Go back to your regular classes as though nothing happened. Accept the fact that you are going to be unsettled. The other students will be talking about and looking at you. But if you can get through the day, things will start to improve. You may get some help from some of the students, and you may not. You may find out who your true friends really are. Don't worry about learning anything, just get through the day. Then, come back here in the last period, and we'll take it from there."

I was trembling as I nodded again. He almost had to push me out of his office and down the hall as the bell rang once again.

I felt like a zombie for the rest of the day. No one said anything to me. The teachers, probably aware of the situation, avoided calling upon me. Everyone steered clear. I didn't see Rob, Hank, or Ralph. At the end of the longest of days, I returned to Mr. Douglas' office. He was waiting for me. I had heard the expression, "Any port in a storm." It seemed to apply to Mr. Douglas.

He greeted me with, "That took some doing. I'm proud that you were able to get through it."

I said, "Thanks. It was flat out terrible."

"Your mother and your sister Julie were in to see me, and I think that everyone has settled down a bit. At any rate, I think you can return home without getting hassled. Julie wants to talk with you, but only if you want to hear what she has to say."

"Julie was here? She said that?" I was totally surprised. Julie and I hadn't ever talked together.

CHAPTER 18

Bottoming Out

I left Mr. Douglas' office and returned home. My mother nodded to me and said nothing. Maybe Mr. Douglas had told her to cool it. I went to my room.

In short order, Julie tapped at my door. In Mr. Douglas' office, I had been surprised when he told me she wanted to talk to me. Now I was astonished when she actually did seek me out. Despite the fact that we had been brought up in the same house for umpteen years, neither of us had ever talked about anything really important. What would she have to say?

Julie came in and sat on my bed. "May I talk?" she asked.

"Sure."

Julie spoke softly and slowly. "I really don't know where to begin. I'm terribly sorry about all of this mess. And I'm so sorry that I haven't been here for you in the past. But we both know that this is the way it works out in this family. I knew that you were in trouble and headed for more, yet I did nothing. That bothers me. And while it's maybe too late in the game to come riding to your rescue, I really want to do something to help out. Is this okay with you?"

I was at a loss. "I really don't know what to say. We've never been close. In the early days, before I wised up, you were right in there with the rest of the pack, eager and willing to make me miserable. Why do you want to help me now of all times?"

Julie said, "Maybe guilt. There were many times when I wished I had someone I could talk with. When the chips were down for me, there was no one there. I know how I suffered in silence for a long, long time. I know how it feels. And for once in my life, I want to be there for someone."

I wondered what that was all about. I couldn't remember Julie ever getting into any trouble. But then, maybe I had been out of the loop. In our family, we don't talk about anything, including the good, the bad, and the ugly.

Julie continued, "You probably don't know anything about it. Once night, when I was about fifteen, dad came home loaded and he caught me coming out of the shower. I had a towel on me, but he pulled it off and looked at me in the strangest of ways. I don't know what he would have done if Mom hadn't come barging into the bathroom. She had heard something and had come to check it out. I've never seen her so mad. She pointed toward the hallway and Dad caught on real quickly. He left without saying a word. Then, Mom handed me the towel and then got right in my face. I can still remember how red her face was. She slapped me hard. I slipped on the wet tile and went right to the floor. Mom kept right on calling me every name in the book. Finally, she turned around and left.

That was the end of that…except that it wasn't. While no one ever talked about it, the chill around the house was 20 below for weeks. I felt guilty even though I had done nothing wrong. It was hell for me. I thought about this and I thought about that. I thought myself into what I called my 'nervous breakdown.' I didn't know what to do. I became so desperate that I finally made an appointment with Mr. Douglas. I came to get along well with him. I talked to him about the slapping episode for a long time, and he listened. I started to talk to him about a lot of other things as well, and it helped. I felt better. We met regularly for three or four months, then I tapered off.

That was four years ago, and I haven't seen him except on a hello-goodbye basis when I see him in town. He's an all right guy. If you're having problems—and you are having problems—go and see him. Lean on him for a while. Things will get better. It worked for me."

I just had to say something. "But I'm so ashamed. And he's a man. Everyone's talking, laughing and showing these pictures around. Have you seen them?"

Julie said, "Yes, I have. They are pretty bad, but they can be dealt with. At least, I think they and your other problems can be handled. For openers, Rob and the other two are in really deep doo-doo. The law is looking for them. They are guilty. You are innocent. Dumb, but innocent. Believe it or not, that is true. And if my experience is any guide, that might take a long time for you to believe it. Talk with Mr. Douglas. Talk with me. Play it along just one day at a time. Things will get better. I'll help you as much as I can. I know what it's like to be alone."

All of this had come on too fast for me. Too much too quickly. That night; school the next day, and even Mr. Douglas intervening. And now, Julie in my bedroom offering to help me. But I heard "one day at a time" loud and clear. That gave me something to go on. With Mr. Douglas urging along those very lines, I'd already survived one day.

Julie sounded both convinced and convincing. As I had no options, I thought that I'd see Mr. Douglas. He did seem okay and he went out of his way to help me on this god-awful day. I'd march right in the very next day, head held high, and make an appointment. As for talking to Julie up the road, I didn't know about that. But like Julie said, "One day at a time." I'd play it by ear.

The next time I saw Mr. Douglas, I was tense; probably awkward and was embarrassed to the max. But he soon put me at ease and I started talking. And I talked and talked; it was as though I couldn't stop. The hour ended too soon. At the end of it, I felt much better even though I couldn't remember hardly anything I had said.

I came back regularly and talked about everything under the sun. During the first month, I talked mostly about that awful night and its consequences. During that time, I came to realize that while it had been bad, it was not earth-shattering. I began to examine other personal issues, my promiscuity, my need for attention, my dysfunctional family, my fine academic credentials, and my future. In regard to the latter, I found it interesting that I had never given any serious thought about what I might accomplish as I lived out my life.

Looking back, I came to see that everything had been done on a day-to-day basis. Living a day at a time could have a serious downside. If the boys were flocking to me, all was great. But if I was rejected by someone, then I had to plot so as to make myself acceptable. My body had been my passport to personal success. That kind of attention remained important to me, but over the course of my counseling, I came to emphasize some of my other strengths. These included my intelligence, academic excellence, and my "street moxie."

All of this was probably pretty routine for Mr. Douglas. He had established rapport with me rather easily. There was something about him that made him seem trustworthy from the very beginning. After the first four or five sessions, I had gone to the library to find out what approach he took to counseling, i.e. what was he up to? As near as I could figure, he was "non-directive." That meant that he could not and would not furnish me with any directions or answers to my problems. This approach was built on the belief that I could develop these on my own if I would but talk and seek these solutions. In the readings he suggested, I came across the word "catharsis" quite frequently. This seemed to me to mean that spilling your guts made you feel better. It really worked. When I talked about terrible things, they would begin to lose their sting.

Mr. Douglas seemed pleased and a little amused when I told him about my extensive readings. As I continued to see him, the focus of the sessions began to change. I came to believe that my past had led me astray, but that was history. When I told him that that was my conclusion, he said that he agreed that, "Your past is like your ass. It's behind you." Every day was born afresh. You wake up each morning to the first day of the rest of your life. Personal goals began to emerge in my talk, e.g. Who was I? Who did I wish to become? In my life, what really mattered? What did I want to be doing in five or ten years? I didn't really nail anything down, but I begun to develop a confidence in myself that I could do a lot of things. The light at the end of the tunnel began to glow more brightly.

While the counseling went well, nothing ever worked out with Julie. While I became friendly toward her and grateful for her advice, the negatives rooted in our upbringing proved to be very deep. We met a few times to talk, but it proved to be awkward. It would have been nice if Julie and I could have become real good friends, but that was not to be. She had been there for me at a most critical time and that's what counted. She had given good advice.

CHAPTER 19

A Second Betrayal

Some said I lucked out when it came to dealing with the consequences of that night. All three of the boys were charged. Rob and Hank were eighteen, so statutory rape was one of the charges. If convicted, they were facing some serious jail time.

I had been scheduled as a witness. I knew and was told repeatedly that they would bring up my "Rosie Roundheels" reputation. I would be painted a bad girl, "Fifteen going on fifty" or as one who had "been around the block so many times that she would run into herself." As a minor, I was not capable of granting consent, but a clever defense attorney could paint a picture of me as the perpetrator and the boys as the innocent victims.

Mr. Douglas and I touched on all these bases before the cases came before the court. I felt reasonably prepared for the onslaught in court even though I knew it would be incredibly rough.

Then came the "lucking out." A wimpy D.A. engineered some sort of plea bargain with them. Rob and Hank received credit for time served. They had spent a week in the local jail before they were released to the custody of their parents. In addition to this, they joined Ralph with a two-year term of probation and 300 hours of community service.

So I never had to testify. I felt very lucky at the time. It would have been sheer hell for me on the witness stand.

But I remained disturbed by this. I had been betrayed, become a nervous wreck, and held up to the scorn of the community. And I remained convinced that an awful lot of people held me responsible for all the trouble; that I had spread my legs apart once too often.

There was one especially disturbing event that bothers me to this day. It involved Rob. After the plea bargains had been arranged and his life was going back to normal, I was in the school cafeteria. He was sitting across the room. I looked at him; he looked at me. Our eyes locked for only a second or two. But in that time, he pointed his finger at me, smiled, and winked. It said, "Gotcha." He had had his way. He had abused me horribly, and he was still enjoying what he had done.

CHAPTER 20

On Hold

It seems strange to say that for two or three years of my high school life had simply been on hold. Perhaps "in limbo" would be a better designation. But that seems to have been what happened. I had been deceiving myself for many years. I thought that I was the belle of the ball. My easy availability had made me very popular, or so it had seemed. Then, after that awful night, my whole life came crashing down on me. My social life went from frenzied feast to famine.

Almost immediately after Rob's plea bargain, the pendulum of my emotional life took a huge swing in the direction of unhappiness and even deep depression. I had been "had" in every since of the word, and society didn't care. The District Attorney's negotiated settlement had said in effect, "She got what she was looking for." Or so it seemed to me.

Had I been referred to a branch of the mental health establishment, I probably would have been diagnosed as suffering from a bipolar disorder. I would have been prescribed medication which may or may not have dealt with my depression. If it did, there would be some tweaking of the dosage from time to time, and I probably would have gotten along. They might have even concluded that I was doing "as well as can be expected under the circumstances." If the prescribed medication did not elevate my mood, some other kind of medication would have been recommended. Sooner or later (more likely later), an effective drug would be determined. The basic ingredients of my personal problems would have remained unaddressed.

As it was, I was very much inclined to lick my wounds and back off from all those who had been important in my world. I really hadn't sat down and fashioned any such strategy. I simply did it.

It's also sad that I withdrew from the counseling of Mr. Douglas as well. The sessions with him had gone very well. He had provided me a safe haven when I desperately needed one. He had accepted me unconditionally as a person of worth. In the cocoon that he'd furnished, I had felt safe and free to express myself in a way I'd never done before. Personal problems were identified and resolved. But after four months or so, there was something of a lull. I came to wonder if continued counseling was really necessary. At least, that's what I told myself at the time. At this stage, I was beginning to touch upon some very deep personal issues. A lot of this was frightening. I came to believe that if I continued, I would reveal things to Mr. Douglas that would lower his estimate of me. He would see through me. He would see me as the worthless bitch I was, rather than as the accomplished and attractive person I presented to him. I convinced myself that it was time to get out of this counseling relationship while I was still ahead. I had improved, but I had not improved enough.

My self-imposed cocoon provided me with a sanctuary that had many advantages. After a relatively short time, I found myself out of the loop. At first, the boys would seek me out as before, but soon became disinterested when I didn't respond. As a loner, I did not hear any of the gossip that undoubtedly circulated about me. Those who had made such a big thing out of that night soon turned to other matters of greater current interest.

My academic performance improved immensely. Essentially devoid of contact with other students, I concentrated on the subject matter and earned great grades once again. And the teachers, probably at the behest of Mr. Douglas, seemed to go out of their way to accept and compliment me. I liked this kind of attention. They saw me not as the slut I had come to believe myself to be, but as a person of considerable accomplishment and great promise. And while really believing that I was only fooling them, it was great to hear what they had to say.

I had found another source of solace, but this one wasn't as constructive as study. It was booze, 80 proof vodka. My usage had kind of snuck up on me. I knew very well I should stay away from it. Both my mother and father were drunk and disagreeable most of the time. Unfortunately, I had liked the impact of liquor and had felt very good on that fateful night until I had overdone it. Home alone after school and on weekends, I had access to vodka anytime I wanted it.

Concealing my drinking was no problem. My parents didn't know where they were most of the time, and they continued to act as though I didn't exist. I found that I could be in a mild and enjoyable La-La Land without anyone catching on. It was good to get a glow on. I came to look forward to it. But at the same time, I was frightened over what might happen if I overdid this drinking and got flat out loaded. I became something of a controlled drinker. I could take it or leave it, or so I thought.

And I learned to take it, quite literally. I didn't stop. Both of my parents were alcoholics by any standard. Both always wanted to make sure that they had an adequate supply. Usually this consisted of four or five quarts of vodka in the cabinet next to the kitchen sink. I dipped into this supply every day. The small amount I took probably would have gone unnoticed, but I was well on the way to developing a protective devious streak. I kept track of the bottles and always knew exactly what the actual content of vodka was in each. For every drop of vodka I took, I added half a drop of water. The dilution went unnoticed by my parents, but I always knew exactly what I was drinking.

While generally unhappy over matters that I could not control, I was pretty much in charge of my drinking, and I was proud of this ability. I was in control of at least one aspect of my life. I was excited by this living on the edge. There was always that chance that I might become drunk or my parents might notice that their booze lacked proper impact.

CHAPTER 21

Free at Last?

I had all the credentials necessary for admission to a nearby university, the University of Wisconsin-Eau Claire (UWEC). This necessitated a move. UWEC was located about 40 miles from my home. No one in the family said much of anything to me after I announced my acceptance. No one seemed to care. I remained convinced that they were glad to be rid of me.

As always, Mr. Douglas was a source of great support. He discussed in infinite detail what I could expect and what would be expected of me. He was a UWEC graduate and had maintained contact with some members of the Psychology Department. He suggested that I conduct a trial run before the semester actually started. I was no stranger to Eau Claire, having visited this city of roughly 60,000 several times on field trips. However, I had never seen, let alone visited, the UWEC campus. Mr. Douglas arranged for some brief meetings with Dr. Moss, the Chair of the Psychology Department, and Dr. Leader, who was a practicing clinical psychologist. They welcomed me warmly and volunteered whatever assistance I might need.

I received no emotional or financial support from the family. A small amount of money from my grandmother's estate paid to get me enrolled and ensconced in a university dormitory named Horan Hall.

Moving in for me was easily accomplished in as much as I was traveling very light. For most other students, the move looked like a disorderly crowd scene. Cars filled with computers, special furniture, and toy dogs disgorged their contents as near as possible to the dorm entrance. I was envious of other students who were being helped by their parents. Some of the co-eds thought that their parents were overly-concerned and overly-solicitous. They couldn't seem to wait until they left. I was moved to tears when I heard them talk that way! What would I have given for one such moment when I would be missed?

I met my new roommate, Sylvia Nelson, and her parents. Sylvia was the last of their offspring to fly the coop. While her parents said facetiously how great the "empty nest" would be, I could tell that they were saddened as this new chapter in their life was about to unfold.

By nighttime, the whole dorm was ready to settle in. There was a "get acquainted" buffet in the first floor rec room. Each of us had a name tag. There was a lot of chatter, people asking where are you from? What's your major? What are the hot spots? We were one happy and excited bunch of girls, or women, as some of them demanded to be called.

After this broke up, Sylvia and I went up to our room where we talked until two in the morning. I learned more about her than she did about me. Distrustful soul that I had become, I just couldn't loosen up and talk freely. I knew that I could and probably should be more trusting.

Then, too, there was so much I really didn't want to talk about. I knew, despite all the ways in which I had changed, that I still had a long, long way to go.

I was pretty much on my own as I registered for various classes I was assigned an advisor, but she didn't seem to want to dispense any advice. With Mr. Douglas' help, I had already decided which courses I was going to take.

A student loan was negotiated with the help of the Financial Aid people, but in order to support myself for the remainder of my first semester, I would have to work. I applied for a job at the university cafeteria. That worked out well for me. In addition to the money, I found myself surrounded by students who were as friendly and excited by university life as I was. And the natives back at the dorm were friendly as well. Initially, as a confirmed recluse, I found the sheer number of all these people to be a bit overwhelming. But little by little, I settled in. I was happier than I had ever been in my life.

I had signed up for a full load of introductory courses. While some of them were very demanding, I believed that with a bit of discipline, I could excel in the work demanded of me. I was beginning to develop a new, positive outlook on life. People around me liked me. I genuinely liked them, and I liked being liked by them. I really wasn't in any seventh heaven, but I felt that I was getting close. My current life was as different as day and night when compared to the long, dreary years of my childhood and adolescence.

On occasion, I'd go out to Oakwood Mall with my fellow "dormites" to shop, nose around, and maybe go to a movie. Sylvia had a car and was happy to fill it with whoever wanted to make the trip.

Then, on what proved to be yet another fateful day for me, we girls decided to go to a local bar, the Bellow Inn, to celebrate the end of the first week.

It was there that I met Curtis Thompson. Some important chapters in my life were about to be written.

Section C

The Confluence of the Tormented Twosome

CHAPTER 22

First Meeting

It had all started innocently enough on a cold, beautiful fall day in 2003. Curtis still hung around UWEC and the Water Street bars although he had dropped out some two years previously. Andre had not been happy with that decision. It had a downside quality about it that did not sit well with him. It ran counter to what Curtis could be accomplishing if he were to live up to the expectations dictated by his "Pygmalion complex." When Curtis started to live with him, Andre appeared to be unconcerned about he did. But then when Curtis really started to roll, Andre increasingly became identified with what he accomplished. As the books say, Andre's "ego involvement" was maxing out. Over the first semester, Curtis saw Andre more and more as a suspicious Svengali than a Rex Harrison character dead set on Eliza Doolittle's improvements.

Once again, as he wrote this, he was little short of amazed at the breadth and depth of his literary background. He really understood Andre in terms of Pygmalion and Svengali. These names had become part and parcel of his extensive working vocabulary. That self-taught vocabulary, his extensive readings, and his considerable writing skills had a downside. He found that he had become regarded as something of a nerd by his classmates. In his beginning days at UWEC, he used to join the other students at the Davies Center for coffee and conversation, and he was definitely the odd man out. They wanted to talk about the Blugold football team, sports, the upcoming dances, who would become Homecoming Queen, etc. He couldn't join in. Curtis wanted to talk about politics, both nationally and abroad; or he'd have loved to have talked about some of the central characters in the classics he had read. His efforts at socialization went for naught. Either he would sit silently or he'd attempt to talk about things that he was interested in. He found his remarks would be met with a stony silence. Others might have been thinking, "Hoity-toity, Christ Almighty, who in the hell is he?" Curtis gravitated more and more to the Water Street bars before and after classes. He was neither learning nor accumulating credits. Dropping out made sense to him. Three weeks passed before he told Andre. He didn't say much, but Andre clearly was not happy.

He had been wondering how long it would last. He was getting older and he knew that Andre preferred younger men. What was he providing to Andre that made Curtis indispensable? The answer was nothing. He may still have been getting his kicks out of the Svengali/Pygmalion thing, and Curtis had indeed made himself special on that count. While he didn't graduate from UWEC, he had blossomed under Andre playing the role of mentor, the loyal friend and advisor of Odysseus. He beamed when Curtis told him that he thought of him in those terms. Curtis was certainly more knowledgeable and literate than most college graduates.

He had profited from the many community connections Andre had. He had a great niche as a landscape architect. When Andre had first provided him with that title, he wasn't sure what it meant, but it had a nice ring to it. It was impressive when Curtis showed his card to prospective customers.

Curtis J. Thompson, Landscape Architect
Thompson Enterprises, Ltd.
2620 Fairfax Avenue
Chippewa Falls, Wisconsin 54729

Phone (999) 999-9999 Email: Thompson@tattoo.com

Now in truth, his actual job wasn't as complicated as the business card might suggest. Andre and his friends would supply him with a diagram showing a house they had built or were building. There would be empty spaces around it that had to be landscaped. Curtis filled these in with lawn, trees, bushes, perennials, annuals, or whatever. He even had rubber stamps that he could use to show where he was going to plant various things. He came to know the names for these. Potential customers were impressed when he presented them with a final planting plan. In their mind's eye, they could see the finished house and its resplendent plantings. From there on in, it was simple to have them sign on the dotted line as they contracted for services.

He made a lot of money doing this. Andre let him keep it all. His savings and checking accounts were substantial. There was every evidence that he would be expanding Thompson Enterprises, Ltd. Over half of his work was already being done in nearby Eau Claire.

He continued to read wildly. He even began to write a novel based on his life.

As Curtis thought about his dropping out over the years, he began to wonder if he'd been bull-shitting himself with all this "odd man out" stuff. In his thinking, he was already the consummate scholar. He thought he read more widely and understood far more than his mere mortal class-mates. With that wondrous self-image established, he truly believed that it was a waste of time to subject himself to the dreary routine of classroom attendance, boring lectures, and test-taking. It became easier to sit at the Bellow Inn and think his own great thoughts. He had been drinking more and more. Curtis was usually able to shape up before he returned home, so his excessive drinking was not a great problem, or so he thought. While Andre had not expressed any concern, he had given him a few hard looks from time to time. Nevertheless, his landscape work went well.

It was late afternoon when Curtis saw Kay at the Bellow Inn. He was occupying one of the back booths. She had just walked in and had taken a seat at the bar. He knew immediately that she was going to be very special in his life. Little did he know how dangerous she would be.

She was a shapely brunette flashing a brilliant smile at the bartender as he poured her martini. She looked around expectantly and continued to stand at the bar.

What was he to do? His track record with women—particularly co-eds—was flat-out terrible. He didn't know how to approach them or what to say to them if he did get within range. Small talk was definitely not his forte. His sexual ambiguity and his relationship with Andre further complicated matters. He just sat there for a while, and then he had yet another drink. After that, he had another one.

The crowd was sparse. She was still standing there alone. She appeared to be waiting for someone. Emboldened by the booze, Curtis arose and headed for the bar. As he ordered yet another drink, he looked in her direction, caught her eye, and asked, "Do you come here often?" Can you imagine that he actually said that? It's a pick-up line that everyone jokes about. But she smiled indulgently as she replied, "Sometimes."

He moved a bit closer as he asked her all sorts of typical questions. "Are you a student? What's your major? Where do you come from?" and on and on and on. He did all of the talking. He bought her a drink. She didn't ask any questions of him. He was clearly striking out in his effort to strike up a conversation en route to an acquaintanceship. She appeared tense and uncomfortable. He was about to haul ass when she offered to buy him a drink. He said yes and suggested that they move to one of the booths. She went along with this. They introduced themselves. Kay Nelson was her name. She was a lot more talkative when they were by themselves. In fact, after a short while, he couldn't shut her up. The drinks were having a considerable effect upon her. It developed that she was supposed to meet a guy in another bar and that he had stood her up. He had done this before. She had finally stalked out and came over to the Bellow Inn.

She seemed depressed as she talked about him. Even though he was in his own blue velvet haze, he thought it strange that she would talk about this with a stranger. And she wouldn't shut up. She went on and on about how unhappy she was about her classes, her major, her housemates, and the guy who had stood her up. "Who does he think he is?" She said repeatedly in the midst of her ramblings. Curtis just sat there, nodding his head at what he thought were the appropriate times. As he'd said before, he was one hell of a listener.

Curtis had to leave. In talking with Andre earlier, he wanted to make sure that he would be home to eat dinner this evening. Although Andre had not ordered him to be home by then, Curtis knew he'd better be there. Probably, Andre was anticipating one of their nights together. So while he wanted to tarry with Kay, he had to leave. They exchanged phone numbers (he had his own private phone) and he headed out. She looked rather lonesome and forlorn as she waved at him as he went through the door.

CHAPTER 23

A Developing Relationship

Over the next few weeks, I was very busy with my landscape work. Andre had a friend who knew a friend whose large housing development was nearing completion. Of course, I had been granted the contract for the landscaping. During the summer, I had met with a lot of people to determine what everyone wanted and where they wanted it planted. Now, I had to get the trees, bushes, perennials and other greenery planted properly while the weather was good. I had to round up my crews and set them in motion. All the plantings had been ordered long ago and were now available at Blackorby's. I didn't have to do any of the actual work anymore. I just had to see that it got done. I enjoyed this. I liked ordering people around. I liked to hear the praise of the customers for a job well done.

When I got home three nights later, there were several messages on my answering machine.

They were all from Kay. It was apparent that she had been drinking. She had a lot to say. She called several times so as to overcome the shortcomings of my answering machine. The gist of her message was, "Why haven't you called? You said that you were going to call. I thought that you were a nice guy. I thought that you were different." She ended each of these with "Call me." She provided her number again. I washed up, ate dinner, and then called her. She wasn't at home. The woman who answered didn't know where she was. I left a message which said I hadn't called because I had been busy. I asked her to call me.

And she returned my call…at 2:00 a.m. She was smashed. She babbled on about how great I was, how different I was, and how she'd like to see me. I listened to this for about ten minutes before I hung upon her after reminding her of the time. She called again at 7:00 a.m. as I was just getting out of the shower. She still sounded rattled. She went on and on about how sorry she was for having called at 2:00 a.m. She asked repeatedly if I was angry with her. I listened and tried to calm her down. She wanted to meet me again. She said that we could meet at the Bellow Inn as before and then go over to her nearby dorm room. Although this was the busy time for me, I agreed to meet her that night at the bar at about 5:00 p.m. She was still thanking me profusely when I hung up on her.

What was I up to? There was no doubt that I had a woman who was hot to trot. She was attractive, had a great body, was smart enough, and appeared troubled. While I was more than content with my arrangement with Andre, I still harbored some anger about it. In a way, it reminded me of my dealings with Lloyd. While there were obviously marked differences, there were marked similarities. While Andre treated me wonderfully in bed and elsewhere, I was still under his complete and impersonal control. Like Lloyd, he never held me or spoke to me in an affectionate way. I could have been almost anyone. I was simply a depository for his semen. I wanted a closeness that he could not or would not supply, and that made me angry.

Did anger play a part in my seeking out Kay even though I sensed that she was probably trouble in the offing? In retrospect, that seems virtually certain that anger-driven retaliation drove me to it. I would betray Andre by sacking in with Kay. How could he be hurt if he would never know? If he ever did find out, then I would be kicked out into a cold, cruel world. I would lose the cushiest of situations. Why? Because I wanted to see if I liked screwing women? That made no sense. But these were my thoughts at that time.

I arrived at the Bellow Inn a half-hour late. One might have expected her to be pissed off at that, but no; she didn't mention it. She grabbed hold of me, kissed me, hugged me, and dragged me into a booth. And I am not exaggerating. She had been drinking. She smiled a lot. She seemed grateful that I had showed up. I ate this up. As a socially awkward man who had little going for me, I luxuriated in the warmth of this reception. I enjoyed the warmth of her embrace. I held her closely in return. Her kiss had stimulated me.

Let the play begin! We had a few more drinks before she suggested that we adjourn to her dormitory. We clutched at one another and kissed en route. When we got to her dorm, she showed me her room. It contained a large bed on which a cat was residing. She shushed the cat out of the room and shut the door. We clutched and kissed a bit before we got down to business. We helped each other disrobe, fell in the sack, and had sex. For a time, she lay passively under me, seemingly inviting me to do anything I wanted. I climaxed early on, a bit too early for her. As I was thinking about so many other things, I didn't get as much satisfaction out of it as I should have.

While I would have liked to relax and enjoy the afterglow, she was at me after a minute or two. She grabbed my penis and rubbed it vigorously. I found this most annoying. I told her to slow down, but she wouldn't. I playfully slapped her hands and said playfully, "No, no. Bad girl!" She persisted, so I slapped her alongside the head. She kept on, so I slapped her with considerable force, and although she stopped, I hit her once again.

She started crying ever so softly. I told her to stop crying. When she didn't, I slapped her again. I then put my arms around her and talked to her. I said, "Let's get a few things straight. I like you. I'm very attracted to you. But when we're in the sack, I'm in charge. It's the way I am. We'll have exciting times together, wait and see." With that, I wiped her tears away, held her tightly, and gave her a deep, prolonged kiss.

I then got on top of her again and did my thing once more. She was responsive and excited, although I wasn't sure if she climaxed. When I asked her about this, she said that she hadn't. She said that she had problems with this. I reassured her that I would help her find the way. I told her, "Different strokes for different folks," and with that, I then pinched her nipples and slapped her again. I told her she would learn to love it and me. When I mentioned that last possibility, she melted in my arms.

Later, when I was home, I started to think about what had gone on. She clearly wanted a relationship with me. She had leaped into the sack immediately where she made every effort to please me. And she had hung in there even after I had hurt her repeatedly. She was one strange broad. I had enjoyed hurting her. I felt like a man. I was surprised by how much I enjoyed it. Next time,

I'd surely do it again. I knew that I could control her very easily. How far could I go? How far did I want to go? If she really cares for me, she'll take just about anything I dish out. I found this exciting.

In our first sex, I set a pattern in motion that kept right on building. She seemed to look forward to the slaps that were part of the sexual foreplay. I started to see how much I could get away with before she'd tell me to stop. I could get by with almost anything after a while. I could twist her arms, push several fingers into her vagina, and slap her face repeatedly. She never cried out. She would often stare at me as though she as daring me to do more.

I had read about masochism. Now, I was face-to-face with it. Both of us really got carried away as I accommodated her. Her breathing would become intense, enduring pain as she experienced multiple orgasms. On at least three occasions, I thought that I had hurt her enough to break or strain something. Often on the day after, she would show me her bruises. Sometimes, I would say, "I got carried away—but we really did it, didn't we?" At other times, I'd apologize. After a while, as she never objected, I stopped explaining and apologizing. But she clearly wanted me to do what I was doing. And in my thinking, I came to the conclusion that she must really love me if she would allow me to hurt her in this fashion. And as I've said before, inflicting pain became an important and rewarding part of my sexual satisfaction. We were really strange, but what we were doing really worked for each of us. Or so it seemed at first.

CHAPTER 24

Two Different Worlds

I started living a double life with all the hazards of that deception. I had to keep Andre from knowing about Kay. If he found out, or even suspected that I was real tight with a girlfriend, he'd hand me my walking papers along with a $3,000.00 check. Bear in mind, I had really gotten to like my cushy situation. It was truly the best of all worlds for me, as it had been for the two young men who preceded me.

Now, here I was, jeopardizing all of this and my future because I wanted to prove myself a man, and that was the sum and substance of it. I truly didn't care for Kay on a personal level. When we did talk, she bored the shit out of me. She would chatter on endlessly about UWEC, what Bob said to Ruth, how boring her professors were, and on and on ad nauseum.

She wanted to know all about me, where I lived, what I did for a living, and where I was every moment I was not with her. When we were together, she would climb all over me. All of this made for complications in my life. I wanted to keep things simple. I wanted to meet with her in her bedroom, do our thing, and then split. She'd then go her way and I'd go mine, kind of like the arrangement that Andre had with me. But she wanted a greater personal involvement early on. She'd call me at all hours, day and night. It was nothing to find more than ten messages on my answering machine when I came home from work. She wanted to know where I lived in Chippewa Falls. What did my apartment look like? Who were my friends? Why couldn't we sack in at my place? And of course, I couldn't tell her any of this. The story I told was full of holes, but she bought it. I told her I lived in an apartment in a three-story house on Superior Street. I drove by it to show her where I lived. I told her that I had a religious nut for a landlady who was dead set against my having any female visitors. When she asked why I didn't move, I told her that I was thinking about it.

Talking about my work was easy. I took her out to my planting site on one occasion, even introducing her to a couple of guys who I had working for me. She wanted a pack of my business cards so that she could distribute them amongst her friends.

What now? I wondered. "What a tangled web we weave, when first we practice to deceive." And here I was in an entanglement. I had proven my limited point about my manhood in the first few weeks. And while enjoyable, I did have some qualms about her enjoyment of all the twisting, punching, and humiliating I was doing as part of our sex. While I had initially enjoyed her holding and hugs, I had soon tired of them. They seemed to be more like evidence of her oddity than healthy expressions of her affection.

And I had kept all of this from Andre, or at least I thought I had.

CHAPTER 25

One World Vanishes

I went home one night as I had many times before. Andre called to me as I entered, summoning me to the living room. He was agitated, striding back and forth in front of the sofa. He looked at me accusingly and asked, "Who is Kay Nelson?"

I was shocked by this unexpected inquiry. It had come completely out of the blue. I didn't know what to say. As I tried to come up with something by way of response, I said absolutely nothing.

"Who is Kay Nelson?" he repeated. It was evident that he knew who she was and the nature of my involvement with her.

I finally said, "I don't know what to say."

He replied, "Then say nothing. I know enough about the two of you already. I also know that you will be out of this house by tomorrow. Any questions?"

I nodded my head.

"Yesterday, your phone kept ringing and ringing and ringing. I thought it might be some kind of emergency, so I went in to answer it. It stopped ringing before I could get to it, but then I checked out your answering machine. There were a bunch of messages on it. Guess who they were from and what they said?

He gave me one last look and strode from the room, saying, "I'll give you my final word on this tomorrow."

In a matter of moments, black had become white. My wondrous world had dissolved. In its place was a great unknown with all its threats and uncertainties. I experienced an incredible sense of loss. I didn't know what to do. I went to my bedroom and lay down for a while. I thought and I thought about what I had done and what was to become of me. I could not come up with a plan as to what I should do next.

I soon found that I had to make some major decisions immediately.

Andre met me in the hallway the next morning. He looked me dead in the eye and said, "Our party's over. You're history. By the time I come back tonight, you will be gone. Incidentally, I'll see to it that Thompson Enterprises is no more by the end of the week.

I was speechless. I had lost everything.

Section D

The Crime and Its Aftermath

What really went on the night of November 2003? Why did it happen? What was involved?

To the extent that the personalities of these central characters have been released to you, the reader, to that extent you will have the ingredients necessary to fashion reasonable and reasoned answers. Of course, your understanding of all of this will be tempered by your pasts as well. The "facts" describing the events of that evening will be selectively perceived in a different way by each of you, and the conclusions will reflect that diversity.

What really went on the night of November 2003? It is unlikely that anyone will ever really know. There will always be lingering doubts. Some of the dark determinants may run very deep, unavailable to even Curtis and Kay. But in individual efforts to understand, each reader can come up with a most plausible story, an account which makes some sense. That may be as close as we get to the "truth" regarding this rape.

As an aside, this may apply to virtually all complex interpersonal involvements, experiences encountered during the course of the reader's life. Absolute truth regarding the important matters in life is not only elusive, it is unattainable.

CHAPTER 26

Kay's Account

The newspaper article (Part A, page 1) provides the salient features of the event. These were provided in her testimony at Curtis' trial as filtered perceptions of the newsman. While certainly not all-inclusive, they were sufficient to provide a general scenario of what actually occurred.

But was there more? Certainly. What were Kay's private thoughts as she endured this controlled onslaught? While undoubtedly some of these were revealed later on, many of her recollections were never fully revealed. She did not report the pain of the slap, the smell of the urine, the cruel, cold wind on her naked body, and a thousand other minor details. It is absolutely impossible to report any event in such a manner that it can be conveyed to another. The great force that is repression will set in almost fully immediately, further complicating a comprehensive report.

One must note that comfort and consolation that she extended to Curtis after she had been so cruelly savaged by him. While she had tackled him on the bridge, she went immediately to assist him when he hurt his head in the resulting fall. She thought that he was having difficulty breathing and gave him artificial resuscitation. Bear in mind, he had just ravaged her in an unspeakable fashion. She brought him back to her dorm that night so that he might have shelter. She cared for him there. She fed him. She slept next to him.

She refused to acknowledge the crime the next day. When asked about the sorry state of her looks, she refused to acknowledge that a crime had been committed. She lied to the police and the faculty at UWEC in order to protect him. A week later, she moved out of the dormitory, moved in with him, lived with him, and ultimately even bore him a child. How could all of this come to pass? It makes no sense, but it must have made sense to her at the time.

Why did she behave the way she did?

It seems likely that Kay's past reached up at this crucial time and bit her in the butt. Her need for him clearly overrode any reasonable reaction on her part. Seemingly she had to have him no matter what. Notwithstanding her many personal insights and UWEC accomplishments, she continued to believe at the deepest of levels of her being that she was a truly worthless person, one who was completely devoid of any personal worth.

One could say that she was suffering from something called "scotoma gargantuan," or humungous blind spots. She could not see the many negative things about him that virtually everyone else saw so clearly. She had come to depend on Curtis, the lover in her life. After all, he had told her he loved her.

It would be useful at this juncture to consider a definition of "love." Monumental decisions often are based on "I love you" without any in-depth consideration of the meaning of this expression. The incredible mix of ingredients included under the vast tent of "love" is rarely, if ever, addressed in depth. A la *Alice in Wonderland*, "I love you" can mean just about anything one wants it to mean. There are as many different meanings as there are people who say or who listen to the expression. These three little words can transport one to the richest of personal and mutual fulfillments. These same three words can also be used by some as a license to dominate, abuse, or even kill their partner. "But you know, no matter what, that I love you," is often employed by someone seeking pardon for their unpardonable behavior. As Curtis used those words, they became a license to enslave her.

On the deepest of levels, she may have felt that she deserved this defilement; that she was at fault. This rape was not simply sexual. All of the fornicating and urinating were means to humiliate and control her. Many believe that the needs to humiliate and control are far more important than testosterone in the commission of rape. This savaging carried with it a resounding statement that Kay was no damn good, that she deserved such treatment. Curtis had been seen by her as her lover and her savior. He had willingly accepted that role, and so did she. "Kay is ca-ca, and ca-ca is Kay."

In the cool gray of the morning after he tried to explain away his actions to her, he said that it really demonstrated his love for her, that he did these things to garner proof of her love for him. In truth, insecurity and presumed betrayal were the triggers. His strong needs to control surfaced immediately. He was insecure and jealous. Bear in mind, he had already had regular access to her every aperture. He needed to express his needs to dominate and control her in special humiliating ways. She would have no doubt as to who really called the shots in their relationship.

The gullibility of an abused woman is something to behold. From Curtis' statements, it followed that if she were not all-important to him, he would never have done these things. She was well on the way to believing this nonsense before they had crossed the bridge that night en route back to the dorm. In the gray of dawn the next morning, shortly before Curtis left, he muttered similar statements. He still couldn't say things too clearly, but he got this message across rather easily.

Why? He was talking into a most receptive set of ears. This was what she wanted to hear. She bought into this bullshit hook, line, and sinker. After all, without him, she was nothing. That was her thinking. Her troubled past, injured pride, poor self-concept, and gullibility took over. She then resorted to damage control; lied about the incident after her roommate had police brought in. She served up a justification for others and for herself. She probably came to believe that all of this was really proof of his love for her, and inferentially, of her own personal worth. This explanation is devoid of common sense, but the roots of such pathological thinking are deep indeed. Her reaction was testimony both to the power and depth of this pathology.

CHAPTER 27

Curtis' Account

Of all people really trying to understand the determinants of this crime, Curtis was the one least likely to be successful. He had been roaring drunk that night. He had no recollection of what he had done. He was forced to accept Kay's version of the events. She couldn't be making this up. But why did he do what he had done? The answers that Curtis provided were ill-considered and self-serving at best.

Truth may be a rarity these days. Some of said that one can expect truth from only three sources: a very young child, an angry woman, and a drunken man. Certainly, Curtis fits the last category.

Was he perversely displaying the truth of how he really felt about Kay and perhaps women in general? Did booze simply unlock his inhibitions? It seems likely that his actions were determined in part by his own insecurity. Devoid of any association with Andre, he saw his own worth now determined primarily by his relationship with Kay. Her casual encounter with another man that night had triggered off this reaction. In his drunken state, Kay's contact, a flirtation at most, had become magnified by him into an example of rejection or impending abandonment. Any such estrangement would be devastating for him. His dependence on her had become incredibly great.

Both Kay and Curtis relied upon the other for strengths that neither possessed.

In his drunken state, long-dormant demons from his past may have emerged. These may have convinced him that he needed proof of her love. He set about putting her to some ultimate test. If she would endure what he was doing to her, this would prove her love for him. This insecurity and hatred for women, fueled by booze, might have impelled him to do what he did. His utterly irrational behavior can only be understood by determinants that are driven by dark, unconscious, and essentially unknowable forces. The explicit reasons for his actions on that night may never be known.

Curtis had really been upset about being dumped by Andre despite knowing his involvement with Kay put him at risk for ending their relationship. He had never had it as good as he had it with Andre. He had been sitting in the catbird seat, in the best of two worlds. Andre made only minimal demands upon him and had set him up for a lifestyle that was great, and he had Kay. Did he ever! She was putty in his hands. There was nothing that she wouldn't do for him. That ranged from shopping for him to complying with his every wish in bed.

Now he felt that he was really lost. It was Kay's fault. Of course, this made no sense, but Curtis was not in a mood for reason. His need to believe this was monumental.

He tried to recall the events of that night. He had called her at her dorm and arranged for her to meet him at around 7:00 p.m. As he had had nothing to do, he got to the Bellow Inn early and began to drink heavily. By the time she showed up, he was well on his way to being loaded.

As always, she was happy to see him. She sat real close to him, smiling at him all the time. But he was in an ugly mood that got darker as the night progressed and the more he drank. A few of her girlfriends wanted to join them, but he was having none of that. She chatted on about school and the problems some of her friends were having. Curtis barely listened. He seemed put-upon and irritable. Kay tried, in her way, to sweet-talk him into a better frame of mind. He kept ordering drinks while she tapered her drinking off. Experience had taught her that heavy drinking exposed a very unpleasant side of Curtis. She wished he would stop but knew that he wouldn't, so she just tried to ride out the storm.

He became very unsteady on his frequent trips to the bathroom. He returned each time more angry and sullen than before. On one occasion, a young man she knew had sidled into the booth while Curtis was gone. When Curtis returned, the shit really hit the fan. He told the guy to get lost, and then he really unloaded on Kay. "Bitch, what are you trying to pull?"

From that point on, Curtis could remember nothing. His next recollection was being awakened by Kay in her dorm room. At that time, he had wondered about what he was doing there.

CHAPTER 28

Reconciliation

Subsequent events irrational as the rape itself satisfied many of the aforementioned psychological needs of both Curtis and Kay. Each was living in a pseudo-community, a Never-Never Land that existed only within his or her head, and that lamentable state of affairs had its satisfactions for them, at least for a while.

Curtis was reassured by her subsequent acceptance of him. After all, she must love him if she would reunite with him after what he had done to her.

Kay too readily came to believe that the violence and Nature of this rape were proof positive of the strength of his love for her. Why would he have done this if he didn't care deeply? Too readily, she accepted his apologizes in an effort to make things go on as they had before. She was secure in her delusion that he loved her and that this love proved to her to be a person of worth.

In the week that followed, Curtis got a day job and rented an apartment. Before Christmas, he convinced Kay rather easily that she should leave Horan Hall and move in with him. She did so willingly. She was pregnant. Several months after the rape, she bore him a child, a tiny girl.

CHAPTER 29

The Break-Up

What passed for a state of bliss for this twosome did not continue. In the seventh month of her pregnancy, she had discovered that he was involved with at least two other UWEC co-eds. She confronted him about this and he denied it.

But the evidence had been overwhelming. She had found some phone numbers that had fallen out of his coat. A couple of phone calls got names and addresses. Kay then dropped over to meet his new conquests. Of course, neither of them had ever heard of Kay and that a child was on the way. Curtis really knew how to spin a story.

She now felt that she was a fool many times over. Once again, she felt helpless and alone. She churned over feelings and recollection in a frightening ruminative process. She would chew things over that bothered her, become distracted, and come back to the original source of trouble. The memories of that night in high school surfaced once again in this process. She had trusted both Rob and Curtis. Each had never really loved her. Each had used her. Each had betrayed her in his own special way. She wondered now if Curtis had laughed behind her back about all that he had done to her. These thoughts continued to surface, recede, and resurface over and over again. Once again, her world was turned upside-down, and now she was about to have a baby.

She moved out as soon as possible. The UWEC Financial Aid Officer, Dr. Komro, dipped into some emergency funds in order to provide her with the necessary food and shelter. He suggested that she get some personal counseling. She didn't pick up on this. She said to herself, "I've got too many things on my mind." Kay had hoped to finish the spring semester if at all possible. Sadly, that was not to be.

Even though she was now fed and housed, she didn't know what to do next. It was the high school scene being replayed. Déjà vu all over again. She even felt like running out into the street again. She couldn't go back to the university dorm in search of some refuge or support. The women there hadn't ever bought into her story, not even a little bit. None of them had liked Curtis. They had called the cops on him. They had told her that she should blow the whistle on him, but she hadn't. They had been right. Admitting all of this to them was too much for her.

And now, she was pregnant and alone.

CHAPTER 30

Kay's Resolution

She had run out of options, much like she had in high school. Desperate and depressed, not to mention dealing with newly-fluctuating pregnancy hormones, she considered suicide in her plight.

After spending four or five days enduring this misery, she experienced something of an epiphany. She wondered why she hadn't considered this before. She made a phone call, borrowed her former roommate's car, and returned to her hometown the next day for a hastily-improvised appointment with Mr. Douglas, her old school guidance counselor.

He was genuinely glad to see her. The previous deep and accepting rapport was re-established immediately, and she needed that level of acceptance desperately at this time. She began talking just as she had done before. He listened to her as before. She spent the first session talking about Curtis, his infidelity, her pregnancy, and the rape. It was as though she couldn't stop.

Even though it was outside of his responsibilities, Mr. Douglas then agreed to see her on a regular informal basis three times a week after school hours. Over the course of two months, they kept to that schedule. He did what he had done before: he provided her with a safe and accepting place and encouraged her to talk. And she talked endlessly. She came to define her problem. The topic of a recurrent self-defeating pattern took center stage early on. She felt better and saw things more clearly. She considered and rejected various actions she might take in resolving problems.

Her anger had to be dealt with. This issue had the highest priority. Curtis had misled her in the same way that Rob and his friends had on that night. That event had never been forgotten or resolved. She was violently angry as she recalled how Rob had gotten off so lightly, and as she recounted the circumstances, she would stride around Mr. Douglas' room, wildly gesticulating as she expressed her hatred for Rob and what he had done to her.

And now, Curtis, equally guilty, had gotten off scot-free. "Hell," she said, "he didn't even have to do any community service." And the more she thought about it, the more she talked about it, and the more determined she became that she would set this matter straight. Neither this understanding nor her resolution came easily. She was angry, frustrated, and hell bent on vengeance. "Hell hath no fury like a woman betrayed."

Back in Eau Claire one October morning after a good night's sleep, she called her former roommate, Sylvia, and made a request that was readily granted. In fact, she was delighted. Finally, Sylvia thought, Kay was waking up and smelling the coffee. Sylvia said to herself, "Kay should have done this the morning after what happened in Owen Park."

Later that very morning, Sylvia drove Kay to the District Attorney's office where she met with the D.A. to discuss how she should go about filing a complaint. Kay then provided the necessary information and signed on the dotted line. After the twosome had accomplished this, they treated themselves to lunch at Jimmy's Pizza. As Kay thought about what she had done, she grew more and more uneasy.

Harold Harms, the District Attorney, had been skeptical initially as he listened to Kay state her case. He vaguely remembered the case and how uncooperative she had been the day after the rape—or shall we now say the "alleged rape." Her story had several strikes against it. Initially, she had denied that a crime had taken place. It was filed months after the incident. She had lived with the alleged rapist subsequently and had born him a child. But this Kay Nelson was one cool customer. She calmly stated her story with an air of conviction that was chillingly effective. Her ability to conjure up precise details of the assault was impressive. He believed her. He knew that a jury would believe her as well.

He felt that the case should be pursued. By nightfall, the proper papers had been prepared.

Curtis was arrested the following morning as he left his most recent girlfriend's house. The charge was rape. To say that he was completely surprised and very disturbed would be the understatement of the century.

The date was October 15, 2004, approximately eleven months after the crime he was alleged to have committed.

Section E

Redemption

CHAPTER 31

Jailhouse Blues

Out of the blue, Curtis found himself behind bars in the Eau Claire County Jail. Believing that his initial upset would pass, he let the shock waves roll over and over as he underwent the required rituals. He'd been there before. The invasive body search, the inventory of his clothes and possessions, the fingerprinting, the whole ball of wax. But he remained cool and calm in the face of all of this for he knew with absolute certainty that the charge would never stick, that he wouldn't go to trial, and even if he did, he'd never be convicted. Denial had set in, and there is no denying the power of denial.

He repeatedly reassured himself as he assessed and re-assessed his situation. "How could she do this to me?" he thought. "I'm the father of her child. She knows that I was out of my head that night. It had happened so long ago. I say forgive and forget!" He thought that she had done that long ago when she had decided to continue living with him shortly after the event. "And now she's out for blood—my blood—but she'll never follow through on all this." He thought about this over and over again. He always came back to the conclusion that this just could not be happening to him, but it was.

He did not sleep that first night, tossing and turning as he thought about himself and his scary situation. He simply could not accept this, but he knew that he must. This endless thinking and re-thinking only tormented and unsettled him. Acceptance is the key, he said to himself again and again. "I've got to calm down. I've got to be cool. I've dealt with worse situations." But in truth, as situations go, they don't get much worse.

After all the jailhouse formalities were finally completed, he found himself clad in a bright orange uniform and free to mingle with his fellow prisoners. Right from the get-go, it was obvious that the surveillance by the "corrections officers" was tight. He'd always wondered as to why they still referred to themselves with that antique and inappropriate title. They may have been officers, but they did precious little correcting. "Warehousers" or "keepers" or "jailers" would have been more on target. But while he had used these expressions in the outer world, he knew now that he'd have to "Sir" them to death.

He was just in time for the evening meal. He wandered into the tail end of the chow line, watching the others so that he would know what to do. A few of them nodded in his direction. He returned the nod as he continued to feel out the situation. After picking and choosing from a small buffet, he sat down and remained silent, as did most of the others, as he finished his meal. There, he downed a Salisbury steak, potatoes, salad, a slice of bread, and a custard desert. Not bad. So far, so good.

After finishing, he had a choice of remaining in the day room or his cell. He chose the latter because a "God Squad" had come into the day room to spread the word and save their souls.

From his cell, he could both hear and see them. He had been around groups like this in the past and regarded the whole business as a solid crock of shit. Every once in a while, a group used to show up at Loring Park in Minneapolis to "save" the gays from their lives of sin. They seemed dedicated to whatever they were doing. High-pitched wailing of the prayers would be answered with an "Amen," or "Right on" by the prisoners. He wondered as to what this was really about. Then a speaker started doing his thing. Tonight's presentation dealt with chemical dependency in all its forms. What were the games that these people were playing? What was really underlying what he considered an out-and-out charade? He eventually tuned it out, leafing through a series of magazines until the God Squad left at about 9:00 p.m., a half-hour before lights out.

He did not sleep well. He was tired and haggard the next morning as he went through the shit, shave, and shower routine before breakfast. He nodded and said good morning to those who looked in his direction and allowed that "It's a good day," to others. But for the most part, he kept aloof from his fellow prisoners. It seemed to be the way to go.

On the second day, he was approached by a Reverend Jesse Grice who made inquiry as to his health and the possibility of joining a group. He was told about the classes the group provided. There was little of the hard sell on the Reverend's part. He simply made an offer. Curtis didn't know about all this but he thought, "What the hell? What do I have to lose?" They seemed sincere, and it did kill time. They might just have something going that could be useful to him.

It was a ten-week program designed to enable the prisoners to learn new ways of dealing with life and the problems they have had. The topics addressed were the usual ones in such programs: the need to change, money matters, marital problems, boozing, anger management, vocational planning, and of course, the need for prayer Bible study and the Christian way of life. Occasionally, special motivational speakers would be invited to lecture the group about the hazards of returning to old lifestyles when they were eventually released. Efforts were made to promote camaraderie amongst the prisoners, trying to invoke a sense of community so that they could help one another. As members of the God Squad were volunteers, the program was loose and informal, even slipshod in character.

Curtis eventually settled into a routine as he awaited his court appearance. Everyone was awakened at 5:00 a.m. They attended to their personal needs, ate breakfast, had a bit of time for personal reflection, exercised in a leisurely fashion if there was need, could go to chapel if they wanted, and then had a class involving the topic of the day. No one was forced to attend classes. If one didn't go to classes, then one just kept out of the way.

After eating lunch at high noon, the inmates would attend several classes before enjoying a bit of leisure time by themselves or with others. Then supper, then another class, a bit of time for leisure, and then off to bed by lights out at 9:30 p.m. There were Huber work release prisoners who did not follow this routine. They would leave the jail to work on weekdays. Upon retiring, they might or might not participate in the classes. Usually, they did not.

Curtis got into the swing of this operation with ease. There was something mildly comforting and reassuring about such a structured program. He knew what was expected of him at all times, and as long as he conformed, the living was easy.

There were some, even amongst those attending the classes, who made fun of the Reverend and what he was allegedly attempting to do. They alighted at him behind his back while behaving properly as he and others conducted classes. They made crude and obscene remarks about the dress, behavior, and purpose of the volunteers. The latter seemed oblivious to this.

Attending classes was good for him. It killed the time if nothing else. Watching TV and thumbing through magazines was only good up to a point. The weekends were without end. He found himself looking forward to Mondays when the classes would resume.

Another break in the routine occurred when his lawyer would show up or call him on the phone. In truth, they had little to talk about. After the police had picked him up and read him his Miranda Rights, he had admitted to virtually everything that Kay had said he'd done. He remembered nothing. She had no reason to lie. His only excuse was his drunken state on that night.

Curtis had accepted the reason for many months. Or at least she seemed to have gone along with it. But now he wasn't so sure. She had him where the hair was short and he knew it. His only way out of this predicament was to have her drop charges or recant her sworn testimony. During the long jailhouse nights, with denial running rampant, he would make himself believe that she would do just that. But in the cool of morning, when the denial defenses would drop, he would admit to being apprehensive and even fearful. He had screwed up. She had become one beady-eyed, vengeful woman. She rejected any notion of plea bargaining. She was out to hang him high.

Maybe if he talked to her he could get her to change her mind. His lawyer advised him to do nothing of the sort.

His court date had been set. Feeling pressured, he wanted to get this over with. He wanted to be found not guilty for once and for all. He wanted out of this goddamn jail. Then he could return to the outer world and pick up the pieces of his life. He felt that he was wasting too much time just sitting around the jailhouse. Denial served him well in maintaining his composure. There was no way in hell that he would be convicted. He said that over and over to himself.

Saying something does not make it so.

CHAPTER 32

The Trial

The less said about the trial, the better. It was mercifully short.

Curtis had been rousted out of bed early on court day and reminded that today was "his" day. He was tossed a suit of clothes, shirt, socks, shoes and tie. These had been purchased at the behest of his public defender attorney. He then shaved, showered, and donned his finery. He checked himself out in the mirror and was pleased with the results. Officers came in a bit later to escort him to the courthouse.

Curtis entered the courtroom and sat next to his attorney. The courtroom was packed with news media and spectators. He had heard that in view of the large crowd outside, they had resorted to a raffle for the available seats. As he glanced around at the assembled, he thought he saw looks in his direction that were typically reserved for cockroaches, slime, and vermin. Jack the Ripper would have been so viewed. He sat quietly, lost in thought. For the very first time, he became aware that this was really happening to him, that it was possible that he would be found guilty and accountable for what it was he was said to have done. He began to sweat. He looked at the man next to him for support and encouragement.

To say that he lacked confidence in his lawyer would have been an understatement. This lawyer was still wet behind the ears when it came to courtroom experience. This was probably his third case. It had been obvious from the outset that he believed Curtis' case to be beyond salvage, that no jury on earth would find him innocent. In the very first session, he asked Curtis if he would be amenable to plea bargaining. When Curtis replied, "No way," his attorney lapsed into silence. This matter was not discussed again.

In subsequent meetings, his lawyer appeared preoccupied with other matters. It was as though counsel was going through the motions of fashioning a defense. At least, that is what Curtis concluded. He had read all the materials that the District Attorney had supplied, including Kay's version of the event, and it was obvious to Curtis that his attorney believed Kay's account without question. To his attorney, his guilt was a foregone conclusion.

The public defender's behavior in court confirmed the worst fears that Curtis had harbored.

The prosecutor first elicited the testimony of Kay's five girlfriends. They had been well-coached. Their answers were short and consistent. They painted a picture of Curtis as a good-for-nothing user and abuser. Curtis' attorney asked only a few perfunctory questions in the cross-examination.

Then Kay took the witness stand. Curtis marveled at the presence she projected. She had changed markedly since she had left him. Gone was the meek and submissive girl that he had known and lived with for a very long time. Her dress was conservative. Her make-up was minimal and effective. She was cool as a cucumber as she sat there awaiting the questioning, and her manner did not change throughout the friendly direct interrogation. She, too, had been well-coached. She listened intently to each of the prosecutor's questions. Then, after a slight pause to collect her thoughts, she answered each fully and with an air of conviction which one would expect of the Lord Jehovah. If requested, she would amplify on her remarks. Her eye contact with the judge, jury, and the District Attorney was good. She had been here and they had gone there. She had done this and he had done that. Her story did not differ one iota from that which had been reported in the newspaper. It seemed to Curtis that each of her answers was a nail in his coffin. Everything she said jibed with the previous testimonies of her friends. She was thoroughly believable.

Her cross-examination was a farce. Curtis' attorney concentrated on her initial denial, her living with him subsequent to the alleged crime, the birth of their child, and the long time that had elapsed before she finally brought charges. She had been well-prepared for this. Her terse answers were invariably on point. These emphasized and re-emphasized her position as a fearful, submissive, guilt-ridden, loving woman who had been savaged by Curtis on the night in November 2003. Why had she taken him back to her dorm room in Horan Hall? Because she both loved him and was frightened by him. The same held true as an explanation for her living with him and bearing his child. Curtis came across as a punishing, frightening tyrant akin to Rasputin or Attila the Hun.

Curtis waited for his attorney to mount a strong counter-attack on her creditability. He knew that she had many weak points. She was a habitual drinker. She had had more than her share of booze on that fateful night. She was certainly not the sweet young innocent that she appeared to be on this day in court. In her early days in high school, she had bedded down with anyone who would show an interest in her. She had a considerable streak of the masochist within her. He could remember how during sex she would whisper in his ear, "Hurt me. Pinch me." She had been excited when he yanked on her hair and pulled her head back. When he had complied with these requests, she then had surged forth in what had seemed to be thunderous climaxes, replete with wailings of "Yes! Yes! Yes!"

They had even laughed together about the bruises she had sustained. A lot of what she reported as a rape on that night in Owen Park differed only in degree from what happened regularly in their love-making. Curtis thought to himself, "I may have been carried away on that night, but what I did was nothing new at all to her."

Curtis was surprised when his attorney said, "That will be all." Important questions had not been raised. She had handled all the others with ease. She had come through what could have been a blistering counter-attack unscathed. On balance, the cross-examination was as effective as the direct examination in establishing Curtis' guilt.

Curtis did not take the stand. His "blackout" of the alleged events would have denied him any semblance of credibility.

The judge then gave his instructions to the jury. Its members then retired for their deliberations. Within two hours, they returned with the verdict. Guilty! Guilty as sin!

Kay was seated in the same spot that she had occupied throughout the trial. She caught Curtis' eye as he was being led out of the courtroom. She said nothing, but her face spoke volumes to him: "You son of a bitch. I got you good."

CHAPTER 33

Conviction

Curtis was in shock as he was returned to the jailhouse. It couldn't have happened, but it did. He'd been convicted of brutally raping Kay.

"I was convicted," he said to himself repeatedly. Such repetitions were not comforting or helpful. He had been had. His future was terribly uncertain. There was no light at the end of the tunnel. He would be sentenced in due time, and the number of years that he was likely to serve was enormous. None of this had truly set in as of yet. He was numb with shock.

Back at the jailhouse, he fell back into the routine. He did what was expected of him. He rocked no boats. Instinct told him that this was the thing to do, the only thing to do. In his shocked fantasy, he seemed to be trying to show that he was really a "good guy," that the trial and the conviction were unwarranted and that he would be set free.

He knew better. He had no control over his destiny. Other forces and factors had taken over which would determine what he would and would not be doing in his life far in the foreseeable future.

Days later, he began to ask around a bit to find out more about what would happen to him. His lawyer was no help. From that person's legal vantage point, he could talk only of length of sentencing and the likelihood of treatment in some sex offender program. He knew from nothing as to what was really involved in all of this.

Curtis went to more basic resources: his fellow inmates. Many of them were unhelpful, but eventually he came upon Herman, a guy who seemed to know something. Herman had received ten years of treatment at a place called Sand Ridge Secure Treatment Center. It was located near Mauston, Wisconsin. Ten years! Curtis had blanched when he'd heard the casual mention of ten years, but he continued to ask questions about this treatment program. And as the story unfolded, there was little to tell. As far as Curtis could tell, the time was spent in ways no different from simple incarcerations. Herman felt it was easier to do the time if one were in such a program.

It was pretty much "three hots and a cot," but the prisoners got a bit more attention. Not much, but a little. After all, in a treatment program, they were considered to be "ill" and the establishment did treat "sick" individuals with a bit more compassion.

On the other hand, Herman said there were some guards who took the dimmest of views of the assortment of sex offenders under their control and they had special ways of expressing these negative attitudes in ways that never made the official records. Herman, who had been in and out of prisons for forgery before his sexual offender conviction, said that the primary difference involved group therapy. The participants were a mixed bag. Some had been convicted of violent, sadistic rape; others for relatively minor offenses. They were herded together daily initially and then once a week later on. There was a psychologist in charge of this therapy. He didn't seem to do too much.

Herman said that one of the guys in his group had referred to the psychologist as a "social facilitator." That was a fancy title for a person who was to get them talking and keep them talking. If anyone asked questions, the psychologist did not reply directly but bounced the ball right back at the questioner by saying that he was to talk. And by talking, he would come to realize both the error of his ways and fashion a better approach to life. The offenders came to realize all too quickly that questions were verboten, that one was supposed to talk. And talk they did; sometimes about their backgrounds, sometimes about their crimes, sometimes about how they wouldn't be caught the next time. After a bit, that got very old for everyone concerned.

CHAPTER 34

The Sentence

The following article appeared in the *Telegram-Observer*, Eau Claire Wisconsin, on March 15, 2005.

"A 24-year-old Chippewa Falls/Eau Claire man was sentenced to 21 years in prison for the rape and battery of a UW-Eau Claire female student in November, 2003.

Eau Claire Circuit Court Judge Betsy Belknap handed down the 21-year prison term to Curtis Thompson, followed by 10 years of extended supervision, and then 10 years of probation.

"I believe this to be a fair sentence given Thompson's history, the extreme violence demonstrated in this case, and the degradation of the victim." District Attorney Harold Harms agreed as he said, "This man should be incarcerated for a very long time. The only way to deal with him is to contain and control him. He should be under the supervision of the Department of Corrections for a long, long time."

The sexual crime took place on the University of Wisconsin-Eau Claire campus in November 2003. Thompson had been drinking most of the night in the company of his victim and a few of her girlfriends.

After he had left a local tavern, presumably angry at the victim, he contacted her by phone. They met outside of Horan Hall, a dormitory on the UWEC campus. He struck her and then dragged her across the Chippewa River Bridge to nearby Owen Park. As they proceeded, he punched and shoved her repeatedly, and then hit her over the head with a beer bottle.

Later, Thompson raped the woman and threatened to kill her, but then ran away from her toward the bridge.

The victim chased and tackled him, injuring him in the process to the extent that he was having difficulty breathing. After the woman gave him mouth-to-mouth resuscitation, they returned to her dorm where they fell asleep on a couch in the recreation area.

The victim suffered bruises and two black eyes. Later on, she denied that she had been abused. She said that she was injured in a car crash.

She continued a relationship with Thompson and gave birth to his child. She decided to file charges against him almost a year later when he threatened to beat her up.

Harris said that the victim had been suffering from "Battered Women's Syndrome." In this, he said, women are dominated, threatened, beaten, isolated, and made to feel responsible for the abuse. Guilt and fear conspire to force them to continue in the abusive relationship.

The District Attorney called Thompson "A wheeler-dealer who maintained complete control of the mother of his child. He has even threatened to harm his own child if the victim did not toe the mark." He added that he hoped that this victim's courageous course of action would encourage other battered or abused women to come forth.

And his effective argument carried the day.

CHAPTER 35

The Aftermath

As oftentimes happens after a sensational trial, the news media completely lost interest as they set their sights on other stories.

Curtis vanished into the treatment center.

Kay dropped out of sight.

And no one seemed to care.

Section F

Past, Present, and Future: An Epilogue

This section is presented as a "stream of consciousness" with chapter headings inserted occasionally to provide some semblance of order.

It presents new ideas and simply firm opinions along with some expressions of skepticism regarding notions that are firmly entrenched in our society and the psyches of its members.

Where do Kay and Curtis fit into all of this? In keeping with the interactive character of this book, it is suggested that the reader should ultimately make his or her own determination.

CHAPTER 26

Control vs. Chance

It is clear that one enters something of a minefield in attempting to address philosophical/religious issues. Much heat and no light are often generated in the resulting discussions, but even though this involves going where "even angels fear to tread," attention to these issues seems to be both interesting and important.

And as a budding tongue-in-cheek Chaoist, I have difficulty assuming any responsibility for anything I say or do, including, most importantly, what I write. The forces and factors that drive me may just not have gotten it right. If my syntax is out of whack or my style verges on the incoherent, you could blame it on Columbus, Stalin, or Jesus. Or if I'm right on target, these and other unnamed sources should be accorded full credit. If you're a student of Chaoist Theory, this may be crystal clear to you. Continue to read if you find it incomprehensible. For those who object violently, I throw myself on your infinite mercy.

It is my belief that CHANCE plays a far larger role in people's lives than anyone truly acknowledges. By definition, Chance indicates that no control is involved. Life is a gamble involving hits and misses.

Let us dwell on CONTROL. Control is a key issue. Each of us has strong needs to believe that we are in control of our lives, that we are the captains of our ships.

Our need to believe we have this control may account for the resistance to consideration, let alone acceptance of Chaos Theory, which clearly states that we have no control, that stuff happens without any rhyme or reason. When some unexpected catastrophic event takes place, we immediately begin to search for its causes. Invariably, we come up far short of a full understanding, but we don't dwell on this shortfall, nor should we. We often settle for exceedingly incomplete understanding as we rattle on in the living of our lives.

Let us assume that Chaos Theory, with its inherent lack of understanding, applies to everything we have ever done, are doing, and will do in the future. We haven't the faintest notion of why we are doing anything. Why are we so ignorant? It is because each of our actions and thoughts are the end result of an incredibly complex and dynamic chain of events, so complex as to be unknowable. It is absolutely impossible to determine with any certainty as to why we do anything. This is a challenging declaration.

And by anything, I mean exactly that. It is easy to concentrate upon catastrophic events and major life decisions, e.g. the death of one's child, choice of profession or marital partner. But I mean everything—every thought and action that you have ever undertaken—has been determined by factors and forces over which you have little or no knowledge—and absolutely NO control. Why are you reading this line in this book at this time? Why did you scratch yourself or fail to scratch yourself just a moment ago? Why are you perhaps speculating as to my sanity in putting forth this proposition? You haven't a clue! At best, your answers have only superficial validity. You have NO CONTROL.

The Scottish poet Robert Burns said something to the effect that "The best laid plans of mice and men oft go astray." And why is that? It is because we don't fully appreciate the paramount role that Chance plays in our lives.

Many may find this lack of control frightening.

It is so fearful that people deal with it by denial. They need to believe that they can live their lives according to their own pre-conceived plan. It is easier to dismiss Chaos Theory as mere balderdash than it is to consider that it may be valid.

Is it indefensible? That possibility exists. But if you think about it, this might just make some sense.

For example, in 1914, a tired, middle-aged mother looks out in the backyard to see her handsome teenaged son, Ross, rough-housing in play with some of his friends. The day is sunny. Everyone is happy and content.

Later that day, she hears that some Austrian Duke has been killed in a far-away place called Sarajevo. This is of little concern to her. She does not know—indeed, cannot know—that this distant assassination will set in motion a complex chain of events that will end in 1918 with her son bleeding to death in the mud in France with his guts chewed to pieces by a German machine gun.

Was this process predictable? No way! Inevitable? In retrospect, it would seem so.

Recently, in connection with highway shootings in Ohio, a woman driver felt responsible for the death of her passenger. She had made a wrong turn. She kept saying, "If I'd taken the right turn, this never would have happened." The guilt that she had assumed became both chronic and unbearable. If beggars had horses, the beggars would ride.

A young woman got out of her car and went back into her house to retrieve something she had forgotten. Ten minutes later, she runs over a squirrel who happened to be crossing the road at the very minute she came driving along. If she had remembered to take her purse, the squirrel would have lived and she would have avoided the sorrow she experienced. The squirrel would not have been the victim of an untimely demise and possibly lived to bury nuts for the next fall.

In the protective cocoon of your privacy, look back upon your life. Think of some truly important choice points that have occurred, times when Chance determined and dramatically changed the fabric of your subsequent life. Auto accidents are a common example. There will be some events that you readily reveal to others, perhaps at every opportunity. These are the times when you got it right. How about those which represent poor outcomes? Maybe some of these were so disturbing that you never reveal them.

Indeed, there may be some that were so bad that they have been repressed, so bad that they have been repressed so much that you cannot summon them to your consciousness. It may be uncomfortable to consider that there may be other choice points that were decided for you, that external forces denied you anything even coming close to "choice."

If there is need to consider further the complexity of this approach to understanding human development, this self-same process occurs in all persons you have known and for all those you have never known. They and their physical environments could have impact upon your life. In truth, many of them did.

Each specific act or thought on your part is the end result of an incredibly complex process that has taken place throughout your entire life, the determinants of which cannot ever be fully understood by you. You began with what you thought was a clean slate, but much of that which was you at the time of your birth was determined by an infinite number of Chance factors. Your conception was determined by Chance. Why that night? Why had your parents linked up so as to produce you in the first place? That decision was determined by the self-same process operative in each of them. Your conception was a Chance event over which no one had any real knowledge of its complex determinants. This was also true of your parents' parents as well and all their forbears, all the way back to the beginning of time.

Throughout all the lives of these individuals, they were subjected to actions on the part of others whose being was similarly determined in a complex and unknowable fashion. As an example of this, it seems possible that an action on the part of a stranger involving an ancient relative could have had a determining effect on anything and everything you do now or have ever done. All of your ancestors, all of the people having interactions with any of them, all of the people having any interaction with any of these interactors could conceivably have impact on you. This has a grandiose psychotic sweep to it for it suggests that in theory, everyone who has ever lived on earth could have impact upon the determination of the person you are as of this moment. All of this flows from Chaos Theory. It could be called "Chance Programming."

If you find this hard to swallow, consider where you'd be if Franklin Delano Roosevelt, Dwight Eisenhower, or your maternal grandmother had never lived. People we've never met mold our lives.

Currently, at this very moment, you are at a special point in the programming process whose determinants can never truly be identified or understood by you. It is a perpetual, dynamic beehive of activity. Within a second or two, you will be a tiny bit different than you are now. You will not know that to be a fact; certainly you will not know why, and this is scary. We all have strong needs to believe that we exert control in determining what we are doing and what is to become of us.

If anyone had been spawned by Curtis' parents and plunked down into the household that was provided, he would have had the potential to get into all sorts of trouble. The exact nature of the resulting problems could not be predicted, but the negative predisposition would be strong and in place. The same thing can be said regarding Kay.

Consider the first time that Curtis met Kay. If either had something else to do on that occasion or if he or she had been late, they would never have met and this whole megillah involving the two of them would never have transpired. If Curtis had never met Andre in Loring Park…if Kay had never met Rob…If, if, if. The list is infinite. After they became personally involved, the list of "ifs" continued to build.

Chance intervened relentlessly throughout their lives. As troubled individuals, they got into trouble with one another and their worlds.

CHAPTER 37

Chaos

For the purposes of discussion, let it be assumed that the whims of Chance got Kay and Curtis to Owen Park that night.

If each had been personally programmed prior to the rape, how was that accomplished? Is a similar program still in place?

There is nothing new about efforts to gain a deeper understanding of events. It is perhaps best exemplified by the endless conjecture about the meanings and true significance of Thornton Wilder's classic, *The Bridge of San Luis Rey*. Most of this contemplation attempted to answer the central question of this book: Why were these five people on this century-old bridge in Peru at the precise moment it collapsed, plunging them to their deaths in the chasm below? A similar question might be raised regarding any one of the thousands of victims of 9/11 or the December 26, 2004 tsunami in Thailand, Sumatra, and Sri Lanka. Why is anyone anywhere at a particular time?

If any of a billion things had been even a little bit different in the lives and backgrounds of Kay and Curtis, the rape would not have taken place. This figure of a billion is clearly an underestimate. Some of these are readily identifiable. For example, if Kay had not been approached by a man at the Bellow Inn or if she had decided to go to a movie that night instead, or if she had decided to attend the University of River Falls rather than Eau Claire, or if Curtis had not taken Andre up on his offer. These are only a few of the really identifiable factors that seem directly related to the crime.

Consider the possibility that everything that ever happened to either of these individuals influenced their behavior on that fateful night. Virtually all of these are unidentifiable. Even if they could be identified, there would be no obvious linkage to the rape.

Did they just bumble along in the course of their lives? Chaos Theory would say yes.

This requires a belief that there is no rhyme or reason in the conduct of one's life. Neither Curtis nor Kay had any choice in their genetic make-up or the environment into which they were born. From the moment of conception, these factors began to have a determining effect upon the persons they were to eventually become. Everything that happened to them along the way influenced everything that happened to them subsequently.

But while this seems reasonable, it represents a line of thought that cannot be employed usefully in any full understanding of any individual. The commission of a single act—be it a rape, a purchase of stock, a selection from a menu, which socks to wear—stems directly from an unknowable mix of prior experiences and genetic differences. This is the essence of Chaos Theory. Its acceptance imposes real limitations on our understanding of people and our ability to predict and control their behavior. It clearly suggests that individuals are pawns, drifting through life at the mercy of factors and forces over which they have absolutely no control. And of course, it follows that if this is true, it is impossible to assign responsibility to an individual for any act they might commit. They had no choice. They never did. Curtis' unique background mishmash dictated each and every one of his acts, and he had no awareness of these determinants.

Similarly, the unique backgrounds of President Bush, Pope Benedict XVI, O.J. Simpson, and John Wayne Gacy impact all of their actions. The end product in each case—and in all others—is produced by an incredibly complex, random process. The person has been fashioned by events and circumstances of which he has no control. Personal responsibility for one's actions would be impossible to establish.

The importance of crucial determinants of an act can only be identified after the fact. That identification is anything but clear-cut. And then it is too late to use them in any constructive, preventative fashion. "If" comes up often in developing useless hindsights.

But in theory, all the events that ever took place in the lives of Curtis and Kay may have programmed them for the rape that eventually ensued. Chance then impacts them.

Some may feel that it is useless to enter into conjecture as to what might have happened if certain things had or had not happened. "If" is an important operative word. "Should" is another. Kay "should not" have done any number of things. "If" Curtis had done this, that, or the other thing, the crime would never have been committed.

We could repeat the old chant:

> "If ifs and buts
> Were candy and nuts
> We'd all have a Merry Christmas."

Or they might say:

> "If should and could
> Were sticks of wood
> We certainly could
> And most assuredly should
> Have a big bonfire."

The rape could not have been predicted at any time prior to the event. No one could have determined what eventually transpired moments or even seconds before it took place.

One can accept the premise of Chaos Theory, that the fluttering of a butterfly's wings in the Amazon might have precipitated Hurricane Andre, but no one could claim an ability to pick the responsible insect at the very beginning of the process.

CHAPTER 38

Alternatives

Alternatives to Chaos Theory are available. Many psychologists, psychiatrists, and psychoanalysts have worked diligently to construct personality theories, and they have produced some wildly different viewpoints as to how a person develops. The people described by one theoretician may seem to be from a different species than those described by another. The same person would be viewed quite differently through the eyes of a Freudian, a Rogerian, or an apostle of some other theorist, but each performs a useful function. Each provides a framework for understanding people, a framework that becomes the basis for providing therapy and even fashioning social policy. You go with what you've got, even though it's not much.

Looking backward may lead to backward thinking. Anyone can check over anyone's personal history and hazard a guess or two about missteps, mistakes, and downright catastrophes that could have been avoided "if" some other course of action could have been taken at the time. This is called "post diction." Such post dictions often fit comfortably into the theory of the theorist making them.

Accurate prediction, so dependent upon Chance, remains elusive, perhaps impossible to achieve.

CHAPTER 39

Religion

Does religion enter into a discussion of control issues? Of course.

While this very brief chapter will single out Christianity in its varying forms as a representative religion, all considerations and questions will apply to other religions as well. These can be mainstream or offshoot in character, e.g. Buddhism, Voodoo, Confucianism, Mohammedanism, Seventh Day Adventists, Mormonism, Jimmy and Tammy Bakker, Al Sharpton, etc.

The Christian God is seen as an omniscient and omnipotent presence who is in charge of everything that goes on in heaven and on earth. "His eye is on the sparrow."

Questions immediately arise in the case of Kay and Curtis. What was God up to? What was His plan for each of them? Why did he allow the two of them to develop as they did? Did Kay "fall away from Him" and thereby justify the punishment she endured during the rape? What was the lesson that she learned? What did God intend to teach Curtis? Could the lives of Kay and Curtis be redeemed if they would have become devout Christians, believe in Him, and live the "Good Life?" Believers have firm ideas already about the plight of these two and their beliefs are all that they need to justify their views. Belief does not demand nor require any rational basis for the answers to these and other relevant questions.

CHAPTER 40

Accountability

The concept of accountability must be addressed. According to Chaos Theory, if Curtis is not truly responsible for his actions in any meaningful sense, how can punishment be justified for him? Regardless of his lack of responsibility, alleged or otherwise, he did commit the act, a true transgression of currently established law. A hard-assed approach is clearly in order. "He did the crime, so he does the time." So what if he is not really responsible for his actions? "Tough titty," or "That is the way the cookie crumbled."

If things had been different, he would have been different. If the laws were different, it would have been different. But they weren't. He is held accountable for his actions regardless of his past. There seems to be no other viable alternative available to the society in which we live. This and other punishments represent a collective judgment determined by members of this society. In another culture, his behavior might have been applauded.

It also follows from the foregoing discussion that "legal insanity" is an insane idea. This concept should vanish from the courts of our land.

CHAPTER 41

The Future

It has been said that those who ignore the lessons of history are doomed to repeat their mistakes. In looking over the personal histories of Kay and Curtis, what has been learned? With the wisdom of hindsight, many of their experiences seemed to have programmed each of them to participate in the rape that took place in Owen Park. Would any of their past experiences at the time prior to their occurrence have allowed for a prediction of this event?

The answer is no.

At this stage of the game, does our knowledge of these two individuals enable us to predict what will happen to them in the future?

The answer is again no.

The answer may be a qualified yes in the case of Curtis. He will be incarcerated in a correctional facility for many years, even with time off for good behavior. But what will happen to him during this time is clearly a matter of conjecture and a matter of Chance. He will undergo "Sex Offender Treatment," whatever that might mean. Presumably, this will be undertaken to correct any tendencies on his part to rape. What will be done for, with, and to him during the course of his confinement? Will he profit from this treatment so as to grow and develop as a person? In as much as acquaintance rape and other forms of rape appear to be quite different, will he receive special treatment that recognizes and emphasizes this difference? Whatever happens, the day will come when he is released into a free society, and what he does from that time on is unknown.

Kay is already operating in a free society, and there would seem to be little likelihood of predicting her behavior as well. It has been said that battered women have an established predilection to seek out men who batter women, e.g. that when such a woman enters a crowded room, she will gravitate immediately toward the man most likely to beat her up eventually. And as is the case in all generalities, there may be modicum of truth to this. Kay is currently carving out a new life for herself. She has distanced herself from all of her Eau Claire friends and acquaintances. Whether or not she is maintaining any contact with her former school psychologist and counselor, Mr. Douglas, is unknown.

CHAPTER 42

Closing Remarks

Both the chaotic and religious approaches highlight the importance of external factors upon the individual, that a person is molded by forces over which he or she have little or no control. If things are going well for him, he should rejoice. He should revel in the glory of the moment. He has either lucked out or a beneficent God is smiling down upon him.

Taking the position dictated by Chaos Theory, everyone is simply dealt a different hand of cards, and in the course of their lives, each of us plays them out. Perhaps Chaos Theory could profit from some form of personification. Having a God who is omnipotent and omniscient, while hard to believe, has marked advantages. One can personally relate and talk to God or His representatives on earth. One cannot relate in a similar way to Chaos.

Perhaps it would be useful to refer to the conglomerate focus of Chaos as "Gus." Maybe such a personalization would help, but you can't argue with Gus, or bargain with Gus, or curry favor with Gus, or gain forgiveness from Gus. Gus simply is! And anyone at any moment is simply the latest manifestation of his or her Gus. Look across the room and locate another person. He or she can be described as a manifestation of Gus. Come back in an hour. Your Gus and that of the Gus of the other person will have changed, and neither of you will know that anything has happened.

Implementing his faith to provide understanding, a religious person might say forgivingly about a criminal or reprobate, "There but for the Grace of God, go I." A Chaoist could compassionately say, "There but for Gus, go I."

A person still undecided as to which of several horses to ride could then say sympathetically, "There but for the Grace of God or Gus or whatever, go I."

As to what becomes of Curtis and Kay, there is no crystal ball. God is said to know. Gus doesn't. Only time—not Gus—maybe God—will tell. Both Gus and God seem to move in very mysterious ways, their wonders to perform.

Part III

Suggestions for "Changelings"

(People Who Want a Happier and More Effective Life)

By

John R. Thurston, Ph.D.

A Changeling's Creed

Be steadfast in your search for truth—and "entelechy," your reasoned potential.
Aristotle & St. Jay (4:24)

When the student is ready, the teacher will appear.
Sufi saying

I think, therefore I am.
Rene Descartes

If you don't think, you aren't———much!
St. Jay (4:24)

Just be yourself; everyone else is already taken.
Oscar Wilde

At a party, Descartes was once asked if he wanted a drink.
He replied, "I think not."
He promptly disappeared.
JJB (2.14.11)

Entelechy uber alles!
St. Jay (4:11)

TABLE OF CONTENTS – PART III

PART ONE

To Fellow Changelings, Welcome!

Changeling: Changeling is a very old word with all sorts of different meanings, some of them having a decidedly negative character. I now propose to endow that word with a new and very positive meaning. It captures who and what I'm trying to emphasize in this book. According to me, "Changeling" can now be defined as "a person aware of the need to address and resolve the inevitable problems one encounters in adjusting to inescapable change."

A Changeling may have looked into his/her psychological mirror and been unhappy with some of what is seen. Some of us become Changelings because we weren't as contented or effective as we think we should be. Even a mild lack of fulfillment may trigger a desire to change. Others are forced to change as they feel themselves crumbling under the stress of some incredible storms they cannot weather.

The title ***Guidelines for Changelings, Those People Who Want a Happier and More Effective Life*** clearly indicates its purpose to provide some practical ideas that can lead to significant personal improvement.

If you are to change, you must modify or replace some of your very personal beliefs. This might be accomplished with minor tweaking, but it could easily come to light that a major overhaul is required. This might require a level of determination that you don't have at your disposal. I'm certainly no Messiah who can by the force of my writings inspire and sustain the necessary motivation. Maybe you'll find in my labyrinth of words something that will set you in motion. Maybe not. Like me, you must go with what you've got. It's my position that if you can't comfortably identify and defend your beliefs, then there may be some question regarding their strength and credibility.

Too many people fail to change in the face of the inevitable and unending changes that life brings to their table. Sad to say, they can probably never become Changelings. Very set in their ways, they remain in an unchallenging, unchanging, and unfulfilling life-long rut. They go along so as to get along. They lack insight into their predicament. Mired in old habits, they go through the motions of living and die without even coming close to realizing their full potential. They would never read this book. If they did, they'd be likely to reject any and all of the suggested ideas.

But then, one never says never! There is always the possibility that some earth-shaking Chance event might jolt those individuals out of their lethargy. Chance is an inescapable factor in personality development. In my wildest, most facetious moments, I'd like to think that a Chance encounter with this book could be considered such a truly "transformative event." Read on. We shall see.

As one optimistic Changeling to another, I bid you welcome and wish you well.

John R. Thurston, Ph.D., Changeling
Clinical Psychologist
Professor Emeritus of Psychology (University of Wisconsin-Eau Claire)

PART TWO

The Nature of Personal Change

Change: Everyone has some knowledge regarding the major, identifiable changes confronting them in their lives, e.g. marriage, death, parenthood, a new job, bankruptcy, etc.

But no one has a conscious awareness of the full range of the tiny, yet significant changes that have taken place—and are constantly taking place—in one's own life. Most personal change occurs in subliminal ways that escape our awareness. The importance of such subliminal changes cannot be overstated. While dramatic change occurs rarely, these minute changes are incessantly taking place. The glacial speed and character of their development denies us awareness that change is taking place. By way of illustration, I believe that you aren't exactly the same person you were when you started reading this paragraph, but as of the moment, I'd be hard pressed to provide hard evidence of that assertion.

Another clearer example might involve how much the expression "I love you" means to you. When did you first hear it? When and how did this expression become so empowered with special, highly-personal meaning?

Now, make up your own examples. The real sources of these are very probably lost in the fog of a very distant past. For all intents and purposes, **they will forever remain unknowable.**

Consider how much you may have changed this very day or during the course of an entire week. Think of the time, concentration, and utilization of your "inner resources" that would be required if you were to try to understand the elements of this process.

Let us suppose that you want to change some negative behavior of yours. The same slow process is involved when eliminating unwanted responses and supplanting them with new ones. Even when one develops a sudden "blinding insight" into one's own problems, the road to redemption is a very long and uncomfortable one. There are many bumps in the road. While understandable, impatience often interferes with the process.

Can you teach an old dog new tricks?

Yes, but it takes a long time, and any new ideas must compete with older habits. "Change" for a Changeling—and anyone else—requires new ideas. Established habits or ways of doing things are resistant to change.

But, as Robert Frost suggested:

Robert Frost (1874-1963). *Mountain Interval*, 1920

The Road Not Taken

Two roads diverged in a yellow wood,
And sorry I could not travel both
And be one traveler, long I stood
And looked down one as far as I could
To where it bent in the undergrowth;

Then took the other, as just as fair,
And having perhaps the better claim,
Because it was grassy and wanted wear;
Though as for that the passing there
Had worn them really about the same,

And both that morning equally lay
In leaves no step had trodden black.
Oh, I kept the first for another day!
Yet knowing how way leads on to way,
I doubted if I should ever come back.

I shall be telling this with a sigh
Somewhere ages and ages hence,
Two roads diverged in a wood, and I—
I took the one less traveled by,
And that has made all the difference.

And Robert Frost was right. To effect Change requires the abandonment or extinction of old ways of doing things. It's far easier to continue to march down a well-worn road than try a new and uncertain one.

An old Russian proverb may bear upon this issue. "Up to the age of five, a person can be shaped. From five until ten, he can be bent. From ten to fifteen, he must be broken. After age of fifteen, the only solution is the grave." Exceptions to this undoubtedly abound, but this saying may point out the need for changes early on.

Do it now! You don't need someone to tell you that you're not getting any younger!

It is clear to me that personal adaptation is part and parcel of an awesome, inescapable, dynamic, and challenging process that begins at the moment of conception and continues until death.

The Limitations of Mental Health Professionals as Resources

Let us engage in an exercise in empathy with a Changeling in search of assistance from a member of the mental health establishment, i.e. psychiatrists, clinical psychologists, psychiatric social workers, etc.

The public is generally unaware as to what is involved in seeking out professional help. They might be shocked to learn of the unavailability of assistance and the unevenness of the quality of service they provide.

One Alone

Many troubled patients report that they feel alone without a clue as to how they should proceed in securing mental health services. The clinic secretaries who respond to their telephone inquiries seem more interested in their finances than in the problems they are having. But in these times, word of mouth is a good way to go when looking for a mental health professional. Hopefully, you will have good friends (which in and of themselves are invaluable resources in time of need) who will help you get through this and other problems en route to happiness (see suggestion 18).

As in many medical matters, insurance companies have an incredible amount of say in determining the nature and the duration of treatment. They insist on a medical diagnosis before they will authorize and pay for any treatment. The companies will routinely limit the number of outpatient psychotherapeutic sessions to six or eight. This determination has nothing to do with the nature of the personal problem or the efficacy of treatment. It has a great deal to do with the type of insurance the patient has. By the time the patient seeks treatment; their problems are so great that they will not yield to the insurance company's very limited number of outpatient sessions. If a patient is hospitalized, the companies have rigid rules as to how many days are permissible, and under what circumstances.

There are a few truths involving the care and treatment of troubled individuals. However, research states clearly that the earlier the intervention, the greater the likelihood of successful treatment. The system, however, is geared to treating heavy-duty psychiatric disturbances. Changelings, those individuals seeking help with minor dissatisfactions, are not well-served.

Patients wonder as to whether they are getting value for the $150-$250 or more they expend in the 50 minutes that is the "therapeutic hour." If patients are starting to improve after the six to eight sessions that the insurance company has approved and paid for, they may terminate the treatment rather than pay those exorbitant charges.

It's clear that within the constraints of ignorance and stratospheric prices, responsible mental health services are unavailable to almost everyone. Insurance companies determine the length and nature of treatment. Their goals involve profit, not responsible, effective treatment. Available treatments are few and far between. The customary prescription of pills is cost-effective while creating the illusion that treatment is being provided. At best, personal problems are quelled rather than cured.

The "treatment" takes the following form:

An introductory medication with a tentative dosage.

In roughly two weeks, a "med check." If patient is satisfied, the dosage is maintained. If not, the medication may be increased or reduced dependent upon patient reaction. Any psychological components of problems need never be identified, let alone addressed. Symptoms are quelled; determinants are ignored. The time allotted for "med checks" is approximately 10 minutes.

In the unlikely event that psychotherapy might be provided, the client must become aware of the vast differences amongst therapists in the quality and effectiveness of the service they provide. These include the therapist's personal characteristics and his theoretical stance. While these differences are of paramount importance, there is no way the patient can come to know about these matters. The therapeutic relationship depends on a special, intimate, interpersonal relationship between the client and the therapist. If the client is very lucky, he might avail himself of a therapist ideally suited to the client and the problem he presents. There is a greater likelihood that this will not happen; that treatment will be merely adequate or even substandard.

Some, especially the practitioners, like to promote themselves as supermen/superwomen who are omniscient and omnipotent. It has been my experience that this just isn't true. How does a client check out the personal and professional credentials of a prospective therapist? The answer is that he doesn't. His knowledge is restricted to what the professional chooses to reveal in his advertisement in the Yellow Pages. There is a clear and present danger that the patient will be drained of his finances, exposed to treatment that is lengthy and ineffective.

By way of example, let us single out psychoanalysis. The approach relies on Father Freud and a few of his markedly disturbed patients who were the basis for his theory developed many years ago. To become a psychoanalyst, one must undergo an extended period of training in this discipline, maybe seven to ten years. Much of what he learns is of questionable use in dealing with the everyday personal problems of our current generation.

Dream analysis is another example of psychoanalytic activity that has no scientific evidence that it's helpful to the patient. The analyst believes that he identifies basic, hidden problems by analyzing the patients' dreams. The demonstrated validity of this happening is virtually nil. Enhancing one's self-understanding by dream analysis is comparable to trying to determine the makeup of the local Elks' club by listening to the wailing whistle of a distant train.

People waste tons of money and years of their lives in this effort.

Sad to say, but there is little that can be said about mental health professionals that is truly progressive. They are saddled with the "medical model" which requires diagnosis as a necessary prelude to therapy. If there is no diagnosis, the insurance company will not pay the providers. The uniqueness and individuality of the person seeking help is lost. The treatment is based upon whatever diagnostic category he has been relegated to by the mental health professional. This accounts for the popularity of pills as the predominant treatment.

If a Changeling were to attempt to gain some assistance from a psychiatrist, clinical psychologist, or psychiatric social worker, they would encounter many problems. Prominent amongst these would be the difficulties that professionals might have in diagnosing him. This would be especially true if he wasn't exhibiting clear-cut symptoms. As an individual, the Changeling is truly unique. It is a truism that a difficulty that is addressed early on has a better prognosis than one that is more thoroughly developed. A system based on diagnoses virtually requires identifiable symptoms of established "illness" before it can kick into gear and attempt to help the patient.

A joke might illustrate the basic problem. A person goes to a clinic to get help with a head cold. He is told that they have no treatment for a head cold, but if he waits and develops pneumonia, he should come back because this is something they can treat.

Changelings seeking to improve themselves may find themselves on their own. "Self-improvement" may in large part be a do-it-yourself project. The ball is in their court.

There is a great deal of significant and unascertainable variation in the quality and effectiveness of psychotherapy or counseling. While one might get lucky, exceptions to this statement are few and far between. When I'm asked to recommend a local therapist/counselor, no one comes to mind. Their services are expensive and prolonged; insurance policies make little provision for compensation for the length of services typically required. I find this sad and unlikely to change.

Changelings might be driven to consider the possibility of self-therapy. This promising approach, emphasizing solitary cathartic and therapeutic talking, emulates what actually goes on in traditional therapy, but without the need for the presence of a therapist. The possibilities of this technique have been explored in a novel, *Sharpening Shadows* (Scobie, Nancy Clark and Thurston, John R., 2002).

PART FOUR

The Twenty Suggestions

For a variety of reasons, I recommend that the Changelings consider The Twenty Suggestions, a current, practical, and effective source of useful counsel and advice. These suggestions are just that: faint hints or indications that may be accepted or rejected with ease and impunity. They are the product of my thirty-plus years of experience as a clinical psychologist and professor of psychology. They are brief and to the point, mercifully free from the pretentious "psychobabble" that too often clutters this area of psychology. My clients and students have found them useful in a variety of highly-individualized ways, and such individualization is important. It must be pointed out that the goals of The Twenty Suggestions are unquestionably worthwhile. There's nothing in them that is antagonistic to the positive attributes of any other belief or approach.

Changelings dealing with complex change find abstract personality theories to be of little use. They want concrete suggestions or directions that will encourage them to think deeply and productively as they continue to fashion a tailor-made strategy for the living of their own lives. As a stimulant to engage in new and constructive thought, I believe that The Twenty Suggestions does just that. Once again, St. Jay the Hypothetical Apostate becomes a spokesman. Importantly, he has little use for psychobabble, a language designed to impress rather than inform.

One, two, or all twenty of the Suggestions could have a significant effect upon one's life. The reader is encouraged to try them on for size. If the shoes fit, wear them. There's no downside to this practice. While one can "break" a Commandment, one can't "break" a Suggestion! There isn't any hellfire awaiting the Changeling who chooses to reject any or all of the Suggestions. If a Suggestion doesn't work out, one's life will simply go on as before. But if one or more of these Suggestions click, a person's life may be altered and enriched to a significant degree. Problems can be avoided or dealt with more effectively. The ideas they suggest may open up new worlds to explore, experience, and enjoy.

These guideposts are now offered freely to Changelings who seek a better life. These pithy pronouncements of The Twenty Suggestions may be helpful. Some people may use these suggestions as a checklist, simply reading through them for ideas as to how they might improve. Some may have their interest piqued by one or two suggestions to the point where they wish to explore them fully. Therapists might encourage periodic readings as part of an ongoing treatment program. Parents might find The Twenty Suggestions as a starting point for a personal dialogue with their adolescent children. Their use as focal points for group discussions appears promising.

In the beginning, there must be questions. Are you a potential believer in what you have read so far? Has it seemed to make more than a modicum of common sense?

Are you a potential practitioner regarding what you have read and what you will read in The Twenty Suggestions? Keep in mind that a practitioner is one who practices rules of conduct that others merely preach.

It is relatively easy to accept principles such as those underlying The Twenty Suggestions. However, diligent application is another matter. Testing them out and then eventually integrating them into one's real life can be a very difficult and continuous process.

Perhaps you might select two or three of The Twenty Suggestions that may deal with your most pressing problems. You may then form a tentative plan to remedy your shortcomings. The Twenty Suggestions often contains gentle reminders of some of these. You know what they are and you may have a great insight into what you should do by way of remedy. This is a highly personal matter.

Specify attainable goals and then set about to achieve them. "Baby steps" are in order; the only way to consume an elephant is one bite at a time. Visit and revisit your goals to celebrate your successes or to change your mode of attack as you deal with your failures. Be reassured that change takes time and application; progress may be measured in terms of the psychological equivalent of millimeters. While perhaps lamentable, these statements are true.

Your involvement with The Twenty Suggestions may be a solitary endeavor. For you, this may be the only way to go; at least, for the time being.

I believe that The Twenty Suggestions can be the focal point for group discussions. You can have the advantages of group therapy without the need for a leader with the prohibitive costs he would impose. Sharing your problem and your progress with others can be enjoyable and productive. Listening to others can often provide new ideas that can be utilized for one's own improvement. It might be advantageous for a group of interested and motivated individuals to meet regularly and devote an entire session or sessions to one Suggestion that appears to be of general interest to the group.

The Twenty Suggestions approach is flexible and can be used in any way the individual or a group chooses.

An Admonition

Before The Twenty Suggestions are presented, there's an important admonition that must be considered. The reader must have a sense of humor, an ability to avoid taking himself too seriously, an inclination at times to poke gentle fun at himself and others. If he's not having fun and enjoyment in his life, he is not living fully. Humorless people are often very set in their ways. Without a sense of humor, a person might encounter difficulty in understanding and utilizing The Twenty Suggestions. The playful wording of the suggestions conveys a light-hearted approach. *In no way does this approach undercut their serious and substantive character.*

Humor serves as a valuable cushion against the jolts and jars of problems one inevitably encounters throughout one's life. If one lacks this characteristic, acquisition of it has the highest of priorities. I use a pseudo-Biblical humorous phraseology in an effort to set the stage for The Twenty Suggestions. Don't take them too seriously, but don't dismiss them too readily.

Now, you may begin. Note the large blank spaces under each suggestion. Fill them with opinions and descriptions of your endeavors as you try them on for size. Placing a date in each of your notations will provide you with a timeline on which you, as a fervent Changeling, can record your progress.

Consider this an adventure. Live fully. Prevail!

The Twenty Suggestions

1. Thou shalt plan.

Identify important personal goals that one must accomplish during the next five years. Determine what one must do today and during the next few months in order to achieve these goals. Don't accept the easy rationalizations that one is too busy or that one will get one's true reward in heaven. And do not be fully dismayed when your plans don't work out for you. You will find that such failures are virtually impossible to avoid. Regroup and keep trying. There's enjoyment and hope in each contemplation and the need for revision. This clearly applies to your use of The Twenty Suggestions.

Date	Notes

2. Thou shalt travel.

A conditional Suggestion, for one should travel only for one's own very personal reasons. Exposure to different people and cultures can enable you to learn a lot, both about them and yourself. While travel can be a rich and rewarding growth experience, some people travel often and widely only to impress other people. They return weary and unchanged because in reality, they have never left home. Your "Bluebird of Happiness" may reside right in your backyard.

Date	Notes

3. **Thou shalt be kind to others and to oneself.**

In addition to being generally kind and considerate to others, one should engage in special acts of generosity from time to time. While both the giver and the participant will profit from this activity, the giver may gain even more by remaining anonymous. It's equally important to do kindness unto one's self that others have not seen fit to do unto one.

Date	Notes

4. Thou shalt spend.

Scrooge should be no one's patron saint. Once prudent plans have been made for immediate and eventual financial security, spend freely of one's time and money for one's own enjoyment and that of others. Admirable charities and food banks are available. Any ultimate measure of one's worth will probably make no sense to one's accountant. Spend yourself. Use some of your time and energy in the service of others who may be less fortunate. You'll be richly rewarded.

Date	Notes

5. Thou shalt not advise.

A conditional Suggestion in that this does not preclude free and generous provision of one's own wisdom upon request. If asked, one must be properly humble and circumspect in the offering of one's own advice and counsel.

Date	Notes

6. Thou shalt not accept advice.

This is a conditional Suggestion that stresses self-reliance and a disdain for allowing others to assume responsibility for one's life. Dr. Phil, his merry band of experts, and others of his mind set glibly provide (at best) tools and a small bit of information. In real life, only the very rich could afford the professional services that Dr. Phil and those like him prescribe. There is little, if any, verifiable evidence of the successes they report. However, critical consideration of advice or adverse opinion from others is acceptable. You must supply the "heavy lifting" required of any improvement.

Date	Notes

7. Thou shalt be genteel.

In increasingly uncivil times, it's to one's personal advantage to behave civilly. If you receive email, snail mail, or phone calls, it is both polite and obligatory that you respond immediately. Even modestly mannerly behavior, politeness, and attention to the sensitivities of others shalt mark one as a truly exceptional individual. In the long run, such gentility will redound to one's own advantage. What goes around DOES come around.

Date	Notes

8. **Thou shalt be kind and helpful to animals and birds.**

One who harms animals or birds or extends dominion over them has his neighbor next on his hit list. It's a rare domestic animal that isn't thoroughly deserving of one's compassionate and unconditional love. The mere presence of a wild bird or animal in one's vicinity can cause one's spirits to soar. Seek out and cherish such experiences. Experience them fully.

Date	Notes

9. **Thou shalt engage in regular physical and mental exercises.**

Do it! There are a host of indefensible reasons for procrastinating. Overriding obstacles is both necessary and gratifying. Fun, good health, growth, and relaxation are some of the rewards. Accept the challenge of pushing the envelope while moving ahead to actualize one's full physical and mental capabilities.

Date	Notes

10. Thou shalt take risks.

A risk-free life provides only a mere existence. Let your memories be full of risks taken and results realized rather than the comforts of hazards avoided. Don't succumb to the temptation to take any softer and easier ways. Dream your dreams—and then go about realizing them.

Date	Notes

11. Thou shalt think.

In an age wherein "experts" and computers are said to provide all the answers one really needs, one must realize that the development of significant challenges and their resolution requires deep, personalized, and avant-garde thought. No one should ever allow anyone else to do one's own thinking.

Date	Notes

12. One shalt converse meaningfully and with civility.

In the course of this exercise, one shalt listen attentively and courteously. Go beyond the commonplace to talk about the weather or sports; risk revealing oneself to others even though they may be disinterested or disdainful. Practice that currently unfashionable, demanding, and rare art of *listening*. Others will benefit from this expression of one's own caring and concern. Personal rewards shall accrue to those who are able to listen with compassion and understanding. Gossipers revel in their prattle in the vacuum that is their lives.

Date	Notes

13. Thou shalt not be fearful of silence.

If one has nothing to say, one should feel free to lapse into companionable silence. Some fear silence as though it were the plague. They waste precious moments in idle chatter or loud, empty, self-servicing trumpeting that would drown out the braying of other asses. Silence can truly be golden. The time saved can be utilized in thought and quiet contemplation.

Date	Notes

14. Thou shalt honor thy past and learn from it.

One should look to the future while realizing the importance of the past as a necessary prologue to it. One who ignores the lessons of personal history may be doomed to repeat one's mistakes. It is clearly counter-productive to remain mired in the past, considering endlessly what might have or should have been done. Similarly, don't waste time making extensive plans for an unpredictable future. It has been said, "If you want to hear your God laugh uncontrollably, you have only to tell Him or Her your plans for the next five years."

Date	Notes

15. Thou shalt not perseverate.

Persevere, but do not perseverate. Keep trying in the face of obstacles and failure, but only up to a finite point. Decide when your efforts are merely perseverative, like hitting one's head repeatedly and unproductively against a wall. If you have been doing that, a change in tactics becomes mandatory. Acceptance of losses and abandoning a losing situation are parts of a winning strategy. The woulda-shoulda-coulda rumination is pointless. One excellent definition attributed to Albert Einstein indicates that one is "insane" if he keeps doing the same thing over and over again with the expectation each time that the results will be different and better.

Date	Notes

16. Thou shalt accept one's lot.

Dwelling on past and current mistakes will unnecessarily constrict, complicate, and diminish one's life. Learn from your mistakes. After accepting a shortfall, move ahead. As Kierkegaard once said, "Life can only be understood backwards; but it must be lived forwards."

Date	Notes

17. Thou shalt exalt creativity, art, individuality, and one's special passions.

If one is creative, this gift should be flaunted and realized fully. If this talent is not in one's Nature, it should be supported fully in others. One must exult in marching to the beat of one's own very unique and distant drum. It's good to dream about one's self and circumstance. To live fully, one must develop a special personal passion for some activity or involvement, and then pursue it to the max. It should be so important that you will cry if you encounter serious problems along the way.

Date	Notes

18. Thou shalt cultivate personal relationships.

One must be highly selective in choosing and investing in the important people in one's life. After that, the effort involving acceptance and tolerance may lead to truly important, deep, and regarding personal relationships with those selected. Such a mind-set may counteract a developing trend, which makes such relationships rare and even unattainable.

Date	Notes

19. Thou shalt not "should" unto others.

Abandon the common practice of telling others what they "should" do. No one has the knowledge or authority necessary to dictate the conduct of another's life.

Date	Notes

20. Thou shalt not allow others to "should" unto one.

One is far better off being a hammer than a nail. One must remain an individual who is free from any domination by others, i.e. having people tell one what he or she should do. One is fully responsible for the conduct of one's own life. That one is YOU! You should exult in your freedom and independence. Sing out your song loudly, proudly, and prolongedly.

Date	Notes

U

W

Y

Personal/Professional Resume
John R. Thurston, Ph.D.

Education

Bachelor of Arts degree (Psychology) Phi Beta Kappa, U of Wisconsin-Madison 1949; Master of Arts degree in Psychology, U of Wisconsin-Madison 1950; Doctor of Philosophy (Clinical Psychology) U. of Iowa 1953)

Military Service

World War II, U.S. Navy 1943-46 Signalman Mostly destroyer duty in the N. Pacific (Alaska, Aleutian Islands, Russia's Sea of Okhotsk, Japanese Kurile Islands) One battle star

Professional Experience

Full time

Clinical Psychologist, Veterans Admin Hosp. Madison, Wis 1953-57
Chief Psychologist Eau Claire Co. Guidance Clinic Eau Claire, Wis 1957-58 Assistant to Full Professor of Psychology University of Wis.-Eau Claire 1958-87(Retired)

Part-time

Principal Investigator, Eau Claire Youth Study (Eau Claire)1958-1972; Principal Investigator, Nursing Education Research (Eau Claire) 1959-71; Clinical Psychologist Northwest Psychiatric Clinic (Eau Claire) 1973-1984; Private Practice 1984-1990

Writings and Publications

More than 60 research articles, pamphlets, and books of a professional nature (1953-1977)

Horse Racing Psychology Book 1987. Co-author Betty J. Thurston

Muses, Music, and More Book 1998. Co-author Nancy Clark Scobie

Primarily Poetry, Pithograms, and Pictures...But a Little Bit More Book 1999.Co-author Nancy Clark Scobie

Meandering With Mariah Book 2000. Co-author Nancy Clark Scobie

A Provocative Potpourri of Poetry, Pithograms, Prose, and Pretty Pictures Book 2000. Co-author Nancy Clark Scobie.

Purposeful Pithograms Book. 2002

Sharpening Shadows Book 2002, Co-author Nancy Clark Scobie

Sides Seldom Seen: A Novella Book 2004. Co-author Nancy Clark Scobie

A Very Full Circle A compilation of Thurston's writings.2004

It Took Two To Tangle: A Rape Explored Book 2005

Contributions to ***Poetica Grandma-tica 2004,2005, 2006-2007, 2007-2008, 2008-2009, 2009-2010, 2010-2011, 2011-2012, 2012-2013, 2013-2014*** Editors: Scobie and Bredeson.

Nuts and Bolts 2006: Mostly Nuts A compilation of Thurston's writings.

The Way of a Reluctant Warrior in WW II A review of wartime navy career of Thurston. 2006

Nuts and Bolts 2007: Mostly Nuts A compilation of 2007 writings by Thurston

The Way of a Reluctant Warrior in WW II: An Addendum Additional material regarding Thurston's WWII navy career 2007

The Old Altoona Public School: A Collection of Memories Book 2008 Memories of those attending this school before 1951 fire

Grandma Had Her "Say" ——and She Said a Lot Booklet 2008

Jesse Jensen, Principal, Coach, Teacher, Altoona Public School, 1921-1943 Booklet Hoyt and Thurston 2008

A Star-crossed Venture: Contributions to The Altoona Star, Altoona, Wisconsin 2007-2009 Booklet 2009

The Red Caboose, A Collection of Altoona, Wisconsin Memories Blackburn, Rasmussen, and Thurston Book 2009

"Partnering" Wisconsin Medical Journal, March 2009

Suggestions for "Changelings, Those People Who Want a Happier and More Effective Life Book,2011

"Effective Doctor/Patient Communication, A Hit or a Myth? Twenty Suggestions for Improvement" Wis. Medical Journal, April, 2012

Ageism—- Solitary Sufficiency Booklet 2012

Doctor-Patient Communication-Partnering-Assessment of Patient Satisfactions/Dissatisfactions Booklet 2012

"An Alternate Form to Determine Patient Satisfaction with Medical Treatment" Wisconsin Medical Journal 2013.

"Reflections: "Taken by Chance" Book 2013

"Nurses' Communicative and Empathic Skills" Book. 2014

"The Thurstonian Theory of Life: There, But for the Mindless Whims of Chance, Go I." Book 2014

Additional writings: Booklets: ***Ago-ing*** (how to write memoirs), ***Expressions of Gertrude McCluskey*** (a tribute to Thurston's grandmother), ***Naval World War II Slang; Past Imperfect, The First 50 Years*** (an unpublished autobiography), newspaper columns (St. Paul Pioneer Press; The Altoona Star), letters to editors, thousands of Pithograms ("thoughts and matters of substance in written form"). Columnist, ***Senior Review*** (Eau Claire, Wis.), 2010-11

Other Pursuits:

Writing, landscape art (a geoglyph of an angel called "Angelhazel," "Alex, the Wonder Underdog" These could only be seen from air),stock car track ownership, dog/horse racing, travel (I have visited 48 National Parks, Africa 4 times, China twice and 6 of the 7 continents), tree farms, baby seals and polar bears, humane societies, speeches, preservation of historical sites, excessive recreational TV viewing, exploring the Internet, research into patient satisfactions/dissatisfactions with medical treatment, nurse and doctor/ patient relationships/communication and memories.

John R. Thurston, Ph.D. Clinical Psychologist, Research Psychologist, Professor Emeritus of Psychology (U.Of Wis.-Eau Claire)
3752 Cummings Street, Eau Claire, Wisconsin 54701
(715.832.0034) E-mail:thurstjr@charter.net Updated 08.12.14

CPSIA information can be obtained at www.ICGtesting.com
Printed in the USA
LVOW03s0451111014

408329LV00003B/3/P